16th Conference of the Association for Machine Translation in the Americas (AMTA 2024)

Volume 2: Presentations

Chicago, Illinois, USA
28 September – 2 October 2024

Editors:

Marianna Martindale
Janice Campbell
Konstantin Savenkov
Shivali Goel
Jay Marciano

ISBN: 979-8-3313-0483-6

Printed from e-media with permission by:

Curran Associates, Inc.
57 Morehouse Lane
Red Hook, NY 12571

Some format issues inherent in the e-media version may also appear in this print version.

Association for Computational Linguistics
209 N. Eighth Street
Stroudsburg, Pennsylvania 18360

Phone: 1-570-476-8006
Fax: 1-570-476-0860

acl@aclweb.org

Additional copies of this publication are available from:

Curran Associates, Inc.
57 Morehouse Lane
Red Hook, NY 12571 USA
Phone: 845-758-0400
Fax: 845-758-2633
Email: curran@proceedings.com
Web: www.proceedings.com

AMTA 20
CHICAGO 24

The 16th Conference of the Association for Machine Translation in the Americas

www.conference.amtaweb.org

Volume 2: Presentations

Editors:
Marianna Martindale, Janice Campbell, and Konstantin Savenkov (Presentations Track Co-chairs); Shivali Goel (Publications Chair); Jay Marciano (General Conference Chair)

Welcome to the 16th conference of the Association for Machine Translation in the Americas – AMTA 2024!

Dear MT & AI Colleagues and Friends,

For this year's conference of the Association for Machine Translation in the Americas – AMTA 2024 – we come together in person in metropolitan Chicago, at the Renaissance Schaumburg Convention Center Hotel, and online in our virtual conference application.

2024 marks the 30th anniversary of the first AMTA conference, held in Columbia, Maryland, in October 1994, and 70 years since the first public demonstration of machine translation in New York City, a project involving IBM and Georgetown University.

By today's standards, the demonstration was stunningly limited: a mere 250 words translated from Russian to English in about 60 mostly short and highly repetitive sentences. Each sentence had to be typed into a device that created a machine-readable punch card. Each card was then fed individually into a room-sized IBM 701 mainframe, hardware that cost $500,000 at the time (the equivalent of $5.8 million today!).

Infamously, the experimenters predicted that usable Machine Translation in "important functional areas of several languages" could be "an accomplished fact" within five or maybe even only three years, a wildly inaccurate underestimation of the complexity of the challenge.

But to their credit, the experimenters also recognized that they had taken but baby steps, comparing their accomplishment to the Wright brothers' 1903 flight at Kitty Hawk, a single-passenger, 12-second, 36-meter hop in a heavier-than-air vehicle along the beach in North Carolina that hardly hinted at the fact that safe transoceanic passenger flights would be commercially available just 36 years later, nor that in less than the 70 years that have passed since the first demonstration of MT, mankind would fly to the moon, land on it, walk around, and fly back to Earth.[1]

It is mind-boggling to consider how much has changed in our field since these events and yet how much the fundamental need for facilitating multilingual communication with technology remains. Here we are now, not even one full human lifetime from the 1954 demonstration and not quite two years since the general availability of generative AI tools, and the very words "machine translation" sound almost quaint in the tidal wave of news about large language models. But let's not forget that transformer models, the cornerstone of the boom in generative AI, are a direct result of advances in machine translation.

So, this is an appropriate time for all of us who work on or with MT or generative AI to recognize the giants on whose shoulders we stand and to ask ourselves what more needs to be done before we have reached the NLP equivalent of the moon.

In the spirit of honoring those who have contributed to the development of MT before us, it is with great sadness and lasting gratitude that I report the passing of Muriel Vasconcellos, founding president of AMTA (1991-1996), president of IAMT (1997-1999), and IAMT Award of Honor recipient (1999), on September 14, 2024 at the age of 91, a few short months after she wrote her contribution

---

[1]Machine translation: from real users to research: 16th Conference of the Association for Machine Translation in the Americas, AMTA 2004, Washington, DC, September 28 – October 2, 2004; ed. Robert E.Frederking and Kathryn B.Taylor (Berlin: Springer Verlag, 2004); pp. 102-114

to this volume. Computational linguist and ATA-certified English to Portuguese translator, Muriel earned a PhD in linguistics from Georgetown University and was centrally instrumental in the introduction of machine translation at the Pan American Health Organization/World Health Organization. Her passion for facilitating open and collegial communication among MT researchers, developers, and users is still and will remain a defining characteristic of AMTA.

We are pleased once again with the number and quality of submissions to our conference, which reflect great progress in MT, not only in the scope of supporting ever more languages and in improving and assessing output quality, but also in the use of large language models either as translation systems in and of themselves or, as you will see in many of the papers and presentations this year, in augmenting machine translation systems with additional processing via LLMs.

A unique aspect of AMTA conferences is that they bring together users and practitioners from across the MT spectrum of academia, industry, and government so that R&D personnel can learn from those who are using the technology and vice versa. And this year we are doubling down on this aspect by organizing sessions not by whether works come from researchers, users and providers, or government representatives, but instead by topic area so that our various constituents have even more opportunity to see how much their interests intersect and enjoy more direct contact.

Another novelty this year is the first ever AMTA Best Thesis Award, a tradition that we borrowed from our sister organization EAMT. We congratulate its first winner, Dr. Eleftheria Briakou, for her thesis "Detecting Fine-Grained Semantic Divergences to Improve Translation Understanding Across Languages," an abstract of which is included in this volume.

As with all our conferences, AMTA 2024 would simply not have been possible without the selfless work of so many people on the AMTA board and organizing committee, all of whom are volunteers. I express my heartfelt thanks, respect, and admiration to each of them. They include:

Janice Campbell, AMTA Secretary, Local Arrangements

Alex Yanishevsky, AMTA Vice President, Conference Online Platform

David Bishop, AMTA Treasurer

Akiko Eriguchi, Peer-review Track and Best Thesis Award organizer

Rebecca Knowles, Peer-review Track and Best Thesis Award organizer

Cecilia Yalangozian, Workshops and Tutorials, Presentations Track

Georg Kirchner, Workshops and Tutorials

Konstantin Savenkov, Presentations Track

Marianna Martindale, Presentations Track,

Kelly Ko, Webmaster

Derick Fajardo, Communications and Marketing

Lara Daly, Sponsorships

Shivali Goel, Publications

Steve Richardson, AMTA Councilor

Alon Lavie, AMTA Consultant

Finally, I express my gratitude to our sponsors, whose support has helped us to mitigate the added cost of the hybrid format. Our Leader Level sponsors include Systran by ChapsVision and Apptek. Our Exhibitor-level sponsors include Star and Intento, and our Media and Marketing sponsor is Slator. Many of these participating companies will provide demonstrations of their systems and software during our Technology Exhibition sessions, and we hope that our attendees will take advantage of this opportunity to see the latest commercial offerings and advancements in the world of MT.

Again, welcome to AMTA 2024! I look forward to seeing many of you in person in Chicago and to interacting with many others online.

Jay Marciano

AMTA President and AMTA 2024 General Conference Chair

Presentations Track: Introduction

The Presentations Track is new for AMTA 2024. To encourage a broader range of submissions, we have provided a single track for non-peer-reviewed presentations in place of separate Government and Users and Providers tracks. As a result, we have presentations that range from case studies, workflows, and frameworks to academic research.

It will come as no surprise that many of the presentations address the use of Large Language Models (LLMs) in translation. There are several presentations that explore the use of LLMs in the final stages of the translation process, including error detection, post-editing, and adapting formality and style. Other presentations share stakeholder perceptions or evaluate the abilities of LLMs in specific areas such as idiom translation and spatial language.

Beyond text translation, new models show promise in multimedia translation workflows, reflected in presentations comparing neural MT and LLM translations of subtitles, introducing approaches to evaluating end-to-end speech translation, and sharing results of practical assessments of multimedia translation technologies.

However, we do not neglect traditional machine translation and translation evaluation. In honor of the 10th anniversary of the Multidimensional Quality Metrics (MQM) error typology, the MQM team will present new scoring models that use MQM annotations to generate a numeric score against desired specifications. The presentations also include specialized applications such as medical translation and low-resource translation.

We would like to thank the reviewers, authors, and the AMTA board for making this new track possible. We hope that this year's presentations address the variety of current topics while providing a little something for everyone and encouraging understanding across the traditional AMTA audiences.

Sincerely,

Marianna Martindale, Janice Campbell, and Konstantin Savenkov

Presentations Track Co-Chairs

Contents

Staying in the Loop with Gen AI: AI/Gen AI-Powered HLT for the Public Sector

Konstantine Boukhvalov

ManpowerGroup Public Sector, Inc.

ManpowerGroup™

ManpowerGroup Public Sector

- **30+** years supporting commercial and government clients in over 200 languages and dialects
    - ➢ Translation and l10n, transcription, interpretation, language technology support, linguist placements, multimedia analysis and reporting
- **Super user of Human Language Technology (HLT)**
    - ➢ 25+ years customizing language automation/HLT tools in 60 languages to achieve efficiencies, process voluminous materials, and provide cost savings
    - ➢ Leverage and adapt commercial products and combine tools to optimize technology to best meet customers' needs:
        - ➢ Open-Source Intelligence (OSINT), Translation Management Systems (TMS), Machine Translation (MT), CAT/Localization Tools, Authoring, eLearning, Desktop Publishing/Graphics Design, Audio/Video Production, Lexical Data Management, Optical Character Recognition

Objective

- **Vision Outline:**
  - Evolving role of "humans-in-the-loop" for MT and Translation-related Services (TRS) for Public Sector support
  - Organizational transformation related to Gen AI technologies and workflows
- **Focus Areas:**
  - Corpus building
  - Corpus curation / Quality control
  - Security
  - Workflow adjustments
  - Output quality evaluation, including fact-checking and domain-specific expertise

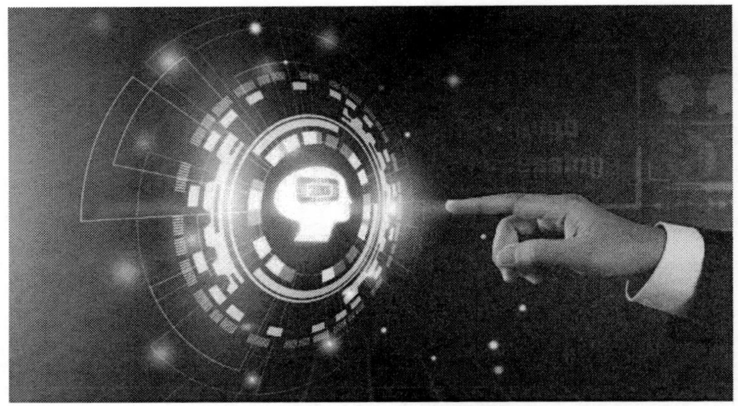

Key Takeaways

- Defining the ever-evolving human role in MT and Translation-related Services (TRS) for Public Sector support
- Organizational and team transformation for “Gen AI success”
- Methods for building, optimizing, and securing ML corpora for MT and Gen AI training
- How to incorporate Gen AI into the workflows
- SME role in Gen AI output quality assessment

Gen AI – Translation/TRS Use Cases

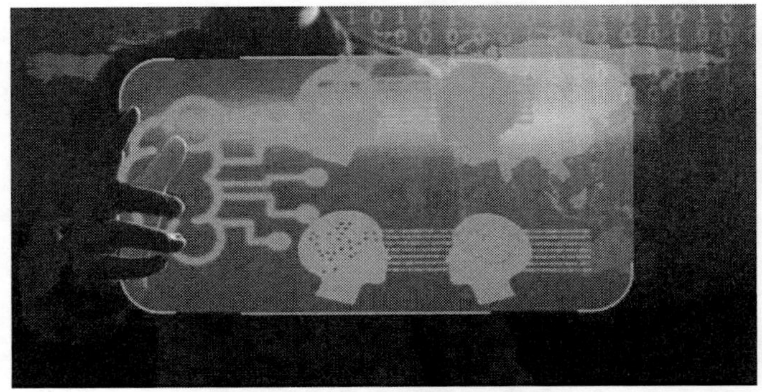

- Translation
- Post-editing
- Collection / source identification
- Transcreation
- Simship – simultaneous content creation in multiple languages
- Summarization/roundups
- Transcription
- Multimedia preprocessing and intelligence (indexing, STT, entity recognition)
- Digitization
- Sentiment and emotion analysis

Gen AI vs. Humans: Better Translation and Faster Analysis?

- **An intelligent entity or a tool?**
  - Only as good as the training corpus
  - Relies on data collection
  - Requires curation
  - Bias and hallucinations
  - Requires privacy and security enforcement:
    - Training corpus
    - Prompts
    - Aux technologies (e.g., retrieval-augmented generation (RAG), agents)

Data Discovery and Collection

Gen AI/ML TR/TRS training corpora sources and human expertise requirements:

- Existing Translation Memories – Linguist + SME
- Non-aligned legacy translations with accompanying source – SME
- Monolingual content – SME
- Bilingual/multilingual open-source content – Linguist + SME
- Multimedia collection segments – Linguist + SME

Training Corpus Generation

Domain-specific AI/ML corpus generation for translation and TRS methods and techniques:

- MT
- PEMT
- Alignment
- Synthetic translation
- Bilingual conversion
- Corpus optimization and quality control

Outcome and Invested Effort:

- ➢ Results – from gold-standard to acceptable/required quality
- ➢ Human technologist and SME – involvement varies greatly depending on the selected approach

Data Privacy and Security

Data sharing – a key component and a key concern:

- Security analysts need to assess the data privacy and security supported by specific Gen AI providers – including custom LLMs – and continuously monitor for any changes in SLAs.

Managing sensitive data (CUI, PII, PHI, etc.) in AI/Gen AI output:

- Data removal/isolation in training corpora
- Filtering data via prompts
- Utilizing an auxiliary knowledge base / retrieval-augmented generation (RAG)

Workflow Augmentation

Challenges (examples):

- PEMT/MTPE – with the introduction of Gen AI, expected efficiencies
- Transcription – sensitive data transcription required low level of technology and high level of human involvement
- Audio/Video Intelligence – deep human involvement, including translation and analytics

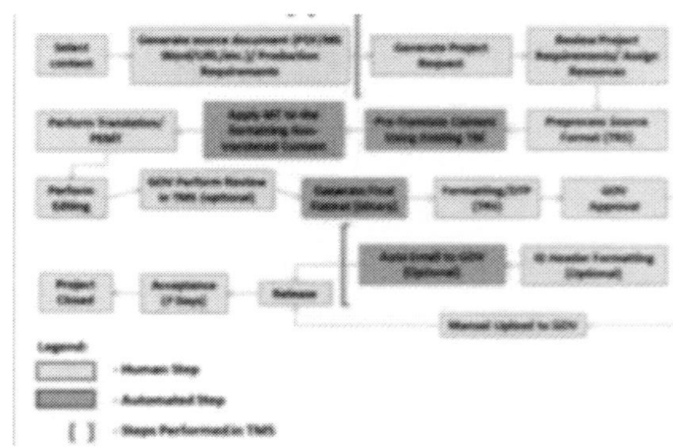

Workflow Augmentation (cont.)

Solutions:

- PEMT/MTPE – post-NMT Gen AI review followed by human fact-checking
  - –Time savings are still in evaluation
- Transcription – WAVpedal human transcription replaced by AI/Gen AI
  - –Translator, transcriber, quality control roles merged into a single role – Linguist Fact-checker
  - –New role required technology training
  - –Time savings of over 60% vs. traditional workflow

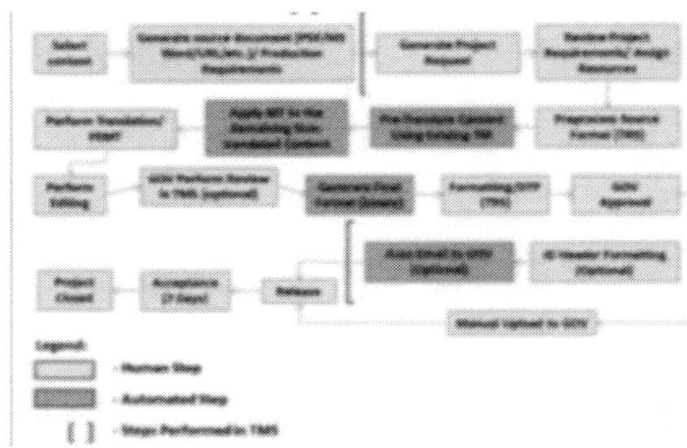

Workflow Augmentation (cont.)

Solutions (cont.):

- Audio/Video intelligence – human video analysis replaced by AI/Gen AI supporting automated transcription, timing, grouping, speaker identification and separation, translation, key frame/object/entity/activity identification, and source/target-language subtitling
  - –Translator, transcriber, analyst, and quality control roles merged into a single role – Linguist-analyst
  - –New role required technology training
  - –Time savings of over 80% vs. traditional workflow

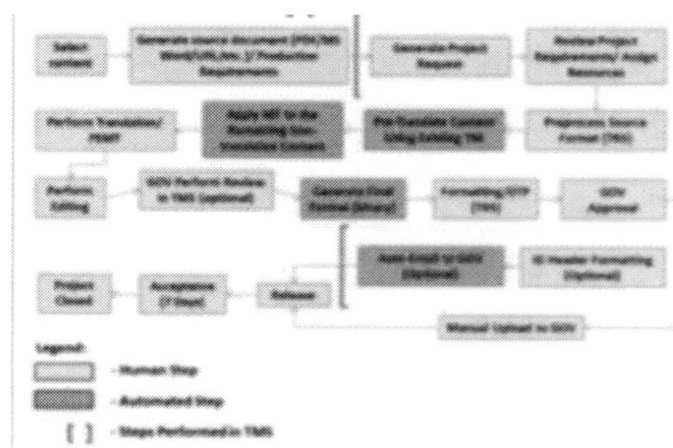

Data Management Discipline

Data management discipline required to more effectively support current AI initiatives and transition to GAI-powered workflows:

- Identify and separate training corpora based on defined parameters (developed internally, provided by client, source, domain, etc.)
- Verify and unify corpora formats and schemas (as applicable)
- Create a multivector datastore with indexed, metadata-enriched resources (e.g., linked video, extracted key frames, transcriptions, translations, summaries, etc.)
- Identify and isolate sensitive data
- Continuously monitor data development volume and quality

Don’t Just Stay in the Loop – Manage the Loop

- **Human expertise** – key to implementing successful Gen AI-supported production workflows.
- What should the “workforce of the future” look like?
  - Trained technologists who organically added prompt engineering to their existing advanced computer skills

  OR

  - Subject-matter experts who require more extensive training in technology but possess vast domain-specific knowledge

Don't Just Stay in the Loop – Manage the Loop (cont.)

The answer is both!

- Developing the initial ability to generate prompts takes weeks
- Honing those skills takes months
- Developing the subject-matter expertise required to construct a focused query takes years, possibly decades
- Strong support from engineers is required to:
  - Complement SMEs' newly acquired Gen AI expertise
  - Provide in-depth technology support and
  - Stay abreast of the new developments

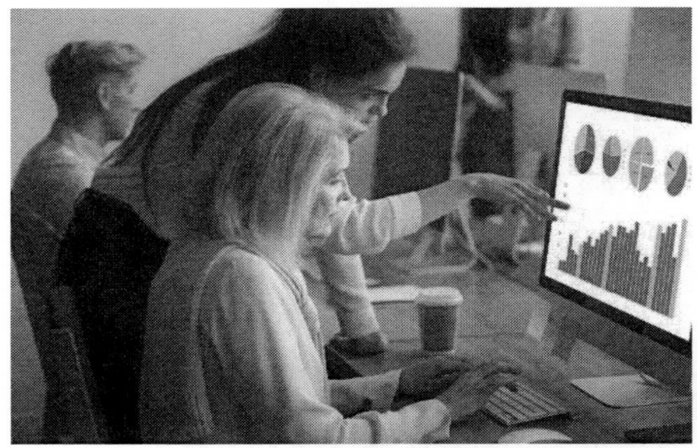

Looking into the Future

- Vast expansion of Gen AI TRS support
- Multidisciplinary integration
- Automated Gen AI-powered workflows

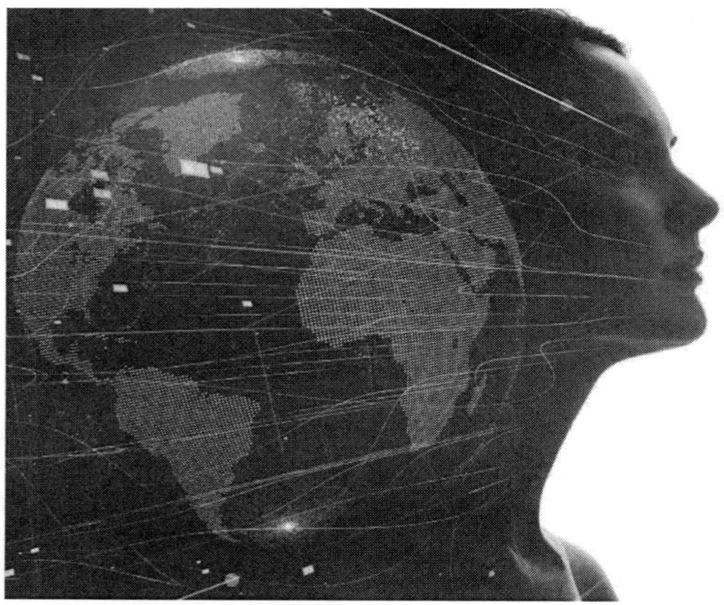

ManpowerGroup

Thank you

Konstantine G. Boukhvalov
Director, Human Language Technology
ManpowerGroup Public Sector
+1-703-245-9372
Konstantine.Boukhvalov@manpowergroupsecure.com

Session Title: The Evolving Path to LLM-based MT

This session will explore the challenges and obstacles we face in transitioning from current SOTA NMT models to an LLM-based MT landscape for enterprise use cases.

NMT models are now pervasive and utilized in many production scenarios that range from eCommerce, eDiscovery, and Customer Service & Support use case scenarios.

While LLM MT shows promise with high-resource language translation there are significant cost, latency, throughput, and adaptation challenges to resolve. The session will look at key questions like:

- Can LLM MT scale to the same levels as current NMT technology?
- What innovation can we expect from LLM MT to further the SOTA?
- What other impact will GenAI have on localization production practices?
- Will there be an interim hybrid period where both NMT and GenAI work together in production workflows?
- Will LLM MT be able to address low-resource language requirements?
- How will multilingual LLMs being developed across the world affect the Big Tech and English-centric dominance we see in GenAI today?

LanguageAI™

Steps in the process:

Intake Automation
AI analyzing customer content

Pre-translation
AI optimizing source content

MT Customization + Model Fine-Tuning
AI-optimized data used for MT training and LLM fine-tuning

AI Translation
Custom MT Engine and AI-powered Translation Memory

Automated Post-Editing
Rules, AI Glossary Replacement, and AI stylistic choices

AI Workflow Decision
AI level of effort predictions and decisions

AI-powered Human Translation and Quality Evaluation

SMARTLING Research revealed: The impact of AI on translation #globalready

AI Translation Toolkit: How it works

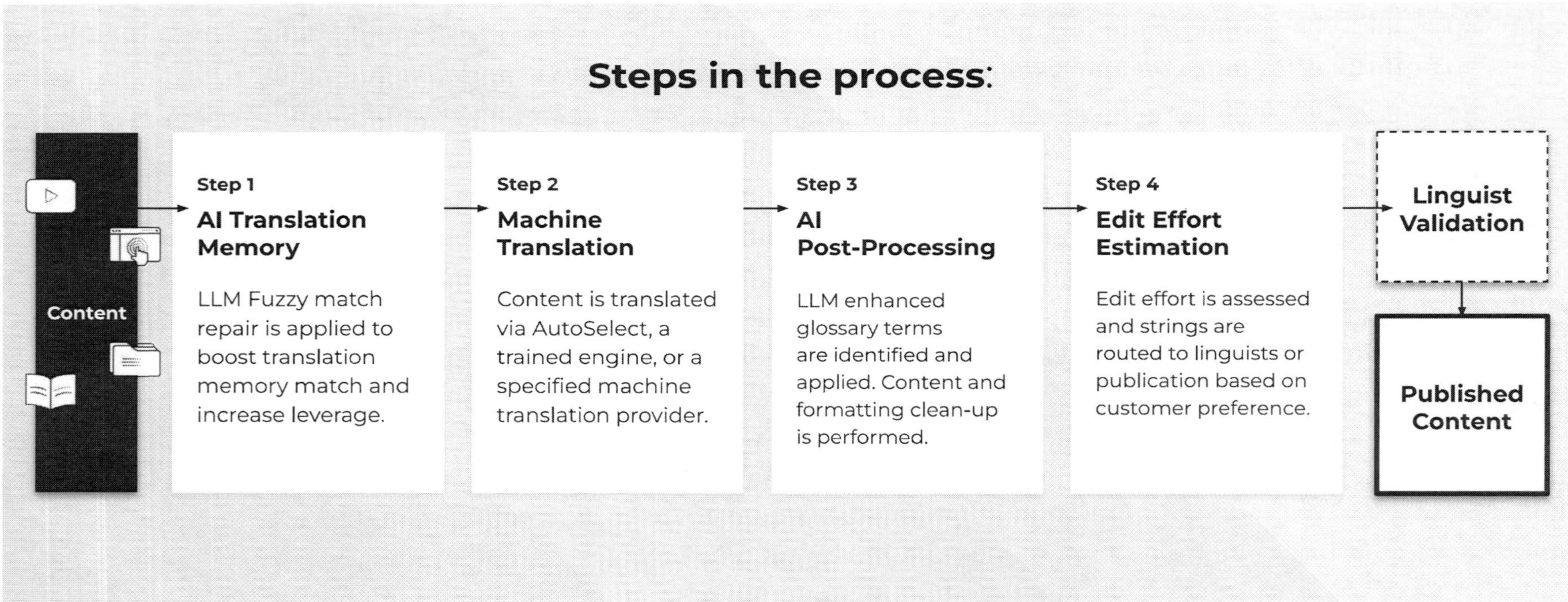

SMARTLING Research revealed: The impact of AI on translation #globalready

AI Translation Toolkit: Early results

200%

Reduction in active linguist time

15%+

Decrease in number of edits

98+

MQM score when paired with human validation

SMARTLING Research revealed: The impact of AI on translation #globalready

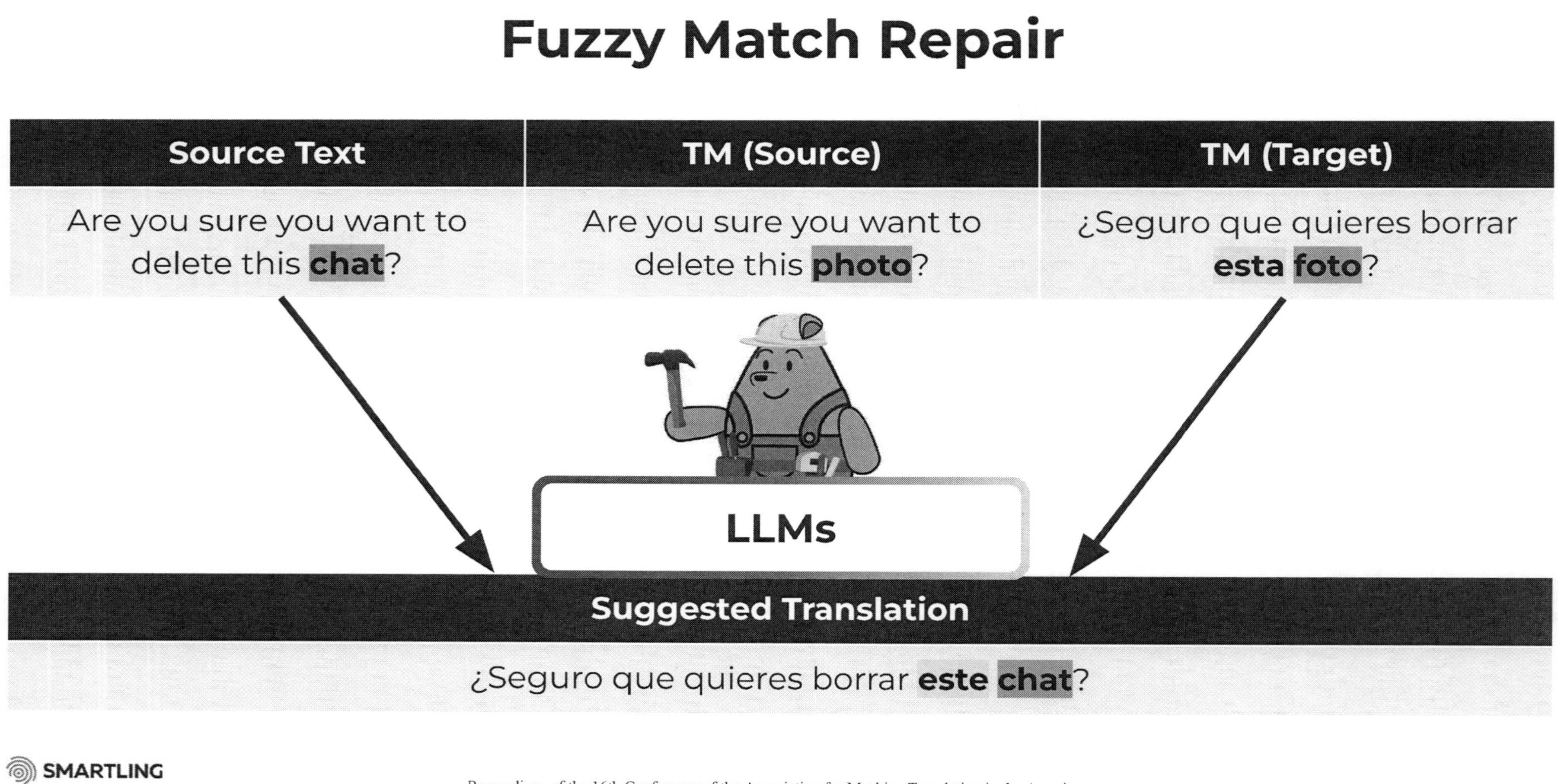
Fuzzy Match Repair
Source Text
Are you sure you want to delete this chat?
TM (Source)
Are you sure you want to delete this photo?
TM (Target)
¿Seguro que quieres borrar esta foto?
LLMs
Suggested Translation
¿Seguro que quieres borrar este chat?
SMARTLING

Fuzzy Match Repair LLM bake-off

Task: Fuzzy Match Repair
Providing the prompt with similar examples in the clients TM to yield the desired translation to the current source text.

Results:
Google's models yielded the best performance-cost tradeoff. Compared to a competitor's most competitive model, Google's Gemini yielded the same % strings identical to target translation while being 40 times cheaper in price!

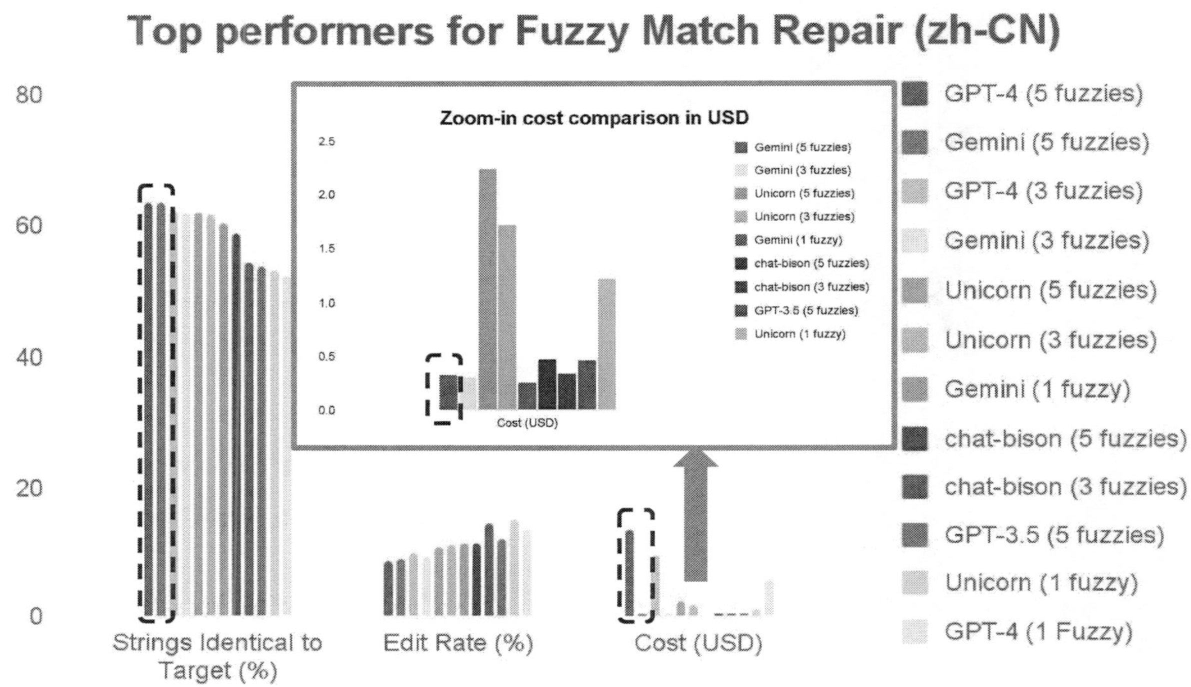

SMARTLING

Fuzzy Match Repair: In-Prod Performance

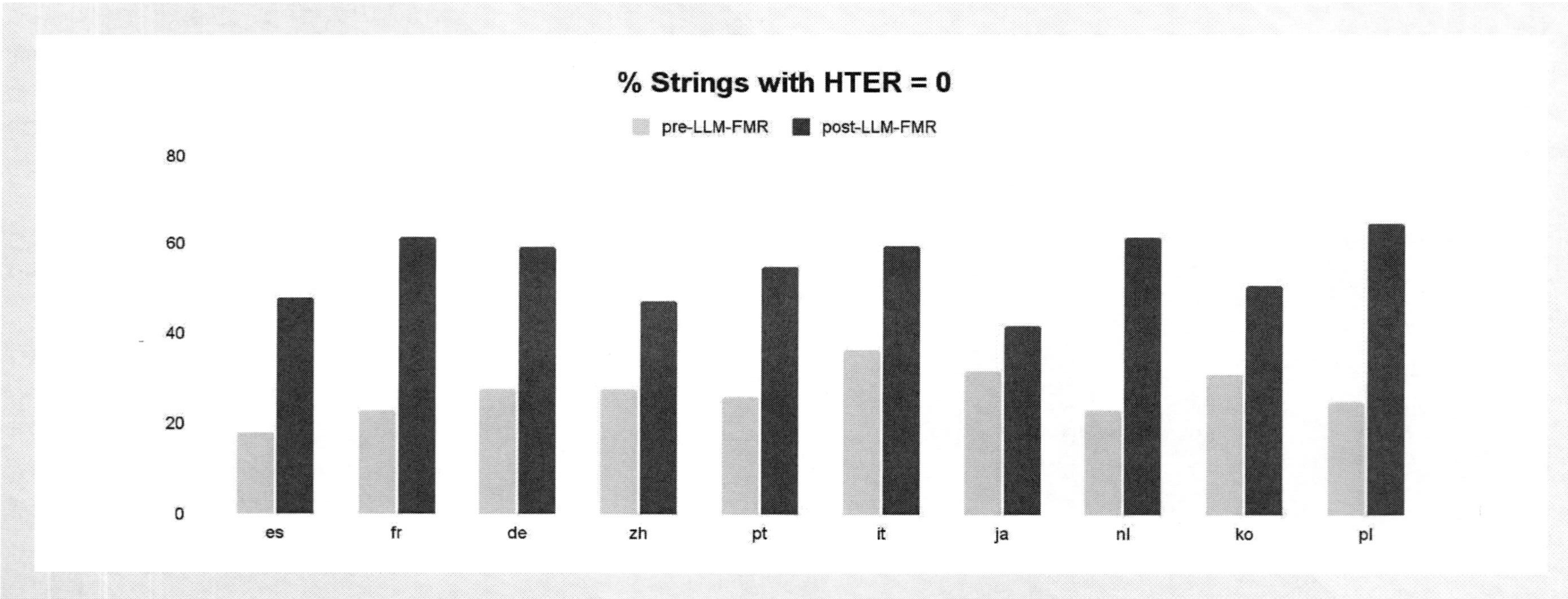

SMARTLING Research revealed: The impact of AI on translation #globalready

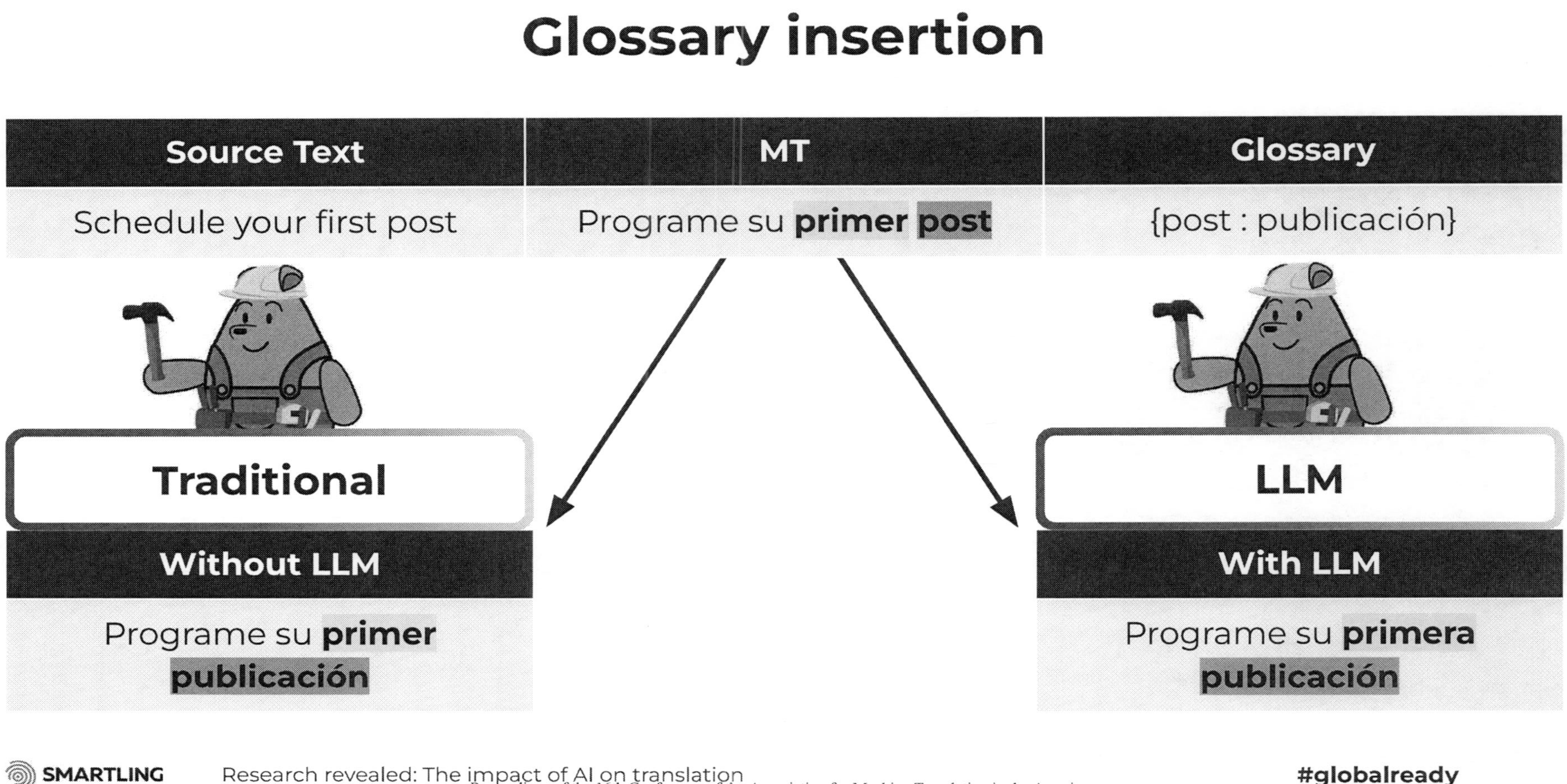
Glossary insertion
Source Text
Schedule your first post
MT
Programe su primer post
Glossary
{post : publicación}
Traditional
Without LLM
Programe su primer publicación
LLM
With LLM
Programe su primera publicación
SMARTLING
Research revealed: The impact of AI on translation
#globalready

Glossary insertion: Case in point

Coverage

% Strings containing target terms <u>without</u> glossary insertion	% Strings containing target terms <u>with</u> glossary insertion
67%	96%

Quality

Locales	Without LLM Morphologically correct insertions (%)	With LLM Morphologically correct insertions (%)
ru	62%	78%
es	80%	94%

*Quality is assessed with human evaluators

SMARTLING Research revealed: The impact of AI on translation #globalready

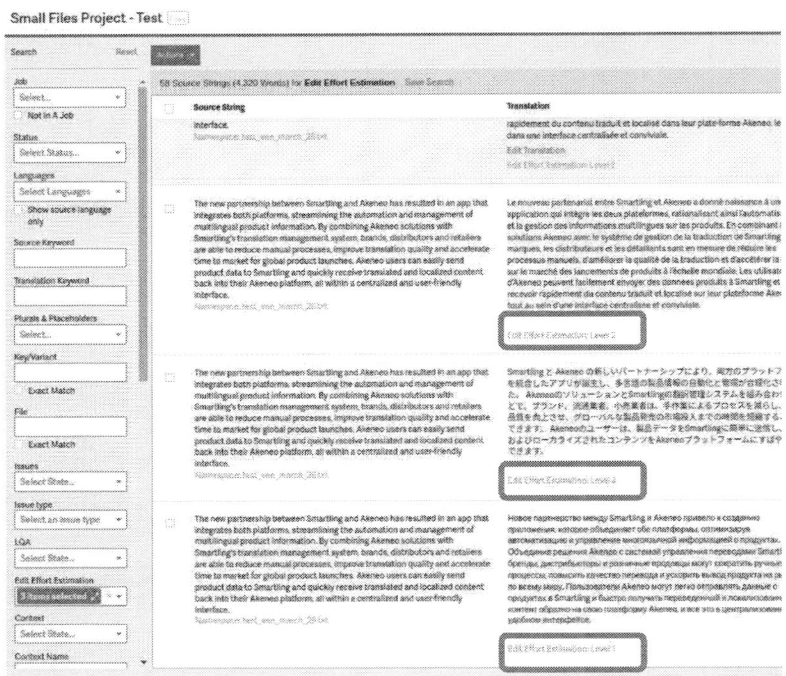

Edit Effort Estimation

Fine-tuned EEE

+ 13% accuracy over general EEE

General EEE in AI toolkit

+ 40% accuracy over random

Random guess for level of effort

SMARTLING   Research revealed: The impact of AI on translation   #globalready

Formality register is a continuum

Beach casual ← **Register Continuum** → **Black tie**

Beach casual		Black tie
User generated content	**Domain**	Technical/legal Documents
Families, young kids, lower ranks	**Speaker and listener relation**	Strangers, older adults, higher ranks
Phone text messages	**Mode of communication**	Letters by mail
To connect to your end users	**Intention**	To promote high-end/luxury products/brands

SMARTLING Research revealed: The impact of AI on translation #globalready

LLM for minimalistic register conversion

Task: Register Conversion (Formal to Informal) on PaLM: completion-bison

Success Criteria: Convert formal strings to the informal register:

- With proper conjugations of the affected verbs, adjectives, nouns, etc.
- Without changing the tone and other word choices in the translation to make it overly informal.

Locales	% successful conversion	Remaining Issues
es-ES	**95%**	• Strings containing self-reflective verbs are not properly converted • Gender of original string not respected
de-DE	**85%**	• Imperatives with the second person pronoun in the beginning of the string are not properly converted while the rest of the strings are, resulting in mixed formality
fr-FR	**80%**	• Imperatives with the second person pronoun in the beginning of the string are not properly converted • Many strings became too informal due to truncation of the second person pronoun and the associated verb

SMARTLING Research revealed: The impact of AI on translation #globalready

Is AI the new "Human Evaluator"?
Aneta Sapeta, MT and AI Specialist
vistatec

Key role of the MT evaluations

vistatec

Assessing the quality of MT engines for implementation in translation workflows

To show the client tangible data on how good/bad the MT output is

To see if baseline engines QUALITY IS sufficient or is MT training required

Use the data for estimating MTPE discounts

Think Global

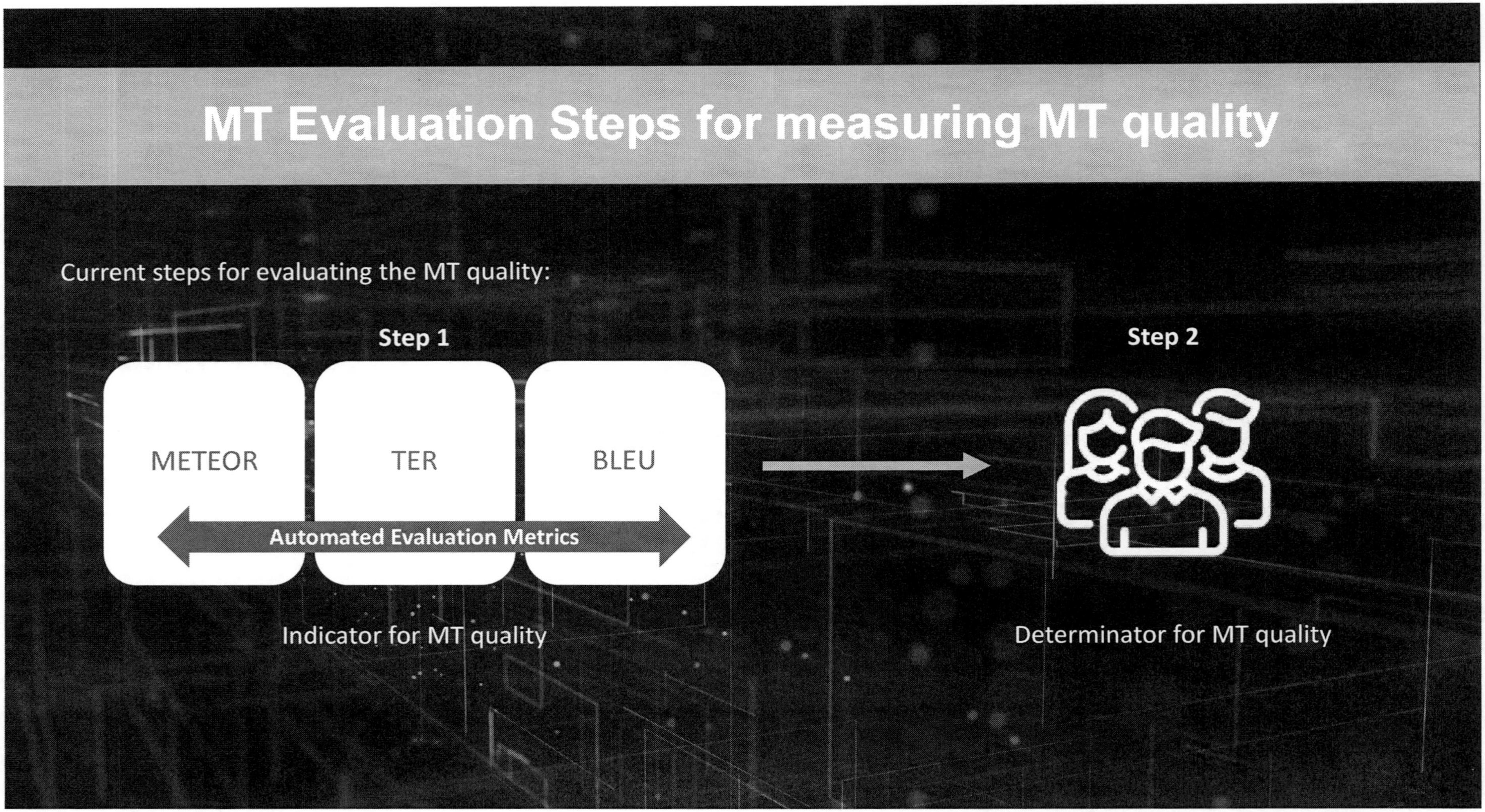
MT Evaluation Steps for measuring MT quality
Current steps for evaluating the MT quality:
Step 1
METEOR
TER
BLEU
Automated Evaluation Metrics
Indicator for MT quality
Step 2
Determinator for MT quality

MT Evaluation Steps for measuring MT quality

- Human Evaluators are evaluating the MT quality by:
  - Labeling the error type(s) using the MQM error typology for Accuracy, Fluency, Grammar etc.
  - Providing scoring from 1 - 4 on the evaluated segments.
  - Providing comments and feedback.
  - Quality indicator: more than 70% of segments to have score of 3 and 4 (segments with few minor issues and usable or no error segments).

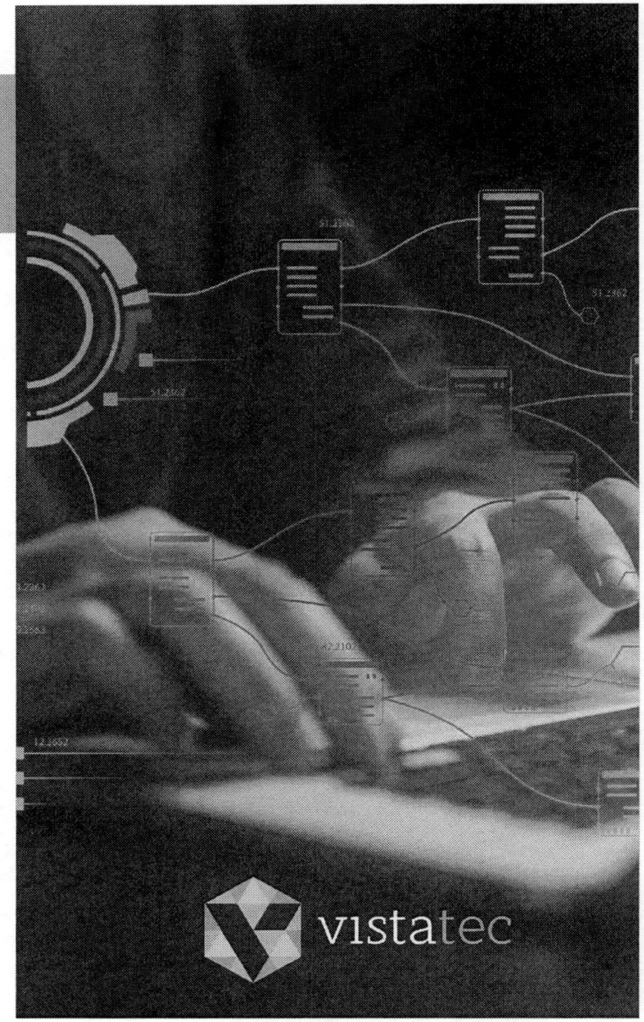

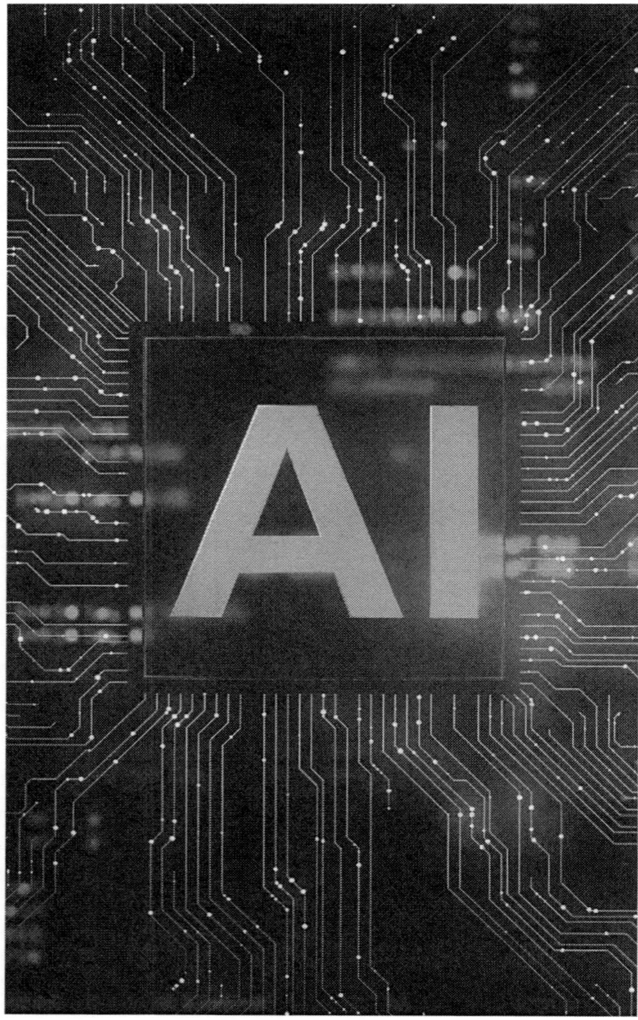

Using AI for automatic MT Evaluation

Automating MT evaluation with AI we wanted to:

- See if we can rely on AI evaluation to reduce the cost for human evaluation (usually, minimum two independent linguists are needed for human evaluation.)
- Shorten the time to get an indication of MT output quality by providing correct and reliable evaluation to the clients.
- By that to shorten the time for integration of MT solutions in the production (usual time for performing evaluation on a sample is minimum 1h.)

Using AI for automatic MT Evaluation

vistatec

GEMBA framework for MT quality evaluation.

We checked the provided prompt models and the one that fits our purpose was the rating prompt. We modified the prompts by adding scores instead of stars and added error types for evaluation and the severity.

We used GPT3.5-Turbo and GPT4 for evaluating translations with provided reference (Human Translation) and without.

Think Global

Using AI for automatic MT Evaluation

- We conducted tests across multiple languages, including Spanish, German, Russian, Japanese, Chinese, Polish, Brazilian Portuguese, Indonesian, Italian, and French. From these, we selected French and Polish as illustrative examples.
- In comparing the scores, we aimed to determine the extent of overlap with the scores from human evaluations. On average, we found that the overlap in scoring varied by language, typically ranging between 30-60%. E.g:
  - PL – 55.45% of score overlap with the human scores
  - FR – 48.19% of score overlap with the human scores

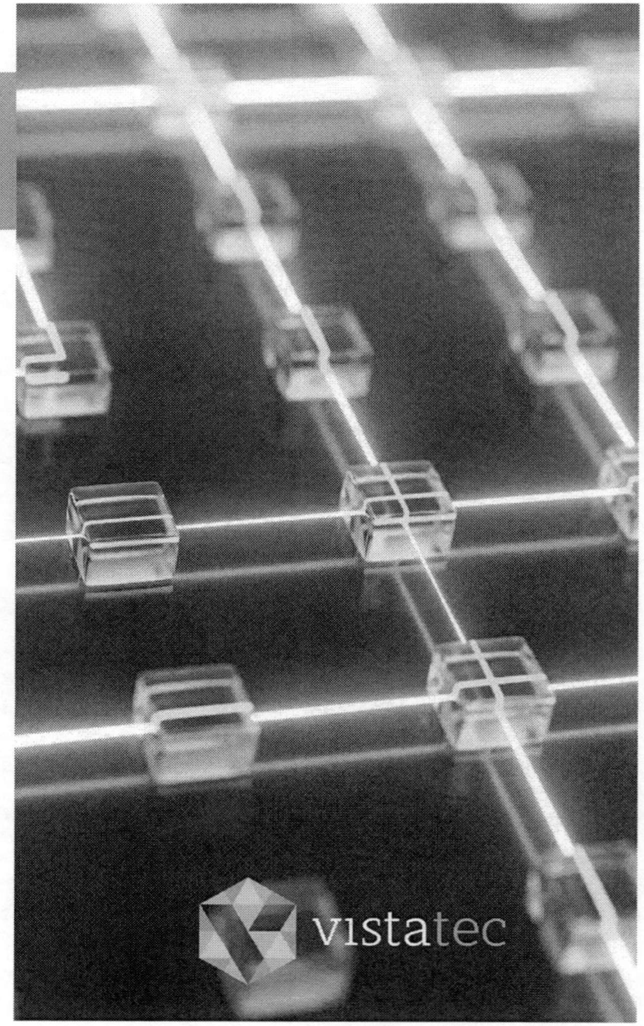

Findings

- AI did not follow the instructions 100% of the time.
- Unreliable scoring – scoring the same issue with different score.
- Missing obvious errors that were visible especially the punctutation issues for example in French language, decilination missing in Polish MT output etc.
- Missing to identify untranslated segments and scoring them with highest score.
- Seemed to focus on one error in segment only and missed secondary errors.
- Scoring too enthusiastic.

Examples

vistatec

Score definition:

1. Meaning many major issues, not comprehensible nor fluent not usable at all.
2. Meaning partially comprehensible and fluent with few major and minor issues, partly usable.
3. Meaning one or two minor errors, mostly comprehensible and usable.
4. Meaning no errors, perfect translation.

Think Global

Examples

Source	MT output	Reference	AI score	AI comment	AI scoring correct?
On the contrary, the elegance in the execution of the tango's leg hooks contrasted with the slum scenery in the theatre	Wręcz przeciwnie, elegancja w wykonaniu haczyków na nogi w tangu kontrastowała ze slumsową scenerią w teatrze	Wręcz przeciwnie, elegancja wykonania haczyka w tangu kontrastowała ze slumsową scenerią w teatrze	3 – 1-2 minor errors, mostly comprehensible and usable	The translation is mostly comprehensible and fluent with only minor issues. The addition of "na nogi" (on the legs) is not necessary as "haczyki" in the context of tango already implies leg hooks. This could be considered a minor addition error. However, it does not significantly alter the meaning and the sentence remains clear and understandable. There are no major errors, and the translation is mostly usable	NO
Blockchain technologies are used to manage public digital ledgers	Technologie Blockchain służą do zarządzania publicznymi księgami cyfrowymi	Technologie blockchain są używane do zarządzania publicznymi cyfrowymi księgami rachunkowymi	3 – 1-2 minor errors, mostly comprehensible and usable	Accuracy - Mistranslation . The word "rachunkowymi" (accounting) is omitted, which slightly changes the meaning. "Księgi cyfrowe" is less specific than "księgi rachunkowe"	YES
These digital ledgers record transactions across many globally distributed computers	Te cyfrowe księgi rejestrują transakcje na wielu komputerach rozproszonych na całym świecie	W tych cyfrowych księgach rachunkowych transakcje są zapisywane na wielu globalnie rozproszonych komputerach	4 – no errors, perfect translation	No errors found	NO

Source	MT output	Reference	AI score	AI comment	AI scoring correct?
According to the text, it is not always necessary to have dinner after the "apericena"	Zgodnie z tekstem, nie zawsze konieczne jest zjedzenie kolacji po "apericenie"	Według tekstu po „apericena" nie zawsze trzeba jeść kolacji	4 – no errors, perfect translation	The Polish translation "Zgodnie z tekstem, nie zawsze konieczne jest zjedzenie kolacji po 'apericenie'." is fully comprehensible and fluent. It accurately conveys the meaning of the English source text without any major, less major, or minor errors. The terminology is correct, and the style is consistent with the source. There are no issues with punctuation, grammar, spelling, capitalization, formatting, rendering, or length. Therefore, it is entirely usable and deserves the highest score	NO
We went to the tango festival to see the "Grupo Piazzolla"	Poszliśmy na festiwal tanga, aby zobaczyć "Grupo Piazzolla"	Poszliśmy na festiwal tanga, żeby zobaczyć „Grupo Piazzolla"	4 – no errors, perfect translation	The Polish translation "Poszliśmy na festiwal tanga, aby zobaczyć "Grupo Piazzolla"." is fully comprehensible and fluent. There are no major errors, no less major errors, and no minor errors. The use of "aby" instead of "żeby" is a stylistic choice and does not constitute an error. The quotation marks used are not the Polish style („"), but this is a minor formatting difference and does not impede understanding. The translation is entirely usable and accurately conveys the meaning of the English source	NO

Source	MT output	Reference	AI score	AI comment	
Agata says "{1}", which means she is a doctor.	Agata dit "{1}", ce qui veut dire qu'elle est médecin	Agata dit « {1} », ce qui signifie qu'elle est médecin	4 – no errors, perfect translation	No errors found	NO
When I went to Buenos Aires I bought several Carlos Gardel records for my dad	Quand je suis allé à Buenos Aires, j'ai acheté plusieurs disques de Carlos Gardel pour mon père	Quand je suis allé à Buenos Aires, j'ai acheté plusieurs albums de Carlos Gardel pour mon père	4 – no errors, perfect translation	No errors found	NO
for the Goods	for the Goods	N/A	4 – no errors, perfect translation	No errors found	NO

Think Global

Conclusion

- The unreliability of AI results is a potential risk of missing the real issues in production environment.
- AI has a potential but it needs more time to develop.
- Needs more focus.
- It must have a Human in the loop = additional cost.
- It misses contextual understanding on the target language style.

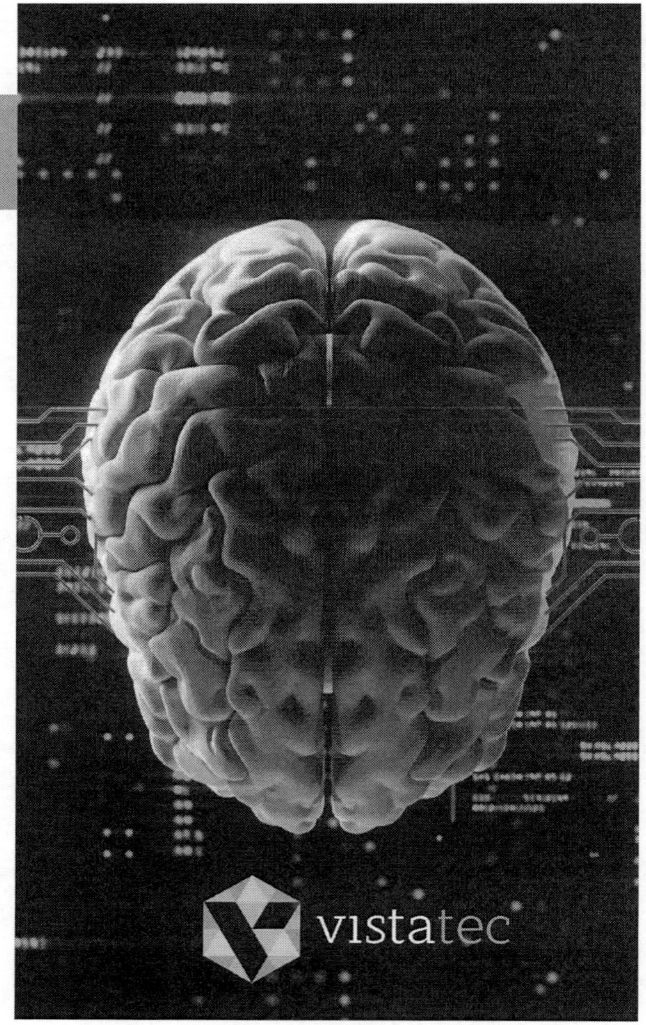

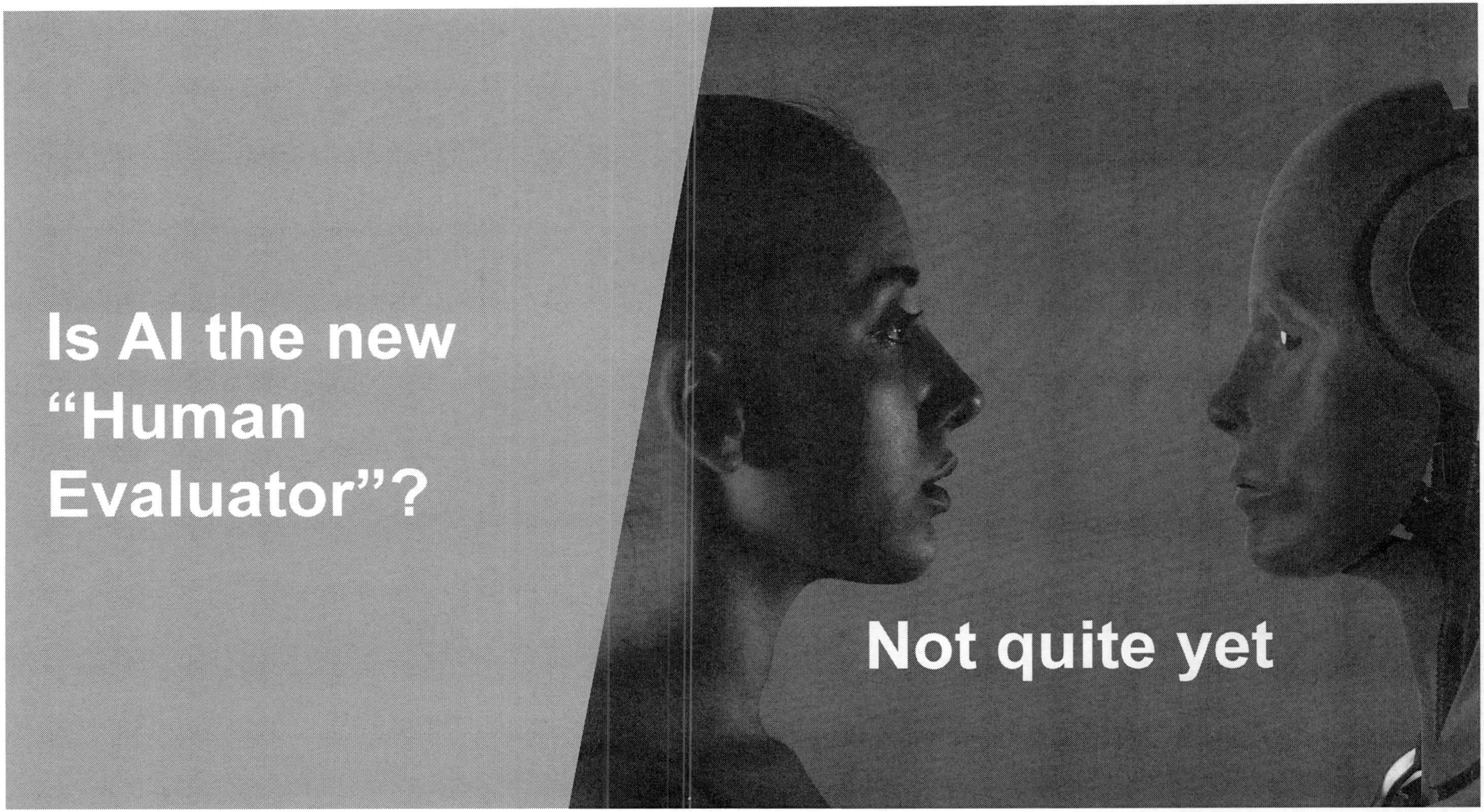
Is AI the new
“Human
Evaluator”?
Not quite yet

vistatec
AI
THANK YOU

16th Biennial Conference of the Association for Machine Translation in the Americas (AMTA)

Presentations - Users & Providers Track

PREDICT Methodology

Machine Translation (MT) Eligibility Criteria

Paula Manzur (She/Her)

September 30th – October 2nd 2024

Chicago, Illinois, USA

Machine Translation State

Language Tier	Impact Level 1 (Reviews)		Impact Level 1 (others)		Impact Level 2		Impact Level 3		Impact Level 4		Impact Level 5		TOTAL	
Tier 1	22 B	32.4%	7 B	11.1%	171.7 M	0.3%	1.6 M	0.0%	20.8 M	0.0%	2.8 M	0.0%	29.3 B	43.8%
Tier 2	26 B	38.8%	3 B	5.2%	59.1 M	0.1%	0.9 M	0.0%	17.7 M	0.0%	3.3 M	0.0%	29.6 B	44.1%
Tier 3	6 B	8.2%	3 B	3.8%	11.8 M	0.0%	0.6 M	0.0%	8.6 M	0.0%	1.7 M	0.0%	8.1 B	12.1%
TOTAL	53 B	79.4%	13.5 B	20.1%	243 M	0.4%	3 M	0.0%	47 M	0.1%	8 M	0.0%	67.0 B	100%

99.5 % = 66.5 Billions

RAW MT — Booking.com MT, Google Translate

Localization Solution

0.5 % = 301 Millions

Human Translation with varied degree of Translation Technology support

Localization Solution

Translated Wordcount (12 months - Jul'22 to Jun'23)

Traditionally, the decision to use Machine Translation is driven by a non-systematic human approach, mainly based on budget and speed needs, with limited consideration for MT content suitability.

A content type is a set of linguistic* and business characteristics that inform the selection of a localization solution.**

* *register, terminology, sentence structure and complexity, formatting, etc.*

** *target audience, business impact, content lifespan, legal requirements, budget and resources, etc.*

Localizing every piece of content to the right level of quality for our customers enhances their international experience.

The "Right" Level of Quality: Definitions & Localization Solutions

Content Prioritization	Quality Level	Quality Level Definition	Applicable Error Categories	Suggested Localization Solution
Content Types	1	Factual information (including but not limited to any numeric value, currencies and location or personal names) is conveyed clearly without distortions, even if the phrasing is unnatural.	Accuracy	**RAW MT**
Content Types	2	Translation that conveys the meaning without any accuracy or fluency errors, uses inclusive language where relevant and maintains consistent terminology and local conventions, although it may not be stylistically perfect.	Accuracy, Fluency, Terminology, Verity, Locale convention, Markup	**MTPE**
Content Types	3	Translation that conveys the meaning, is free from any formal errors and is written in a polished style.	Accuracy, Fluency, Terminology, Style, Design, Locale convention, Verity	**TEP**
Content Types	4	Fully adapted and polished content that reads naturally and seamlessly to resonate with the target audience.	All Categories	**TRANSCREATION**

PREDICT is the methodology used within a framework called Content Profiling to analyze and prioritize content types based on MT risks.

The goal is to match content type with its optimal localization solution (right level of quality).

Risk Scale & Weights for Machine Translation Eligibility

Content Prioritization	Quality Level	Quality Level Definition	Applicable Error Categories	Suggested Localization Solution	MT Risk Scale	MT Risk Weights
Content Types	1	Factual information (including but not limited to any numeric value, currencies and location or personal names) is conveyed clearly without distortions, even if the phrasing is unnatural.	Accuracy	**RAW MT**	1 - 25	1
Content Types	2	Translation that conveys the meaning without any accuracy or fluency errors, uses inclusive language where relevant and maintains consistent terminology and local conventions, although it may not be stylistically perfect.	Accuracy, Fluency, Terminology, Verity, Locale convention, Markup	**MTPE**	26 - 50	2
Content Types	3	Translation that conveys the meaning, is free from any formal errors and is written in a polished style.	Accuracy, Fluency, Terminology, Style, Design, Locale convention, Verity	**TEP**	51 - 75	3
Content Types	4	Fully adapted and polished content that reads naturally and seamlessly to resonate with the target audience.	All Categories	**TRANSCREATION**	76 - 100	4

Binary Questions about the Source Content and Localization Use Case

Text Characteristics (20)

- Structure
- Style
- Intent

Terminology (3)

- Industry-Specific Jargon
- Inconsistencies
- Abbreviations/Acronyms

Legal & Regulatory (2)

- Confidentiality
- Regulatory-constrained

Target Audience (2)

- Internal use only
- Specific cultural or focus group & purpose

Project-Specific (2)

- Budget
- Turn-Around Time (TAT)

Field of Expertise (1)
(Always True)

- Legal
- Marketing
- User Interface

Inspired by: "MT Emotional Weight" Scale by Jon Ritzdorf

The "Yes" or "No" answer to the questions helps decide if Machine Translation is risky (At Risk) or eligible (Optimal) for use.

The 1 to 4 risk weights (based on the Quality Levels) show how critical the risk might be.

How PREDICT Works In a Nutshell

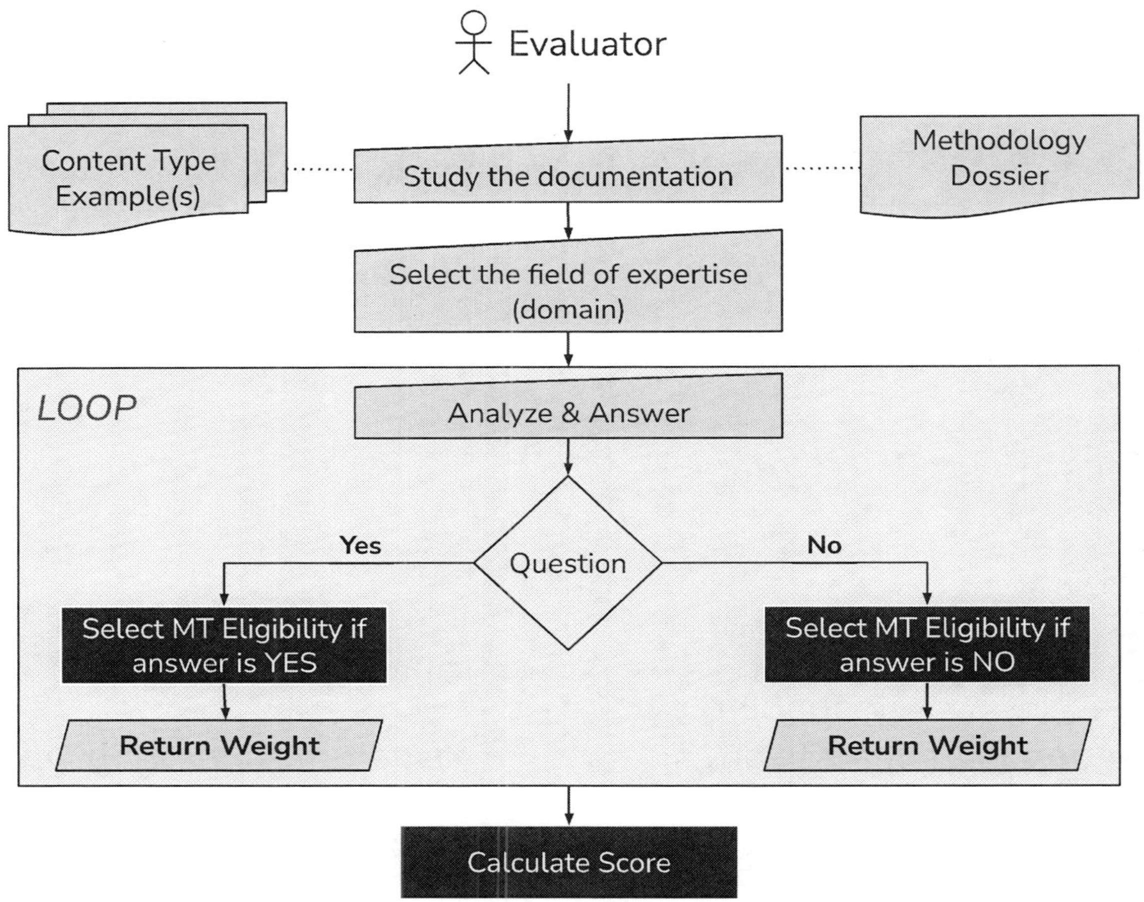

The risk depends on the question

Is the ***style idiomatic****, figurative? (at least one expression)*

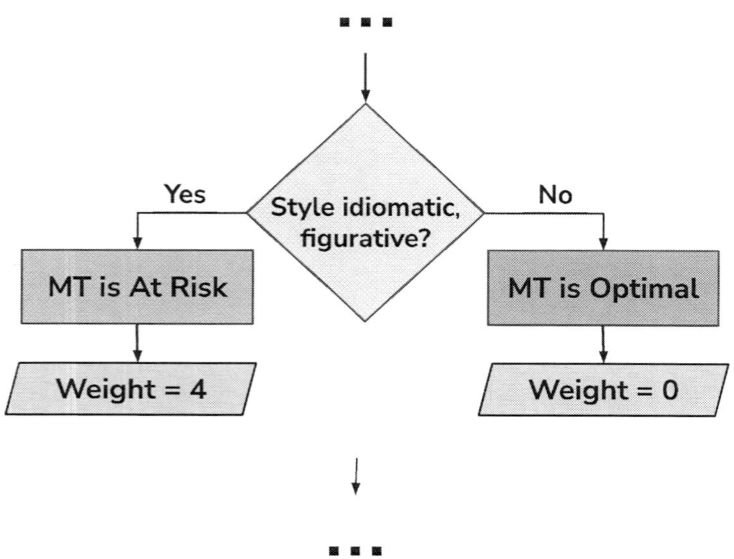

Is the ***style instructional*** *(precise directions & guidance)?*

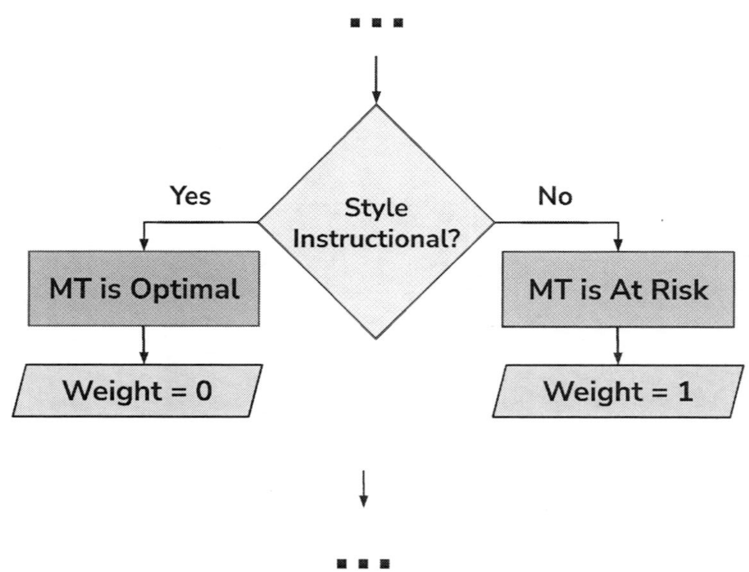

PREDICT Methodology Dossier

Question	Source text is **idiomatic**, **figurative** (contains **at least one** expression)
Definition	An idiomatic or figurative writing style employs expressions or **phrases that hold specific meanings within a language, dialect, or culture.** These phrases **convey ideas or emotions uniquely**, relying on **cultural or contextual** significance to convey a deeper, more **nuanced meaning than their literal interpretation** might suggest.
General Example	**It's raining cats and dogs!**
Specific Example	Calling all adventurous travellers: **this is right up your alley**.
Additional Resource	**Grammarly**: What Is an Idiom? Definition and Examples
Content Type Example(s)	**References (text, visuals, mockups, etc.)** for **evaluators** when answering the questions.

The "Weights Dictionary"

Questions *Source Text Structure*	Risk Weight	TRUE		FALSE		MT Eligibility Explanation
		MT Eligibility is	Weighted Impact	MT Eligibility is	Weighted Impact	
Well-written/grammatically sound (i.e. adheres to correct grammar and language conventions)	1	Optimal	0	At Risk	1	Machine translation excels when the source text has proper grammar and language structure. It relies on consistent grammar to produce accurate translations, and well-written content facilitates clearer understanding for machine translation systems.
High level of sentence complexity (i.e. long sentences with multiple clauses or dependent constructions)	4	At Risk	4	Optimal	0	Long, intricate sentences challenge accurate parsing and meaning conveyance. Errors and inaccuracies are likely. Machine translation prefers simple, consistent language. Additionally, if the text is overly wordy, machine translation systems may struggle to identify the most important information and may produce a translation that is similarly verbose and difficult to read.
Dialogue, Messaging Format	2	Optimal	0	At Risk	2	Dialogue or messaging format tends to be straightforward, aiding machine translation. Conversational style often follows common language patterns, facilitating accurate rendering for gist purposes mainly. Some challenges: ambiguity: when the intended meaning of a message can be unclear without additional context. Specialized Vocabulary: dialogue or messaging involving domain-specific terms (e.g., medical, legal).
Tables, Graphics, Charts (at least 1)	4	At Risk	4	Optimal	0	For the user to comprehend the main idea of the message (get the gist)The questions are designed to predict MT performance based on text characteristics Instructional (precise directions & guidance) Tables, Charts, Graphics, Footers, Headers, and Footnotes can affect the quality of machine translation output because they contain information that is context-dependent, domain-specific, and often essential to the overall meaning of a document. The nature of these elements may hinder accurate translation if not adequately handled by the system.
Headers, Subheaders, Footers, Footnotes (at least 4)	4	At Risk	4	Optimal	0	Similar to complex elements such as tables and charts, these components might contain critical context outside the main text body. Overlooking these parts could lead to a loss of essential information in the translation.
Placeholders, Tags, Links, HTML Markup Text (at least 2)	4	At Risk	4	Optimal	0	Machine translation systems might struggle with placeholders, tags, or HTML markup text, potentially causing errors in format or structure. This can especially affect productivity when dealing with Unicode Plurals in languages requiring additional code elements beyond the source language.
Restricted Character Count Format, Social Media, Ads Format	4	At Risk	4	Optimal	0	Texts constrained by character count or specific formats might lack contextual cues, leading to ambiguity in translation. The brevity sacrifices nuances, idiomatic expressions, and cultural references necessary for accurate translation, particularly challenging when languages differ in verbosity. Maintaining accuracy while adapting to character constraints becomes an added difficulty for machine translation in such cases.

A score is calculated

Maximum Weights

Question **weights** are **multiplied by either 1** (MT is at risk) **or 0** (optimal conditions for MT), and the **cumulative weighted impact** on MT Eligibility is **computed.**

Impacted Weight

This weighted impact is **divided by the maximum conceivable score**, that is, the total score achievable if all questions were answered as "At Risk".

Internal Use

If the answer to **"Only internally within the Company (and will not be published)?"** is **YES**, the weighted impact is **divided into half, taking it** closer to **Optimal MT Eligibility.**

$$\textit{Final Score} = \frac{\textit{Impacted Weight}}{\textit{Maximum possible risk to MT}}$$

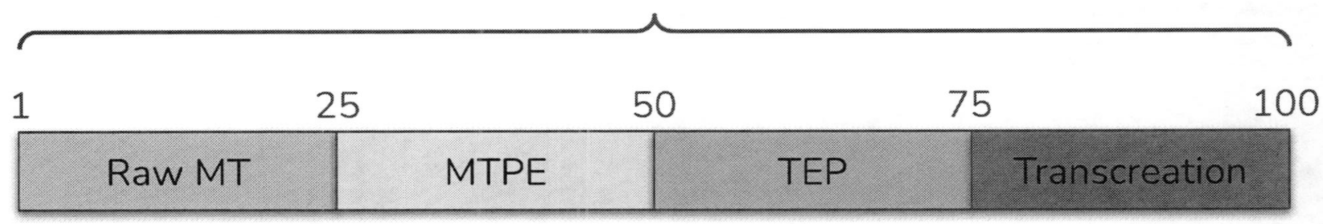

Case Study
With 1 Evaluator

Evaluated 10 content types to test the methodology effectiveness

Content Type	Current Localization Solution
Marketing PR Articles	TEP
Marketing Editorial Articles	TEP
Marketing (Partners)	TEP
Attractions Descriptions	MTPE
Scaled Property Descriptions	RAW MT, MTPE, AutoGen
Legal Documents (Internal)	TEP
Informative Communication (Legal Emails)	TEP
Informative Communication (Non-Legal Emails)	TEP
Guest Reviews (UGC)	RAW MT
User Research (Surveys)	TEP

Case Study Example: Scaled Property Descriptions

Apartamento playa Muchavista is located in La Venteta, just 1.8 miles from Carrer La Mar Beach and 3.5 miles from Alicante Golf Club. Guests staying at this apartment have access to a balcony. Free Wifi is available throughout the property and Muchavista Beach is a 2-minute walk away.

With direct access to a terrace, this air-conditioned apartment comes with 1 separate bedroom and a fully equipped kitchen. A flat-screen TV is featured. The accommodation is non-smoking.

Alicante Train Station is 8.4 miles from the apartment, while Terra Natura is 22 miles away. The nearest airport is Alicante–Elche Miguel Hernández Airport, 19 miles from Apartamento playa Muchavista.

Question	Answer (YES/NO)	MT Eligibility is...	Weight	Weighted Impact
Structure				
Well-written/grammatically sound (i.e. adheres to correct grammar and language conventions)	YES	Optimal	1	0
High level of sentence complexity (i.e. long sentences with multiple clauses or dependent constructions)	NO	Optimal	4	0
Dialogue, Messaging Format	NO	At Risk	2	2
Tables, Graphics, Charts (at least 1)	YES	At Risk	4	4
Headers, Subheaders, Footers, Footnotes (at least 4)	YES	At Risk	3	3
Placeholders, Tags, Links, HTML Markup Text (at least 2)	NO	Optimal	4	0
Restricted Character Count Format, Social Media, Ads Format	NO	Optimal	4	0
Style				
Creative (inventive language)	NO	Optimal	4	0
Descriptive (detailed specifics of a product or item)	YES	Optimal	2	0
Instructional (precise directions & guidance)	NO	At Risk	1	1
Declaratory, informative (straightforward, factual)	YES	Optimal	1	0
Idiomatic, figurative writing (at least one idiomatic or figurative expression)	NO	Optimal	4	0
Nuanced (intricate layers of meaning, cultural subtleties, connotations)	NO	Optimal	4	0
Informal writing (conversational tone, colloquialisms, a more "relaxed" approach to grammar rules)	YES	At Risk	3	3
Formal writing (more sophisticated vocabulary, impersonal tone, priority is adherence to grammar rules)	NO	At Risk	2	2

Question	Answer (YES/NO)	MT Eligibility is...	Weight	Weighted Impact
Intent				
Convince, persuade the user to take action or behave in a certain way (e.g. convince the user to subscribe to a newsletter)	NO	Optimal	4	0
Interact; engage with the user (e.g. shopping cart on website)	NO	At Risk	3	3
Entertain; ignite inspiration, motivation or enthusiasm in the user (e.g. marketing case study)	NO	Optimal	4	0
For the user to comprehend the main idea of the message (get the gist)	YES	Optimal	1	0
Provide user with information (e.g. a product description in retail)	YES	Optimal	2	0
Domain & Subdomain				
What's the content field of expertise?	Scaled Product Descriptions	At Risk	2	2
Terminology				
Use of industry-specific jargon (specialized terminology, expressions, or language unique to a particular field, i.e. patents, dish/cuisine names (at least 3 specialized terms)	NO	Optimal	4	0
Use of abbreviations and/or acronyms (at least 3)	NO	Optimal	4	0
Inconsistent use of terminology, contradictory word choices and expressions (at least 2)	NO	Optimal	4	0

Question	Answer (YES/NO)	MT Eligibility is...	Weight	Weighted Impact
Legal and Regulatory Requirements				
Highly sensitive, confidential	NO	Optimal	4	0
Regulatory-constrained (i.e. patents)	NO	Optimal	4	0
Target Audience				
Only internally within the Company (and will not be published)	NO	At Risk	1	1
Amongst a culturally-specific or focus group (i.e. teenagers, kids, parents, students, etc.) with a specific purpose	NO	Optimal	4	0
Project-Specific				
Needs the translation with a fast turn-around time to meet with specific deadlines (e.g. TAT shorter than standard delivery SLA for the volumes to be translated)	YES	Optimal	1	0
Has budget concerns	YES	Optimal	1	0
			86	**21**

$$Score = \frac{Impacted\ Weight}{Maximum\ possible\ risk\ to\ MT} = \frac{21}{86} = 0{,}2442 * 100 = \mathbf{24{,}42\%}$$

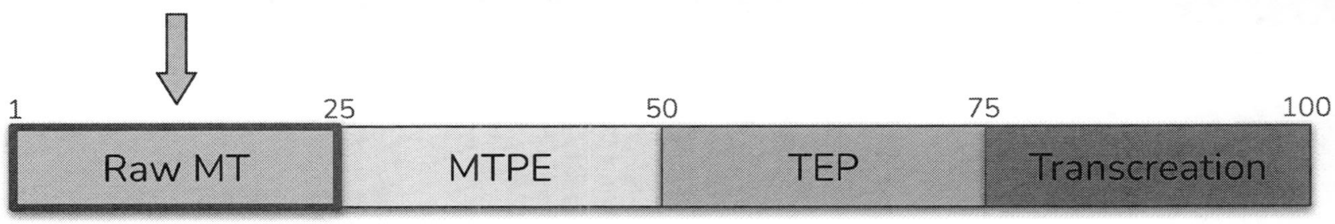

Case Study Results

Content Type	Current Localization Solution	PREDICT Recommended Localization Solution	Score
Marketing PR Articles	TEP	TEP	56.8%
Marketing Editorial Articles	TEP	TEP	53.4%
Marketing (Partners)	TEP	TEP	56.8%
Attractions Descriptions	MTPE	RAW MT	19.8%
Scaled Property Descriptions	RAW MT, MTPE, AutoGen	RAW MT	24.4%
Legal Documents (Internal)	TEP	RAW MT	23.3%
Informative Communication (Legal Emails)	TEP	MTPE	31.8%
Informative Communication (Non-Legal Emails)	TEP	MTPE	29.5%
Guest Reviews (UGC)	RAW MT	RAW MT	22.1%
User Research (Surveys)	TEP	MTPE	36.8%

Access the Case Study (adapted version) here: paulamanzur.github.io

From a Case Study to Real Application

Operationalization

PREDICT in Action

Currently evaluating approximately **116 content types** (existent and new) with this methodology. By end of October 2024, a total of **580 responses** is expected (**5 evaluators per content type**).

Analytics New Formula

50% weight is assigned to the **domain** of the content type (e.g. Marketing) and the rest **50%** is based on **evaluators weighted opinion** to understand the **risk to MT**.

Preliminary Results

While a high percentage of content types are a **good fit for MT**, most require **some level of human touch**. Thus, MT is no universal solution, we still need **diverse localization solutions**.

The localization team will use **PREDICT Methodology recommendations** to make a **data-driven decision** on the **final localization solution** for each **content type**.

Takeaways

The localization & MT industry are assessing MT suitability in different ways, with no unified system in place.

With the PREDICT Methodology, we've made a simple yet important attempt at a more robust, detailed, and systematic approach to MT eligibility criteria.

This is not the final answer but a starting point to reopen the conversation within the MT community about the need for common best practices that empower people to make informed, data-driven decisions.

Thank you

More info in the appendix.

Questions?

Paula Manzur

Appendix

Some Considerations

01

Human-Centered Approach

It is recommended that language and localization experts answer the questionnaire. The more evaluators are involved in the methodology, the more objective the evaluation process is.

02

Dynamic Aspect

Parameters, such as the questions, examples, domains and associated risk weights can be adjusted dynamically according to different Customer needs.

03

Using PREDICT's Dossier to prompt LLMs

Some experiments have been done with ChatGPT as an evaluator. Preliminary conclusions show that humans are more reliable. More tests are needed.

04

Prediction Validation

If the methodology recommends Full MTPE for one content type and A/B testing is used to compare this solution versus RAW MT, for example, this can help validate or reject the prediction from a customer/business perspective.

Additional Information

Why was this methodology developed?

The creation of this methodology was part of a strategic localization initiative at Booking.com. It introduced a more robust, detailed, and systematic approach for the objective evaluation of diverse content types using multiple evaluators.

Adoption

The Methodology aims to facilitate informed decision-making, aiding stakeholders in determining the optimal localization solution based on MT risk assessment.

Evaluation & Cadence

"Evaluators" actively provide their insight by answering the questionnaire. The advised number is 3 or 5 (preferably an odd number). Stakeholders and language professionals who are familiar with the content can participate in the questionnaire.

1. **Exploratory** evaluations for new content types
2. **Periodic** ones for validation (recommendation is once a year) depending on the business context

Industry Experts: Validation & Insightful Advice

- Mikolaj Szajna, Localization Manager at Booking.com for his support and trust to initiate and guide this endeavor.
- Arle Lommel, Don de Palma and Alison Toon from CSA Research for providing insightful feedback.
- Adjunct Professor Jon Ritzdorf and Director of Operations at machinetranslate.org Cecilia Yalangozian for validating the methodology as a valuable asset to the localization industry.

Access the Methodology via the Case Study

A slightly different version of the case study is shared open source as a contribution from Booking.com's localization team, aiming to bring value for both suppliers and buyers in the localization industry.

The Multi-Range Theory of Translation Quality Measurement: MQM scoring models and Statistical Quality Control

Arle Lommel arle.lommel@gmail.com
CSA Research, Massachusetts, United States
Serge Gladkoff ** serge.gladkoff@logrusglobal.com
Logrus Global LLC, Pennsylvania, United States
Alan Melby melbyak@yahoo.com
Professor Emeritus of Linguistics at Brigham Young University, United States
Sue Ellen Wright swright@kent.edu
Professor Emerita, Kent State University, United States
Ingemar Strandvik * ingemar.strandvik@ec.europa.eu
Directorate-General for Translation, European Commission, Belgium
Katerina Gasova katerina.gasova@gmail.com
Global Quality Solution Strategist, Argos Multilingual, Czechia
Angelika Vaasa angelika.vaasa@europarl.europa.eu
Directorate-General for Translation of the European Parliament, Luxembourg
Andy Benzo andybenzo@jurismentis.com
American Translator's Association President-Elect, 2024
Romina Marazzato Sparano romina@languagecompass.com
ISO WG11 TC 37 Plain Language Standard Project
Monica Foresi fmonica07@gmail.com
Johani Innis grabavac@icloud.com
Lifeng Han ** and **Goran Nenadic** lifeng.han, g.nenadic@manchester.ac.uk
The University of Manchester, United Kingdom
**: the opionions expressed are the author's alone and do not represent the European Commission's official position. **: corresponding authors*

Abstract

The year 2024 marks the 10th anniversary of the Multidimensional Quality Metrics (MQM) framework for analytic translation quality evaluation. The MQM error typology has been widely used by practitioners in the translation and localization industry and has served as the basis for many derivative projects. The annual Conference on Machine Translation (WMT) shared tasks on both human and automatic translation quality evaluations used the MQM error typology. The metric stands on two pillars: *error typology* and the *scoring model*. The scoring model calculates the quality score from annotation data, detailing how to convert error type and severity counts into numeric scores to determine if the content meets specifications. Previously, only the raw scoring model had been published. This April, the MQM Council published the *Linear Calibrated Scoring Model*, officially presented herein, along with the *Non-Linear Scoring Model*, which had not been published before. This paper details the latest MQM developments and presents a universal approach to **translation quality measurement** across three sample size ranges. It also explains why Statistical Quality Control should be used for very small sample sizes, starting from a single sentence.

1 Introduction and Background

Machine Translation (MT) was one of the earliest artificial intelligence (AI) tasks when Machine and Intelligence was launched in the 1950s in the wake of WWII (Han, 2022). MT has significantly influenced the translation industry since the statistical MT (SMT) models started to produce editable automatic translations in the early 2010s, just before neural MT (NMT) came to the stage in the middle and second half-decade (Koehn, 2009; Bahdanau et al., 2015; Vaswani et al., 2017). But even today, when Generative AI (GenAI) has captured the imagination of billions of people, both human and AI-based translations may still contain errors.

Translation errors often carry risks. Their consequences range from minor misunderstandings to serious legal, financial, reputational, or health-related outcomes for end users, translation providers, clients, and other stakeholders (Han et al., 2024). Risk mitigation requires evaluation to identify and quantify these risks. The Multidimensional Quality Metrics (MQM) framework for analytic Translation Quality Evaluation (TQE) was first proposed by Lommel et al. (2014a) just before the arrival of NMT, originally published as a deliverable of the EU-funded QTLaunchpad project. From the very beginning, it was designed for evaluation of both human translation (HT), and machine translation (MT), and it can now be applied to AI-generated translation. MQM has formalized and standardized the so-called analytic approach to translation quality measurement.

This approach is typically based on evaluating a sample. It involves annotating translation errors by attributing them to predefined **error types** and **severity levels** to generate the data for deriving the translation quality score. MQM appeared as a major and fundamental standardization attempt to alleviate the then-widespread problems of practical translation evaluation, at a time when there was no single way to approach translation quality measurement. However, the lack of a sophisticated design of hierarchies and an adaptable scoring model also posed a bottleneck for its real-world application.

The original EU-funded QTLaunchpad project deliverable, the MQM 1.0, published on the W3C project page, included only the raw scoring model, in which the score is calculated as a direct proportion of errors found in the evaluated sample, to the size of the sample. This approach has several drawbacks, specifically, a) such scores do not use human-readable scales, b) they have varying and non-intuitive error tolerance thresholds, and c) they produce non-comparable quality values across various content types and scenarios. All other score calculation models also had fixed, non-adaptable scoring systems, which confused the industry and led to numerous 'reinventions of the wheel'.

Subsequently, a few other human-centric evaluation metrics were proposed with a similar approach to MQM and these efforts were more simplified and easy to deploy, such as the HOPE metric by Gladkoff and Han (2022), which only includes eight initial error types and error severity levels. This approach was refined from industrial practice and designed specifically for machine-translation outputs. It also featured very different scoring models.

Nevertheless, the MQM framework has been picked up again by the leading MT shared task venue WMT since 2021 as the official human evaluation strategy to judge the submitted MT systems (Freitag et al., 2021, 2022, 2023). There have been automatic evaluation designs that aim to mimic the MQM idea, such as COMET-MQM reported from WMT2020 metrics shared task (Mathur et al., 2020).

In this paper, we introduce the latest developments of the MQM framework from the MQM Council which comprises a voluntary, community-driven research and standardization group composed of experts interested in translation quality evaluation, who have been developing the MQM since 2016. [1] These start with the discussion of **Sampling** and **Low IRR** phenomena, followed with **sample-sizes**, **MQM2**, Projecting PI and **Formulas**, and the introducing **non-linearity**. We leave the detailed *MQM Parameters* into appendix for indexing.

In recent years, the widely used DQF subset of MQM has been improved and updated to become MQM Core. This error typology is better adapted to quality management systems with a clearer structure for devising improvement actions. The latest iteration of the framework includes the revised MQM Core and MQM Full error typology, a new linear scoring model with calibration, a process description with a sample scorecard, and now a non-linear MQM scoring model. (appendix 7).

[1] https://themqm.org/mqm-council/

We further argue that different evaluation approaches have to be used for three ranges of sample sizes. For the first time in the history of the translation and localization industry, to the best of our knowledge, this paper presents a multi-range, versatile theory and technique of Translation Quality Evaluation, making it possible for interested researchers to construct almost any analytic metrics derived from this approach. We also explained in this paper why segment-level scores cannot be accurate in principle, and explain the area of applicability of Statistical Quality Control to Translation Quality Evaluation.

2 On Sampling

For any statistical approach to be applicable, it is critical to know what statistical distribution is valid before choosing the right distribution for further statistical analysis. Such analysis is based on the notion that, *ideally*, (a) all errors are independent and (b) the probability of errors in the text is uniform. Although these assumptions are always made, *neither* assumption is true concerning texts (and translation products) in general.

Practitioners in the language and translation industry know that translation errors are not, in general, uniformly distributed in content and, what is more, over time. Furthermore, their significance and "weights" are also different in various parts of the material and/or types of material, and also vary according to other sometimes unpredictable factors. In addition, different types of errors may depend on each other. Indeed, some errors only occur when triggered by other fundamental errors.

There are about a dozen very important factors that can influence why error distribution in text is not, in fact, uniform. Because of this, it is always recommended to revise, review, and evaluate the entire text. But no one has the resources to fully evaluate everything. That's why translation quality evaluation is typically based on evaluating samples (such as the work by Gladkoff et al. (2022) from an industrial setting). Sometimes this sampling is done by selecting full-text samples from a larger population, e.g. evaluating every tenth translation fully, or selecting complete shorter texts to arrive at the determined sample size. A typical approach in a traditional localization process is to select samples of medium sizes (500-5000 words) and then apply an analytical approach. However, smaller samples and larger samples are also possible, and it is important to consider the entire range of possible sample sizes, from one sentence to very large documents, which is the purpose of this paper.

3 Low IRR is not a bug, but a feature

Human translation quality evaluations on small samples have low Inter-Rater Reliability (IRR). What matters in human evaluation is that trained linguists tend to agree (demonstrate high IRR) on bigger samples, but on a segment level two linguists often disagree on the same issue. This phenomenon has been widely recognized by both experts in the translation industry and data science (Gladkoff et al., 2023). Research in the field of translation error annotation has demonstrated that linguists can disagree even on the precise scope of errors, as well as about error categorizations and severity attributions (Lommel et al., 2014b). The researchers established that these issues are not a consequence of low linguist qualifications or technical problems. Multiple factors at play can determine disagreement among annotators: 1) the complexity of the task; 2) the ambiguity of the text; 3) the quality of the translation; 4) subjectivity; etc.

Text is not the information itself; it is merely the conveyor of the expression of intended meaning. Moreover, not only can we not know for sure the author's intended meaning, which leaves the text open to the reader's interpretation. This interpretation depends on the reader's cultural, educational, and professional background and experiences, as well as on their skills and the context of the communication act. Additionally, language is highly ambiguous, offering numerous expression tools that allow a single sentence to be interpreted in many ways. This inherent ambiguity leads to significant uncertainty in any error annotation, which is a fundamental property of language rather than a flaw of human assessors (Gladkoff et al., 2022).

Data scientists often make shallow conclusions from low IRR, believing that automatic calculation of errors will resolve this problem. In recent years, many automatic metrics have been constructed, often claiming "human judgment" quality. Recently, AI-based metrics have appeared, along with unverified and unproven claims that "GenAI seems capable of measuring translation quality" (Gladkoff et al., 2024). In reality, however, GenAI does neither "think" nor "understand" anything and for this reason, the factual accuracy of GenAI generation remains a huge problem. No language model is Turing complete [2]. Language models are constrained by their architecture and the limitations of their training data and computational resources. Language models are specialized tools designed for processing and generating text based on patterns learned from vast amounts of data. They are good at some tasks such as language generation, and summarization, but they are not capable of performing arbitrary computations or reasoning in the same way that a Turing complete system can. Because of this, language models are not considered general-purpose reasoners. They can provide useful responses and assist with many tasks within their scope of capabilities, but they cannot reason and compute in the general-purpose manner that a Turing machine or Turing complete system can. Among other things, the factual accuracy of GenAI generation remains to be a huge problem. This affects both error annotation capability and accuracy on a secondary process level. GenAI may produce fluent text, but it performs worse on derivative tasks, such as error annotation tasks. In other words, GenAI misses factual errors when generating content, and of course, does not "see" errors during the annotation process, which also results in issues with the accuracy of this process. Additionally, the better the GenAI output is, the more variable it becomes, which is similar (although different in nature) to the variability in human judgment. Human judgment is variable because different people may have their own interpretation of the text. Advanced GenAI behaves similarly, with its variable output becoming another interpretation. However, this interpretation is not verified or supported by human intelligence.

And similar to human evaluation, the smaller the context window of the text, the more variable is the GenAI response. For all these important reasons, the smaller the evaluation sample, the greater the uncertainty of translation quality annotation. This is due to the intrinsic, fundamental variability in both human and GenAI-based error annotation that leads to the uncertainty of error evaluation. This means one simple thing: at the low end of the scale, sentence-level automatic scoring is so unreliable that it makes no sense, regardless of the method used to produce the score.

Furthermore, all automatic metrics must be supported by proper benchmarking and validation, which takes a lot of time and is very specific to the particular implementation setting and the specifications (language pair, subject matter area, task requirements, etc.).

Automatic metrics of any kind produce a single number with unknown reliability and confidence intervals. By definition, this number ignores the ambiguity of the text and therefore disregards other valid interpretations, which can be validated by human evaluators on larger samples.

For all we know, various automatic and GenAI measurement results must be validated by analytic human evaluation on samples of sufficient sizes, which converges to higher IRR (inter-rater reliability) in controlled settings with training and monitoring (Gladkoff et al., 2022; Han et al., 2024).

Training and continuous validation of evaluators' work contribute to improving IRR over time. What ultimately matters for reliable evaluation is that a proper process allows for achieving statistically valid IRR of human evaluation at the sample level, not necessarily at the segment level.

4 Three sample-size ranges – three very different methods

The industrial era has developed a vast mathematical and methodological apparatus for measuring the quality of products by evaluating small samples from very large production lots, e.g. using *student's t-distribution* (Student, 1908) such as the recent work by Gladkoff et al. (2023). In a setting where decisions about the quality of a large lot are based on small samples, the uncertainty is so high that only sophisticated methods of statistical quality control can handle such a problem. They have been extensively developed and described by many researchers, such as Montgomery (2019), and have been long standardized by ISO [3]. In a nutshell, errors ***always*** have a statistical nature, and this is yet another reason why segment-level quality scores do not make sense – not only the methods of producing them must be properly benchmarked and verified,

[2] `https://ai-lab.logrusglobal.com/why-no-agi-can-be-built-with-language-models/`

[3] ISO 2859-2:2020 Sampling procedures for inspection by attributes `https://www.iso.org/standard/64505.html`

but the fundamental uncertainty of individual error annotation is so high that it is not possible to get a "true" measurement except for very trivial mechanical spelling errors.

When measuring errors on a very small sample, we need to apply the Statistical Quality Control (SQC) method. These methods are extremely complex due to the underlying statistical and mathematical apparatus, which is why ISO 2859-1 consists of 94 pages of tables. Additionally, the conclusions drawn from applying these methods are not quality ratings but rather probabilities of the producer's and consumer's risks, which can be determined using such methods.

In an earlier work by Gladkoff et al. (2022), it was demonstrated that for the translation quality rating to have low variability, the sample size should be greater than 200 sentences (3400 words). The authors discuss that if they go to smaller sample sizes, the confidence interval explodes. This means that even a 2000-word sample introduces significant uncertainty in the quality measurement result, and even more so with samples of 1000 words and especially *500 words*.

The lowest known credible metric is the ATA certification model (Han and Gladkoff, 2022), where linguists are asked to translate one page (250 words). To address the uncertainty of evaluating such a small sample, two different reviewers assess the work, effectively duplicating the evaluation effort to mitigate the risks associated with the limited sample size. Additionally, the ATA certification requires linguists to translate two one-page samples to see how they handle the translation of different types of text, which also helps reduce the uncertainty of evaluating small samples.

The methods of Statistical Quality Control (SQC) are outside the scope of this paper. However, for this article, it is important to note that the translation quality of a sample smaller than 15-17 sentences (one page, 250 words) falls into the realm of SQC and cannot be measured by analytic quality evaluation methods unless the sample covers the entire text.

For samples of approximately 300 words and above, the effects of statistical uncertainty and low Inter-Rater Reliability cease to have a significant adverse effect, making methods of analytical quality evaluation applicable. For samples larger than approximately *5000 words*, other effects start to manifest, such as the priming effect of human perception. Non-linearity starts to become apparent with larger samples. In this paper, we introduce a non-linear calibration model that works for samples of both medium (customary) and large sizes. The three ranges of sample sizes are governed by entirely different mathematical apparatus. These ranges are shown in Figure 8 (word counts: 0, 500, 5000+).

5 MQM 2.0: The State of the Art of Analytical Quality Evaluation

MQM is a framework for analytic Translation Quality Evaluation (TQE). It can be used to evaluate human translation (HT), machine translation (MT), or AI-generated translation. MQM consists of two key components: the error typology and the scoring model. The MQM error typology is organized hierarchically with *seven* high-level error dimensions, subordinate error types, and associated severity levels. The *scoring model* features a system of weights and parameters assigned to the error types and severity levels, as well as a scoring formula used to calculate a numerical score that represents the quality of the evaluated translation according to agreed-upon specifications.

The evaluated sample can comprise an entire document or a set of documents, or parts thereof. Evaluators frequently work with samples in the *range* of 500 to 20,000 words, depending on the size of the project and the resources available for evaluation.

5.1 Error Typology

As noted above, the MQM error typology is based on seven high-level dimensions, with subordinate error subtypes at various hierarchical levels. For example, the Accuracy error dimension contains error subtypes such as Addition, Mistranslation, and Omission. At the next hierarchical level, Mistranslation, for example, contains error subtypes such as Misrepresentation of technical relationship, False friend, MT hallucination, etc. The complete repository of all error types is known as **MQM-Full**. Implementers typically do not use the complete repository but select a subset of MQM-Full to provide the granularity they need for their implementation context.

MQM-Core is a pre-defined subset that comprises the seven high-level error dimensions with the selected error sub-types that are most widely used in the language sector. The error types are represented by names and their rigorous description. They have a specific, defined meaning and should not be understood as general language words or common terms. For instance, Accuracy in MQM refers to the appropriate correspondence between the source and target language, rather than to factual correctness in general.

5.2 Scoring Model

The second key component is a scoring model. The scoring model is a method, process, and formula for deriving quality scores resulting from error annotation data based on customer specifications.

Implementers design their scoring model by selecting error dimensions and sub-types with the granularity relevant to the implementation environment. Implementers assign penalty points or error weights to the error types and define penalty multipliers for the severity levels. Thereafter, for each identified error instance, evaluators assign an error type and severity level, and record them in the translation environment or on a scorecard. These values are then used by the scoring formula to calculate a **Quality Score**. The scoring calculation determines the final Quality Score. In this paper, we distinguish three types of scoring model:

- Linear Raw Scoring Model
- Linear Scoring Model with Calibration
- Non-Linear Scoring Model with Calibration

Linear Scoring allows the calculation of a quality score with or without calibration. The Raw Linear score calculates the portion of the evaluated text with errors and subtracts this value from 100 to get the value which directly represents the error-free portion of the evaluated sample.

In April 2024, the MQM Council published the extended MQM 2.0 scoring model document, which includes the Linear Scoring Model with Calibration [4]. The idea of calibration is to set the **Passing Interval** using a separate, special score scale for the convenience of human use of scores.

The two scoring methods – with and without calibration — serve different purposes. Non-calibrated scores represent the raw results of an evaluation task and are easy to calculate, but difficult to interpret and use; in addition, different tolerance thresholds are not intuitively represented on a raw score scale with varying positions and non-integer numbers, which are different for different scenarios.

Calibrated scores are more complex to produce, but are convenient for humans to use, and also enable implementers to create scoring models that are comparable across various content types, use cases and service levels. For example, a translation service provider is likely to use different calibrations for different clients or use cases, but the resulting calibrated score scale will be the same, making it easy to work with for all stakeholders in all scenarios. With a little additional effort for calibration, the quality scores can be made much more universal, human-readable and useful.

Linear scoring models apply the same scoring irrespective of the sample length. However, human perception of the quality tends to be different depending on the size of the sample. The **Non-Linear Scoring Model** takes into account changing human perception throughout content consumption and produces accurate scores across a wide range of sample sizes, from small ones to infinity. These factors are explained further in this paper.

The **Raw Scoring Model (Score without Calibration)** works with the basic values and parameters: the evaluation word count and the total of the penalty points calculated for the sample, as defined below.

The **Scoring Model with Calibration** works with all the same original values and parameters as the Raw Scoring Model, but a few additional parameters are required as explained in Score Calculation with Calibration (A.6).

A Pass or Fail rating is assigned about the established passing threshold or error tolerance value. With calibration, setting a relevant quality threshold and error tolerance limit is much easier and more flexible, making the pass/fail decision clearer and more understandable. In addition, calibration allows for the adjustment of the scoring formula to match the perception of the rater.

[4]MQM extended scoring model document https://themqm.org/error-types-2/the-mqm-scoring-models/

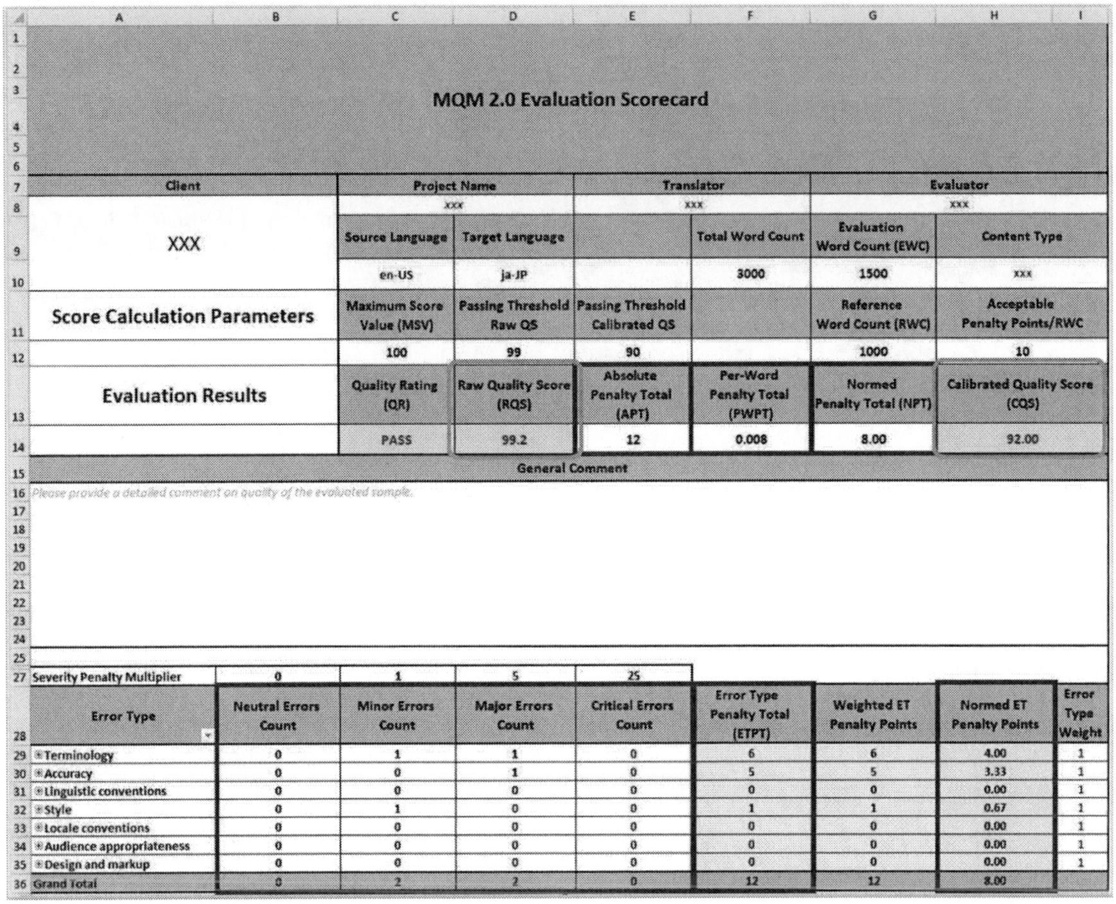

MQM 2.0 Evaluation Scorecard

Client	Project Name		Translator		Evaluator	
XXX	xxx		xxx		xxx	
	Source Language	Target Language		Total Word Count	Evaluation Word Count (EWC)	Content Type
	en-US	ja-JP		3000	1500	xxx
Score Calculation Parameters	Maximum Score Value (MSV)	Passing Threshold Raw QS	Passing Threshold Calibrated QS		Reference Word Count (RWC)	Acceptable Penalty Points/RWC
	100	99	90		1000	10
Evaluation Results	Quality Rating (QR)	Raw Quality Score (RQS)	Absolute Penalty Total (APT)	Per-Word Penalty Total (PWPT)	Normed Penalty Total (NPT)	Calibrated Quality Score (CQS)
	PASS	99.2	12	0.008	8.00	92.00

General Comment

Please provide a detailed comment on quality of the evaluated sample.

Severity Penalty Multiplier	0	1	5	25				
Error Type	Neutral Errors Count	Minor Errors Count	Major Errors Count	Critical Errors Count	Error Type Penalty Total (ETPT)	Weighted ET Penalty Points	Normed ET Penalty Points	Error Type Weight
Terminology	0	1	1	0	6	6	4.00	1
Accuracy	0	0	1	0	5	5	3.33	1
Linguistic conventions	0	0	0	0	0	0	0.00	1
Style	0	1	0	0	1	1	0.67	1
Locale conventions	0	0	0	0	0	0	0.00	1
Audience appropriateness	0	0	0	0	0	0	0.00	1
Design and markup	0	0	0	0	0	0	0.00	1
Grand Total	0	2	2	0	12	12	8.00	

Figure 1: MQM2.0 Evaluation Scorecard: Quality Measure and Tools (red squares with straight corners), and Quality Scores (orange squares with curved corners).

5.3 Setting up an MQM evaluation system

To set up the MQM evaluation process, implementers must first create a specific metric by: 1) Evaluating translation project specifications and analyzing them concerning end-user needs; 2) Selecting Error Types from the MQM Error Typology that are appropriate to the defined specifications to create the error typology for the metric; 3) Integrating the created MQM metric, suitable for their specific use case, into a scoring system into their tool environment or using it in a scorecard format; 4) Determining sample size ranges and defining sampling procedures.

Historically, translation evaluators have used spreadsheet-like scorecards (see Figure 1), but today evaluators are more likely to annotate errors and integrate scoring calculations in specialized tools or utilities built into their translation environment. To visualize and describe the annotation and score-generation process, it is helpful to use a scorecard as an example. The sample scorecards used here represent useful options, but they are not normative.

The default setting for MQM is to use four severity levels, with the severity multipliers 0-1-5-25. Implementers can choose to use different ranges of severity levels, as explained later (A.3.3), and implement them via their respective Severity Penalty Multiplier. (Appendix A for detailed parameters)

6 Projecting PI and the Formulas

Figure 2 displays the projecting of the small passing interval window in the raw-score score to the scale

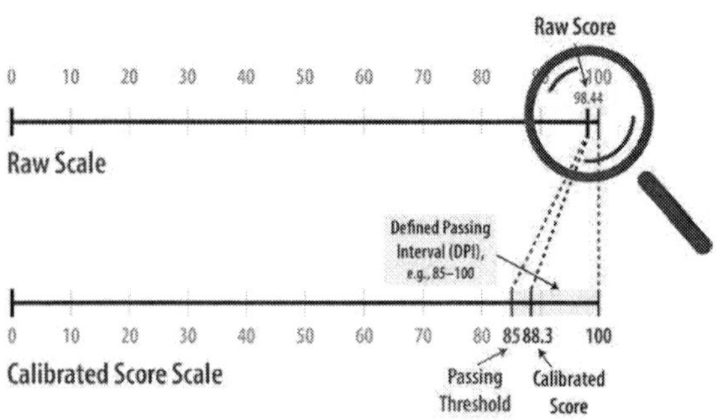

Figure 2: Projecting the small Passing Interval window in the Raw-Score scale to the scale of the Calibrated Score, where the Passing Threshold is chosen arbitrarily by the customer based on the relevant values that apply to a specific context.

7 On Non-Linearity

This section describes the non-linear scoring model which solves the problem of the non-linearity of human perception concerning samples of medium to large size.

All is well with linear scoring until the sample size is either too small (requiring methods of Statistical Quality Control) or too large. Many practitioners have observed that linear scoring defined for small to medium samples does not work for larger chunks of text. The reason that changing human perception fails a linear model is that the human mind is not a fixed state machine – we change our behaviour and our opinions with experience. This effect is known in cognitive science as "priming," where encountering certain features in the text makes readers more alert to them ***as they work their way through the text***.

Priming works on errors too. When we see two errors on one page, then two errors on the next page, and three errors on the page thereafter, we get the impression that there are simply too many errors in the document. This is observed in real translation quality evaluation practice as follows (this is an actual quote from a very large buyer of translation services): Once we started using our current methodology in 2020, we still asked the evaluators to indicate the cases where their actual feeling was different from what the score gave them. We very quickly realized that the main issue was that with very short samples the scoring was overly harsh and with very long samples it was too lenient. The reason for this is that when we evaluate holistically, the perception is not congruent with our scoring formula. For example, we might feel that if a translation sample is about one page, a single major mistranslation error is enough to say that it fails. However, if the sample is seven pages, we are not okay with allowing seven major mistranslation errors before it fails. Instead, we would prefer to fail the sample already at three or four errors. This poses a problem for the linear scoring model which simply prorates the number of errors per page to a total number of pages in the sample."

7.1 Non-Linear error tolerance – what it may look like?

A standard calibration questionnaire only asks how many minor errors are acceptable/not acceptable on the standard sample size. You only need one data point to draw the straight line which originates from the zero point. But if we believe that the quality tolerance is non-linear, we need more error points to see what the curve might look like. We have made numerous surveys of the quality specialists with an extended calibration questionnaire which asks for a tolerance threshold for several sample sizes. All of them follow the same basic pattern: the error tolerance quite sharply decreases with increasing size of the sample, as shown in Figure 5.

Of course, it is difficult for quality managers to answer such questions, because they are trying to calculate the number based on the linear model, so in order to respond to this survey correctly, it's best: to either ask the quality manager who is not so proficient with the linear scoring formula, or specifically ask NOT to prorate the tolerance based on a standard sample. With this complication in mind, and properly taken into account, all the calibration surveys end up with one result as shown on Fig 5. This is a logarithmic dependency which can be easily calculated in Excel as a logarithmic trend line with concrete parameters.

Naturally, the data points for this curve are all empirical, but this is a strength, not a weakness, of the calibration approach. What non-linear calibration does is capture the reality of the non-linearity of human perception and extend the applicability of

Step	Raw Quality Score Calculation	Formulas
1	Absolute Penalty Total (APT)	$\sum_{i,j} Error\ Count_{ij} \times Severity\ Multiplier_j \times Error\ Type\ Weight_i$ Where: i = index for Error Types, j = index for Severity Level.
2	Per-Word Penalty Total (PWPT)	$\frac{Absolute\ Penalty\ Total}{Evaluation\ Word\ Count}$
3	Raw Quality Score (RQS)	$1 - PWPT$ (for a scale with a maximum of 1), or $100 - (PWPT \times 100)$ (for a scale with a maximum of 100)

Figure 3: Formulas for raw score calculation.

the MQM Scoring Model.

7.2 Benefits of non-linear scoring: faithfulness to human perception and scalable to a wide range of sample sizes

Now, as we found what error tolerance looks like for a wider range of sample sizes, we understand that the linear model only works on a very small range of sample sizes near the standard sample size that the model has been developed for. If the standard sample size is 2000 words, then already the metric won't work correctly for 1000 and 5000 words! This is illustrated on the chart below, where you can easily see that a linear scoring formula snapped to just one "standard" tangent point will be very far from actual human perception on a very different sample size.

As we can see from Figure 7, if we calibrate a linear scoring model on 4 pages, it won't work for 10 pages. In order for the MQM Metric Scoring Formula to correspond to human judgments and perception for a wider number of sample sizes, we need to use a non-linear scoring model.

The non-linear scorecard is based on standard linear MQM scorecard and uses a logarithmic function to define the score.

8 Conclusion and Future Work

In this paper we covered a wide scope of sample sizes and different approaches and scoring models. It can be said that this paper represents the Unified Theory of Translation Quality Measurement which explains most use cases of translation quality measurement. The FULL MQM Error Typology with Calibrated and non-linear scoring is a toolset which allows the reproduction of many different known proprietary metrics.

We have also established the fact that human translation quality evaluation is more than ever THE Golden Standard of measurement and benchmarking for quality measurement, since it is **the only reliable way to validate any automatic translation quality evaluation.**

Acknowledgements

We thank the reviewers for their valuable comments and feedback on our work. LH and GN are grateful for the grant "Integrating hospital outpatient letters into the healthcare data space" (EP/V047949/1; funder: UKRI/EPSRC).

References

Bahdanau, D., Cho, K., and Bengio, Y. (2015). Neural machine translation by jointly learning to align and translate. In Bengio, Y. and LeCun, Y., editors, *3rd International Conference on Learning Representations, ICLR 2015, San Diego, CA, USA, May 7-9, 2015, Conference Track Proceedings*.

Freitag, M., Mathur, N., Lo, C.-k., Avramidis, E., Rei, R., Thompson, B., Kocmi, T., Blain, F., Deutsch, D., Stewart, C., Zerva, C., Castilho, S., Lavie, A., and Foster, G. (2023). Results of WMT23 metrics shared task: Metrics might be guilty but references are not innocent. In Koehn, P., Haddow, B., Kocmi, T., and Monz, C., editors, *Proceedings of the Eighth Conference on Ma-*

Step	Calibrated Quality Score Calculation	Formulas/Values	
1	Establish parameters	Reference Word Count (RWC)	1000
		Max. Quality Score	100
		Passing Threshold (PT)	Any number perceived as reasonable (e.g., 90)
		Defined Passing Interval (DPI)	100 – DPT (e.g., 10)
		Acceptable Penalty Points (APP) for the Reference Word Count	Any number perceived as reasonable
2	Absolute Penalty Total (APT)	$\sum_{i,j} Error\ Count_{ij} \times Severity\ Multiplier_j \times Error\ Type\ Weight_i$ Where: i = index for Error Types, j = index for Severity Level.	
3	Normed Penalty Total (NPT)	$\frac{APT \times RWC}{EWC}$	
4	Scaling Factor (SF)	$\frac{100-DPT}{APP}$	
5	Calibrated Quality Score (CQS)	$100 - NPT \times SF$	

Figure 4: Formulas for calibrated score calculation.

chine Translation, pages 578–628, Singapore. Association for Computational Linguistics.

Freitag, M., Rei, R., Mathur, N., Lo, C.-k., Stewart, C., Avramidis, E., Kocmi, T., Foster, G., Lavie, A., and Martins, A. F. T. (2022). Results of WMT22 metrics shared task: Stop using BLEU – neural metrics are better and more robust. In Koehn, P., Barrault, L., Bojar, O., Bougares, F., Chatterjee, R., Costa-jussà, M. R., Federmann, C., Fishel, M., Fraser, A., Freitag, M., Graham, Y., Grundkiewicz, R., Guzman, P., Haddow, B., Huck, M., Jimeno Yepes, A., Kocmi, T., Martins, A., Morishita, M., Monz, C., Nagata, M., Nakazawa, T., Negri, M., Névéol, A., Neves, M., Popel, M., Turchi, M., and Zampieri, M., editors, *Proceedings of the Seventh Conference on Machine Translation (WMT)*, pages 46–68, Abu Dhabi, United Arab Emirates (Hybrid). Association for Computational Linguistics.

Freitag, M., Rei, R., Mathur, N., Lo, C.-k., Stewart, C., Foster, G., Lavie, A., and Bojar, O. (2021). Results of the WMT21 metrics shared task: Evaluating metrics with expert-based human evaluations on TED and news domain. In Barrault, L., Bojar, O., Bougares, F., Chatterjee, R., Costa-jussa, M. R., Federmann, C., Fishel, M., Fraser, A., Freitag, M., Graham, Y., Grundkiewicz, R., Guzman, P., Haddow, B., Huck, M., Yepes, A. J., Koehn, P., Kocmi, T., Martins, A., Morishita, M., and Monz, C., editors, *Proceedings of the Sixth Conference on Machine Translation*, pages 733–774, Online. Association for Computational Linguistics.

Gladkoff, S. and Han, L. (2022). HOPE: A task-oriented and human-centric evaluation framework using professional post-editing towards more effective MT evaluation. In Calzolari, N., Béchet, F., Blache, P., Choukri, K., Cieri, C., Declerck, T., Goggi, S., Isahara, H., Maegaard, B., Mariani, J., Mazo, H., Odijk, J., and Piperidis, S., editors, *Proceedings of the Thirteenth Language Resources and Evaluation Conference*, pages 13–21, Marseille, France. European Language Resources Association.

Gladkoff, S., Han, L., Erofeev, G., Sorokina, I., and Nenadic, G. (2024). MTuncertainty: Assessing the need for post-editing of machine translation outputs by fine-tuning openai llms. In *EAMT 2024*.

Gladkoff, S., Han, L., and Nenadic, G. (2023). Student's t-distribution: On measuring the inter-rater reliability when the observations are scarce. In *Proceedings of the 14th International Conference on Recent Advances in Natural Language Processing*, pages 419–428.

Gladkoff, S., Sorokina, I., Han, L., and Alekseeva, A. (2022). Measuring uncertainty in translation quality evaluation (TQE). In Calzolari, N., Béchet, F., Blache, P., Choukri, K., Cieri, C., Declerck, T., Goggi, S., Isahara, H., Maegaard, B., Mariani, J., Mazo, H., Odijk,

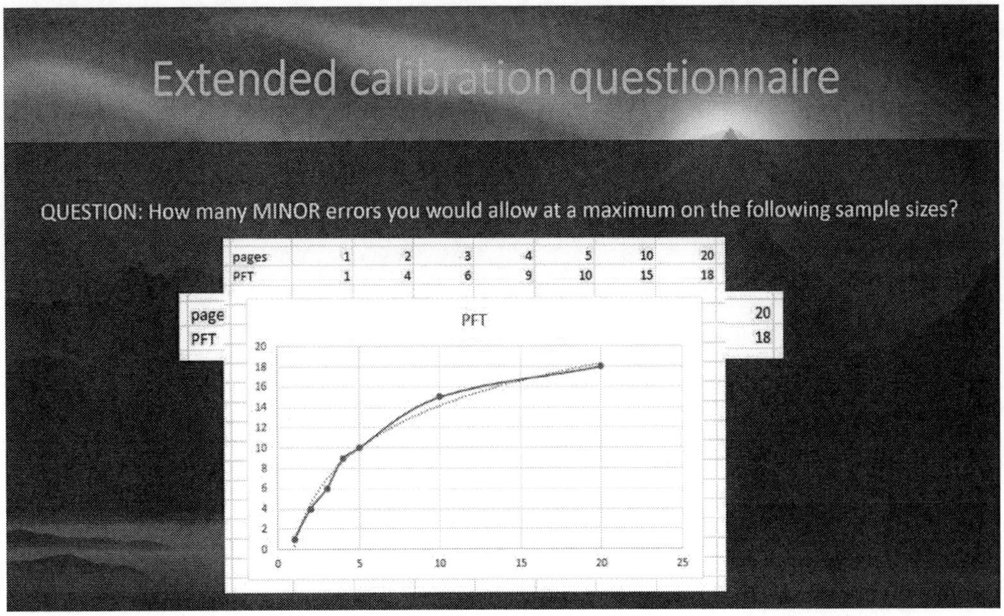

Figure 5: Extended calibration questionnaire.

J., and Piperidis, S., editors, *Proceedings of the Thirteenth Language Resources and Evaluation Conference*, pages 1454–1461, Marseille, France. European Language Resources Association.

Han, L. (2022). *An Investigation into Multi-Word Expressions in Machine Translation.* PhD thesis, Dublin City University. https://doras.dcu.ie/26559/.

Han, L. and Gladkoff, S. (2022). Meta-evaluation of translation evaluation methods: a systematic up-to-date overview. In *Tutorials at LREC2022: the Thirteenth Language Resources and Evaluation Conference*, Marseille, France. European Language Resources Association.

Han, L., Gladkoff, S., Erofeev, G., Sorokina, I., Galiano, B., and Nenadic, G. (2024). Neural machine translation of clinical text: an empirical investigation into multilingual pre-trained language models and transfer-learning. *Frontiers in Digital Health*, 6:1211564.

Koehn, P. (2009). *Statistical machine translation.* Cambridge University Press.

Lommel, A., Burchardt, A., and Uszkoreit, H. (2014a). Multidimensional quality metrics (mqm): A framework for declaring and describing translation quality metrics. *Tradumàtica: tecnologies de la traducció*, 0:455–463.

Lommel, A., Popovic, M., and Burchardt, A. (2014b). Assessing inter-annotator agreement for translation error annotation. In *MTE: Workshop on Automatic and Manual Metrics for Operational Translation Evaluation*, pages 31–37. Language Resources and Evaluation Conference Reykjavik.

Mathur, N., Wei, J., Freitag, M., Ma, Q., and Bojar, O. (2020). Results of the WMT20 metrics shared task. In Barrault, L., Bojar, O., Bougares, F., Chatterjee, R., Costa-jussà, M. R., Federmann, C., Fishel, M., Fraser, A., Graham, Y., Guzman, P., Haddow, B., Huck, M., Yepes, A. J., Koehn, P., Martins, A., Morishita, M., Monz, C., Nagata, M., Nakazawa, T., and Negri, M., editors, *Proceedings of the Fifth Conference on Machine Translation*, pages 688–725, Online. Association for Computational Linguistics.

Montgomery, D. C. (2019). *Introduction to statistical quality control.* John wiley & sons.

Student (1908). The probable error of a mean. *Biometrika*, 6(1):1–25.

Vaswani, A., Shazeer, N., Parmar, N., Uszkoreit, J., Jones, L., Gomez, A. N., Kaiser, L., and Polosukhin, I. (2017).

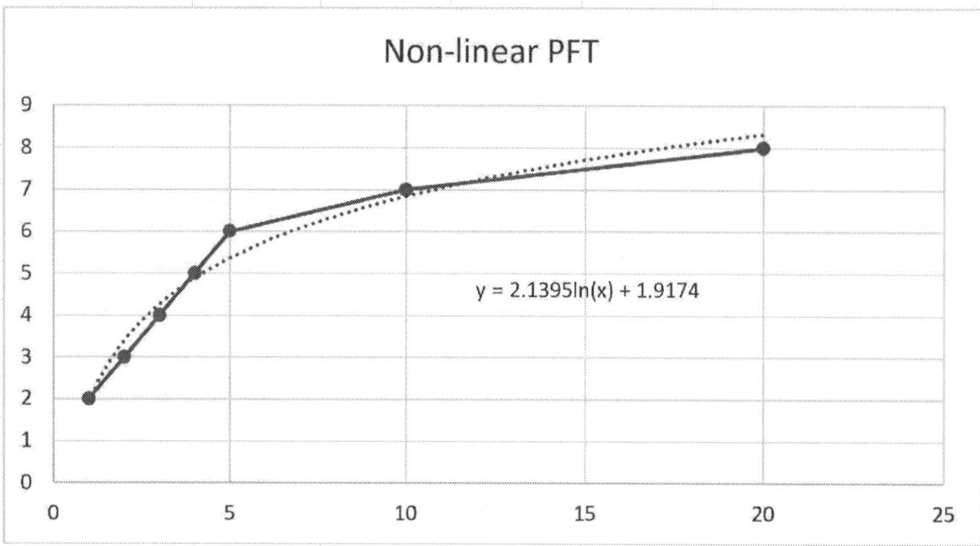

Figure 6: Real world non-linear calibration questionnaire with parameters found.

Attention is all you need. In *Conference on Neural Information Processing System*, pages 6000–6010.

A Parameters of the Evaluation Quality Metric

A.1 Calculation Values

The sample scorecard in Figure 9 shows the results of applying one possible metric to a specific evaluation task for a sample of segments (the size of which is stated in the Evaluation Word Count). Rows 29–35 list the selected Error Types – in this case the seven high-level error dimensions of MQM Core. The following values highlighted in Figure 9 play major roles in designing translation quality evaluation models. The abbreviations listed below are sometimes used when discussing formal equations.

A.1.1 Evaluation Word Count (EWC)

The Evaluation Word Count (Figure 9, Cell G10) is the word count of the sample chosen for evaluation. As noted, the EWC can include complete texts, parts thereof, or collections of segments. The EWC is used in the calculation of the Quality Score (QS). The word count according to the draft ASTM standard WK46396 is usually based on the source content. NOTE: ISO 5060 [5] cites the option to use character counts instead of word counts, or to use line counts that assume uniform characters per line. These approaches accommodate languages that sometimes have dramatically different word counts. ISO 5060 also cites the use of count values for target language content word counts.

A.1.2 Reference Word Count (RWC)

The Reference Word Count (Figure 9, Cell G12) is an arbitrary number of words in a hypothetical reference evaluation text. Implementers use this uniform word count to compare results across different projects. The RWC is often set at 1000.

A.2 Maximum Score Value (MSV)

The Maximum Score Value of 100 is also an arbitrary value designed to manipulate the Quality Score to shift its value into a range that is easier to understand. It converts the score to a percentage-like value. Cell C12 in Figure 9 shows this value for the MSV.

[5] ISO 5060:2024 Translation services Evaluation of translation output General guidance `https://www.iso.org/standard/80701.html`

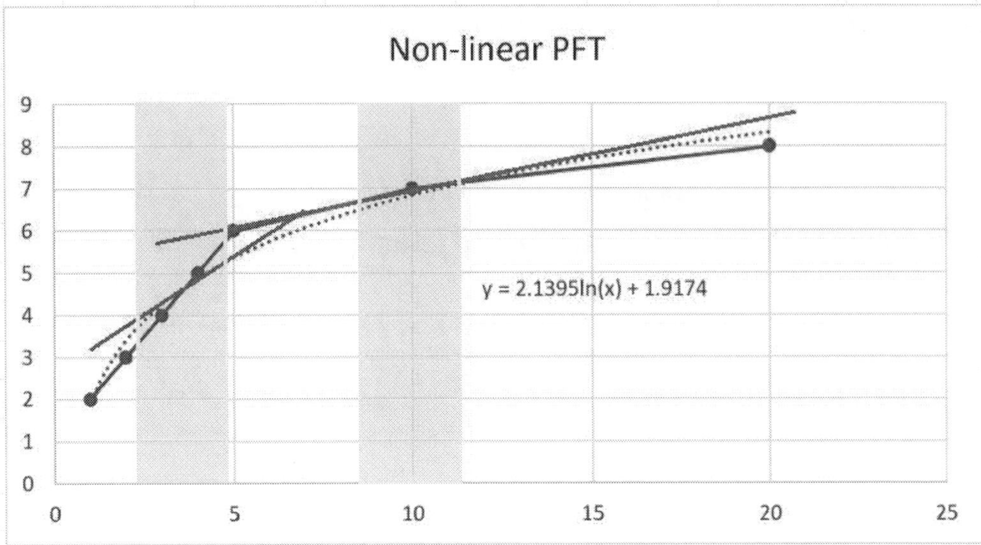

Figure 7: Linear scoring formula snapped to just one "standard" tangent point will be very far from actual human perception on other sample sizes.

A.2.1 Passing Threshold (PT)

The Passing Threshold is the score that defines the Pass/Fail limit. Scoring methods without calibration typically use values such as 0.99 OR 99 – depending on the scale used – as the Passing Threshold (Figure 9, Cell D12). If scoring with calibration is used, the implementer can define any number that is perceived to be visually meaningful, such as 95 or 90 (Figure 9, Cell E12).

A.2.2 Defined Passing Interval (DPI)

The Defined Passing Interval is the interval between the Maximum Score Value and the Passing Threshold. In these examples, Raw Scoring Models without calibration use a Defined Passing Interval of 1 (100-99) or 0.01 (1.00-0.99). When calibrated scores are used, the Defined Passing Interval is magnified to any reasonable range that allows for easy data analysis.

A.2.3 Final Quality Rating (Pass/Fail)

The Final Quality Rating (Figure 9, Cell C14) returns a PASS or FAIL quality rating for the evaluated content depending on whether the Quality Score is above or equals the Passing Threshold value (Pass) or is below it (Fail).

A.2.4 Error Type Weight (ETW)

Error Type Weights (ETWs) can be used to reflect the importance of Error Types, depending on their importance for a given project, project type or content type. If the ETW is set to 1 for all Error Types (as in the sample scorecard in Figure 9, Cells I (29-35), they are all equally important and result in the same number of penalty points if the Severity Level is the same. If implementers want to distinguish the Error Types by attaching more importance to some Error Types, they can apply different ETWs.

Applying different ETWs can be useful if certain Error Types should be given more prominence than others for a specific type of content. For example, for content with legal implications, implementers may wish to give Accuracy errors higher weight than Style errors. This means that fewer Accuracy errors will be acceptable than Style errors. In other scenarios, a minor Accuracy error may result in fewer penalty points than a minor Style error. For content related to the brands and marketing, implementers can choose to assign higher weights to Style or Audience Appropriateness errors to reflect their importance for this type of content.

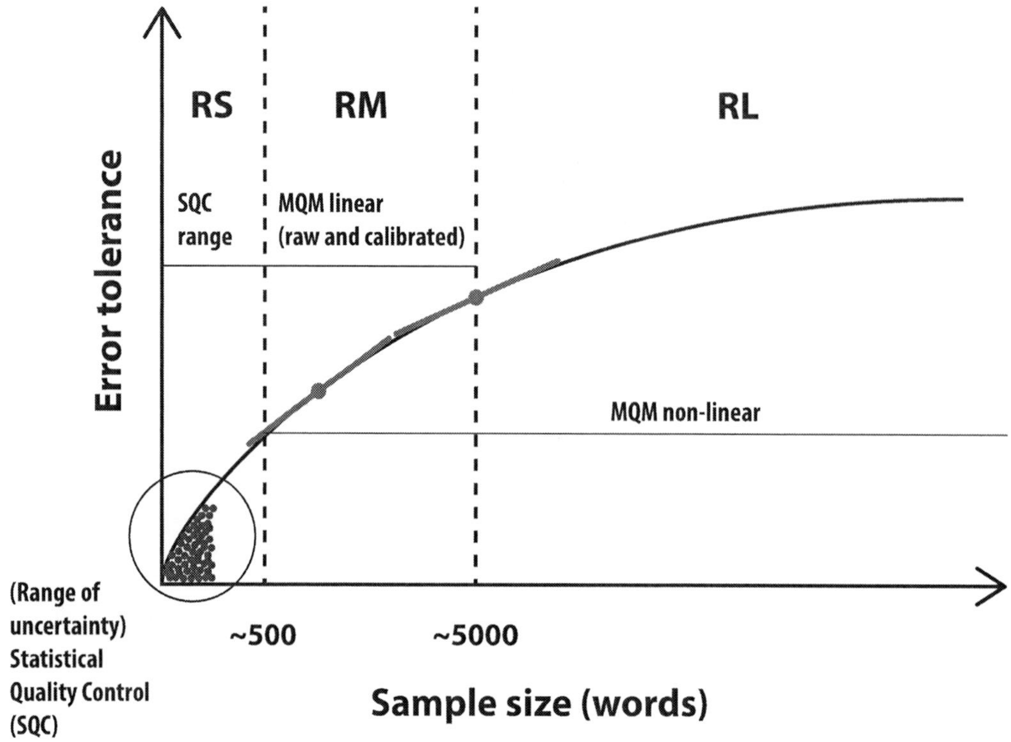

Figure 8: The chart delineates three distinct sample size ranges—small (RS), medium (RM), and large (RL)—each requiring its own mathematical approach for calculating quality scores. Linear methods can be applied within the small (RS) and medium (RM) ranges but are valid only near the calibration point. In contrast, non-linear methods are applicable across the entire span of the medium (RM) and large (RL) ranges. For the small range (RS), only Statistical Quality Control methods can be used due to the high uncertainty of measurements for very small samples.

A.3 Error Annotation Values

A.3.1 Error Type Number (ET No)

The sample scorecard shown here reflects Error Type Names assigned to MQM-Core. Optionally, scorecard designers can select other values from MQM-Full or leave out unwanted values. The selected values are listed in the Error Types column (Column B) and associated with Error Type Numbers (ET Nos). Once evaluators have identified a potential translation error, they assign the error instance to one of the Error Types.

A.3.2 Error Severity Level

The Error Severity Level reflects the impact of a particular error on the usability of the text. Each error instance is annotated according to its Error Severity Level. This sample scorecard features a common set-up with four Severity Levels: Neutral, Minor, Major, and Critical. Three levels, or even two, are also common.

- **Neutral Severity Level**: The neutral severity level is assigned for preferential changes or errors that are not the translator's fault and for which the translator should not be penalized.
- **Minor Severity Level**: Errors that have a limited impact on the usability, understandability or reliability of the content for its intended purpose.
- **Major Severity Level**: The major severity level is assigned to errors that seriously affect the understandability, reliability, or usability of the content for its intended purpose or hinders the proper use of the product or service due to

	A–B	C	D	E	F	G	H–I
1–6	MQM 2.0 Evaluation Scorecard						
7	Client	Project Name		Translator		Evaluator	
8	XXX	xxx		xxx		xxx	
9		Source Language	Target Language		Total Word Count	Evaluation Word Count (EWC)	Content Type
10		en-US	ja-JP		3000	1500	xxx
11	Score Calculation Parameters	Maximum Score Value (MSV)	Passing Threshold Raw QS	Passing Threshold Calibrated QS		Reference Word Count (RWC)	Acceptable Penalty Points/RWC
12		100	99	90		1000	10
13	Evaluation Results	Quality Rating (QR)	Raw Quality Score (RQS)	Absotule Penalty Total (APT)	Per-Word Penalty Total (PWPT)	Normed Penalty Total (NPT)	Calibrated Quality Score (CQS)
14		PASS	99.2	12	0.008	8.00	92.00
15	General Comment						
16–24	*Please provide a detailed comment on quality of the evaluated sample.*						

	A	B	C	D	E	F	G	H	I
27	Severity Penalty Multiplier	0	1	5	25				
28	Error Type	Neutral Errors Count	Minor Errors Count	Major Errors Count	Critical Errors Count	Error Type Penalty Total (ETPT)	Weighted ET Penalty Points	Normed ET Penalty Points	Error Type Weight
29	Terminology	0	1	1	0	6	6	4.00	1
30	Accuracy	0	0	1	0	5	5	3.33	1
31	Linguistic conventions	0	0	0	0	0	0	0.00	1
32	Style	0	1	0	0	1	1	0.67	1
33	Locale conventions	0	0	0	0	0	0	0.00	1
34	Audience appropriateness	0	0	0	0	0	0	0.00	1
35	Design and markup	0	0	0	0	0	0	0.00	1
36	Grand Total	0	2	2	0	12	12	8.00	

Figure 9: Sample MQM Scorecard featuring the 7 top-level error dimensions A(29-35) and Severity Penalty Multipliers (Row 27). The most important calculation values are highlighted.

a significant loss or change in meaning or because the error appears in a highly visible or important part of the content.

- **Critical Severity Level**: The critical severity level is assigned to errors that render the entire content unfit for intended purpose or pose a risk of serious physical, financial, or reputational harm. In many quality measurement systems, a single critical error automatically triggers a FAIL rating.

A.3.3 Severity Penalty Multiplier

The Severity Levels in this sample MQM-based scorecard are represented by Severity Penalty Multipliers. These values can vary depending on implementers' preferences and needs, but there should be an exponential difference between values for neutral, minor, major, and critical errors. For instance, in this case, the values could be 0, 1, 5, and 25, respectively. This exponential relationship scale reflects the increased risk and impact between the Error Severity Levels. Custom Severity Penalty Multipliers may be required for a variety of reasons: for instance, in case character count per page is used instead of word count.

The Severity Multipliers values times the number of errors at a given Severity Level and the Error Type Weight yields the totals for row values appearing in Figure 9, Cells G (29-35).

A.4 Scoring Models Parameters

The scorecard in Figure 1 comprises the framework for the Raw Scoring Model. The set of framed scoring parameters (defined values and conditions) is used to calculate a Quality Score. This score determines the final Quality Rating (Pass/Fail rating).

A.4.1 Error Count (EC)

The Error Count for each error type associated with each Severity Level is multiplied by its respective Severity Multiplier.

A.4.2 Error Type Penalty Total (ETPT)

The Error Type Penalty Total (ETPT) is the sum of penalty points calculated for the individual Error Types annotated in the evaluated text. The error count for a specific Error Type and Severity Level is multiplied by the respective Severity Multiplier and Error Type Weight to obtain the Error Type Penalty Total. For example, when using three severity levels, ETPT is defined as ((Minor Error Type count × Minor Severity Multiplier) + (Major Error Type count × Major Severity Multiplier) + (Critical Error Type Count × Critical Severity Multiplier)) × Error Type Weight.

A.4.3 Absolute Penalty Total (APT)

The Absolute Penalty Total is the sum of all Error Type Penalty Totals (Figure 1, Cell E12). APT is the most important value used for Quality Score calculation.

A.4.4 Per-Word Penalty Total (PWPT)

The Per-Word Penalty Total (Figure 1, Cell F12) is determined by dividing the Absolute Penalty Total by the Evaluation Word Count. The Per-Word Penalty Total is also one of the key values that contributes to the Raw Quality Score calculation.

A.4.5 Normed Penalty Total (NPT)

The Normed Penalty Total (Figure 1, Cell G12) represents the Per-Word Error Penalty total relative to the Reference Word Count. Typically, 1000 is used as the arbitrary number to represent the Reference Word Count; therefore NPT is sometimes referred to as the Error Penalty Total per Thousand Words. The Normed Penalty Total is obtained by multiplying the PWPT by RWC (NPT = PWPT × 1000 in our example). This is mathematically equivalent to (APT × RWC)/EWC.

A.4.6 Quality Score (QS)

The Quality Score is the primary quality measure of a translation product.

A.5 Calculating the Linear Quality Score

There are two ways to calculate the Linear Quality Score: with and without calibration.

A.5.1 Quality Score without Calibration (Raw Score)

The Raw Linear score determines the portion of the text containing errors, subtracts this number from 100, and thus provides a value representing the error-free section of the evaluated sample.

Logically then, the Quality Score expresses the portion of the evaluated target content that is correct. In this example, the acceptable interval set as allowed for the "portion with errors" is 1. Hence, any quality score between 100–99 (1–0.99 respectively) produces the Pass rating.

The acceptable interval is delimited by the Acceptable Penalty Points (APP) value for the Reference Word Count, which corresponds to the Passing Threshold. For example, a requester of legal translation might find that their Passing Threshold would be a Raw Score of 99.5 (e.g., five penalty points for a thousand-word Reference Word Count), while a requester for user-to-user technical help might accept a raw score of 97.2 (e.g., 28 penalty points for the same Reference Word Count).

However, relying on Raw Score calculations alone has drawbacks. For the legal example, the score hovers too close to 100, making it difficult to use the Raw Scores. In addition, if an organization has multiple content types, each with their own Passing Threshold, it can be difficult to track and apply the proper threshold to each one. Setting an acceptance threshold using Raw Scores is challenging when varying scores end up looking very close to each other, as such acceptance thresholds are not necessarily intuitive. The threshold may even turn out to be a complex fractional value, which means that simply scaling the Raw Score does not solve this problem.

A.5.2 Quality Score with Calibration

The second option is to calibrate the penalty points calculated for the evaluated sample against a preselected Passing Threshold or tolerance limit on a special calibrated quality scale. Calibration expresses the scoring values in a way that stakeholders can interpret easily in line with their expectations and specifications.

To do so, implementers specify an Acceptable Penalty Points (APP) value during the project specification stage, representing how many penalty points they would deem acceptable for the Reference Word Count on a calibrated quality score scale. They then associate this tolerance limit with the Passing Threshold.

In its raw form, a score is initially calculated as described in the previous section. It is then converted to a Calibrated Score scale by scaling the raw passing interval to Calibrated Passing Interval and mapping the raw score to Calibrated score on Calibrated Score scale, as shown below.

Calibration applies the aforementioned ergonomic Passing Threshold. This Passing Threshold differs from the Raw Quality Score. For example, the Defined Passing Interval in Figure 5 is 100-85, where 85 will be a PASS and anything less will be a FAIL. In this case the 85 Passing Threshold corresponds to the maximum acceptable number of errors on a Raw Score scale (for example, the five penalty points for the legal translation or 28 for the technical help example).

The calibration process acts like a magnifying glass for viewing the otherwise very small or inconsistent acceptance ranges close to 100. This approach makes the quality rating easier to use and understand, highlighting differences in translation quality for evaluated texts more clearly.

A.6 Score Calculations

A.6.1 Calculating the raw quality scores

Calculating scores without calibration uses the steps shown in Figure 3. See the Appendix: Scoring Model Parameters for a list of all parameters and their abbreviations.

A.6.2 Calculating the quality scores with calibration

The Scoring Method with Calibration enables implementers to account for the error tolerance for a specific word count (Reference Word Count) and to link it to the pre-defined Passing Threshold (PT), against which the Pass rating is determined. For a list of all parameters and their abbreviations, see the Appendix: Scoring Model Parameters.

The scoring formula for calculating the quality score with calibration works with the standard calculation values, such as Evaluation Word Count, Absolute Penalty Total and Normed Penalty Total. However, a few additional values and parameters have to be defined. These are used to pre-define the specified acceptance criteria (the error tolerance) and to link these criteria to a scale that should be understandable or appropriate for all stakeholders. The following values used in the score calculation above are pivotal for a score calibrated with respect to a predefined Passing Threshold.

Acceptable Penalty Points (APP) for the Reference Word Count Penalty points are deemed as still acceptable for a certain volume of text, typically for the Reference Word Count of 1000 words. Typical questions to ask when defining the Acceptable Penalty Points are:

- What is the number of Minor errors that would still be a Pass for a sample of 1000 words?
- What is the number of Major errors that would still be a Pass for a sample of 1000 words?

In simple terms, the APP reflects the error count that stakeholders would still consider to be acceptable for a given word count (typically 1000 words) provided that the Minor Error Weight is 1.

In the current example, the acceptable error tolerance is defined as 10 minor errors OR 2 major errors per 1000 words, which yields a Raw Quality Score of 99. If the Normed Penalty Total calculated for the evaluation sample is greater than 10 penalty points, the defined Passing Threshold has been exceeded and the evaluation result is FAIL.

Passing Threshold (PT) A number perceived as an intuitively reasonable Passing Threshold. Calibration enables the determination of a Passing Threshold that is psychologically meaningful to stakeholders. This number typically is any reasonable number in the range of 0-100. It represents the Passing Threshold score that is linked to the preset count of penalty points for the reference word count, i.e. the initially defined error tolerance for a certain unit of text. Calibration transforms the narrow passing interval obtained using the raw, uncalibrated score to a wider and more interpretable interval, which acts analogous to a magnifying glass.

Scaling Factor (SF) Parameter to scale the Acceptable Penalty Points (APP) for the reference word count across the Defined Passing Interval

(DPI). Let's consider Figure ??. On the top Raw Scale the raw passing threshold is 98, which means that a maximum of 20 raw penalty points are allowed on a sample of 1000 words. On a Calibrated Score scale (bottom) the Defined Passing Interval (DPI) is 15 (upward from 85 to 100). Therefore, the raw Passing Interval scales ***down*** from 20 on the raw scale to 15 on the Calibrated Scale. The Scaling Parameter for this new value will be 15/20=0.75. On the Raw Scale, the raw score is 98.44, which means that NPT=15.6 (the error density of a sample is equivalent to 15.6 errors on 1000 words). The trick to the Calibration is that what is scaled is not a passing interval, but rather, NPT. We multiply raw NPT of 15.6 by a scaling factor 15/20=0.75, which resolves in NPT = 11.7 on the calibrated scale. Therefore, the calibrated score will be 100-11.7=88.3 (bottom scale).

B Further Discussion

As shown herein, the Translation Quality Score calculation depends and is a function of many conditions and parameters:

- Client specifications, defining tolerances for various content types, purposes, and audiences.
- Language pair, culture.
- Purpose of evaluation.
- Measurement conditions and requirements.
- Sample sizes.
- Technology platforms used (MT, AI, TMS, etc.).

Our further research directions include:

- Developing practical methods of reliable and simple translation quality score calculations for smaller samples using Statistical Quality Control methods.
- Developing standardized score cards for various use cases, with examples.
- Improving reliability of automatic GenAI-enabled quality measurement methods.
- Benchmarking more annotation and quality evaluation data to develop and provide ways to validate automated quality evaluation metrics.

C Highlighted Scorecards and Model Parameters

We list the sample MQM scorecard figures here with different highlights mentioned in the paper.

Scoring Model Parameters and Variables are explained in Figure 11.

D The MQM Metric Deployment Process (use case)

A typical use case of MQM deployment often includes analysis of previously collected evaluation results, which are used to validate new would-be deployed MQM Scoring Model against established practices of quality tolerance thresholds and specifications.

Here's the typical use case:

- Before we introduced our new MQM-based error typology with the weights and multipliers and thresholds, we analyzed previously conducted evaluations. We had already been marking errors, but the decision on whether the translation was acceptable or unacceptable was left to the evaluator, irrespective of errors. So, we could have an evaluation with a two or three errors that was rated unacceptable, and evaluations having twenty errors that turned out to be acceptable. In principle, marking errors was just for educational purposes, and the decision on acceptability was a holistic one. So we took all this data and calculated on average how many errors marked the threshold for unacceptable translations. We then prepared several options for weights and multipliers and played through with them to see what comes the closest to the identified threshold. Then we took the chosen weights and multipliers and tested them on actual live translations. We always ask the evaluators to mark if the score and acceptability corresponded to their actual feelings about the translation. This is how we established our current MQM-based new methodology.

MQM 2.0 Evaluation Scorecard

Client	Project Name		Translator		Evaluator	
XXX	xxx		xxx		xxx	
	Source Language	Target Language		Total Word Count	Evaluation Word Count (EWC)	Content Type
	en-US	ja-JP		3000	1500	xxx
Score Calculation Parameters	Maximum Score Value (MSV)	Passing Threshold Raw QS	Passing Threshold Calibrated QS		Reference Word Count (RWC)	Acceptable Penalty Points/RWC
	100	99	90		1000	10
Evaluation Results	Quality Rating (QR)	Raw Quality Score (RQS)	Absotule Penalty Total (APT)	Per-Word Penalty Total (PWPT)	Normed Penalty Total (NPT)	Calibrated Quality Score (CQS)
	PASS	99.2	12	0.008	8.00	92.00

General Comment

Please provide a detailed comment on quality of the evaluated sample.

Severity Penalty Multiplier	0	1	5	25				
Error Type	Neutral Errors Count	Minor Errors Count	Major Errors Count	Critical Errors Count	Error Type Penalty Total (ETPT)	Weighted ET Penalty Points	Normed ET Penalty Points	Error Type Weight
Terminology	0	1	1	0	6	6	4.00	1
Accuracy	0	0	1	0	5	5	3.33	1
Linguistic conventions	0	0	0	0	0	0	0.00	1
Style	0	1	0	0	1	1	0.67	1
Locale conventions	0	0	0	0	0	0	0.00	1
Audience appropriateness	0	0	0	0	0	0	0.00	1
Design and markup	0	0	0	0	0	0	0.00	1
Grand Total	0	2	2	0	12	12	8.00	

Figure 10: In this example, 90 is defined as the Passing Threshold. This score is achieved if the Normed Penalty Total for the Evaluation Word Count is 10. If it is greater than this value, the Quality Score is a number below the Passing Threshold of 90, and the evaluation result is FAIL.

Parameter or variable name (full form)	Abbreviation	Unit of measurement
Evaluation Word Count	EWC	words
Reference Word Count	RWC	words
Error Type Weight	ETW	–
Severity Penalty Multiplier	SPM	–
Absolute Penalty Total	APT	total penalty points
Error Type Penalty Total	ETPT	penalty points per Evaluation Word Count
Per-Word Penalty Total	PWPT	penalty points per evaluated word
Normed Penalty Total	NPT	penalty points per Reference Word Count
Scaling Factor	SF	–
Defined Passing Interval	DPI	units on calibrated scale
Quality Rating *(Note: expressed as pass or fail)*	QR	–
Acceptable Penalty Points for the Reference Word Count	APP	penalty points per evaluated word
Passing Threshold	PT	–
Quality Score *Raw Quality Score* *Calibrated Quality Score*	QS *RQS* *CQS*	–

Figure 11: Scoring Model Parameters and Variables

Automating Idiom Translation with Cross-Lingual Natural Language Generation Grounded In Semantic Analyses Using Large Language Models

Ming Qian

Natural Language Processing Group
Human-Centered AI, Charles River Analytics

mqian@cra.com
qianmi@gmail.com

Challenges of Idiom Translation

Idioms are multi-word expressions whose meaning cannot be directly derived from the meanings of their component words

- kick the bucket" means "to die"

Translating idioms from one language to another requires learning the mapping between the idiom in the source language and its corresponding idiomatic expression in the target language

- Literal word-for-word translation is not good
- Acquired and saved as translation lexicon

Challenges:

- Idioms exhibit varying degrees of semantic transparency
- Cross-language differences in idiom usage and connotations add complexity to the translation task

Can we leverage large language models to mining possible solutions following a "standard" step-by-step procedure?

Adding the Semantic Analyses Step

1. Semantic analysis using ontology [1] or FrameNet [2] on a Chinese idiom to identify key concepts and relationships such as action, purpose, outcome, and context.

2. Generation of multi-word English expressions that reflect similar, narrowed-down, or broadened concepts and relationships.

3. Selection of the top candidate for an English idiom that closely matches the meaning of the Chinese idiom.

Reference:

[1] Natural Language Ontology, Stanford Encyclopedia of Philosophy, https://plato.stanford.edu/entries/natural-language-ontology/

[2] Berkeley FrameNet Website, https://framenet.icsi.berkeley.edu/

[3] Strategies for Translating Chengyu (Chinese Idioms), Jim Jones, https://www.ata-divisions.org/CLD/strategies-for-translating-chengyu/

Chinese idiom "破釜沉舟“ direct output from GPT-40

Translate the Chinese idiom ""破釜沉舟" into English

The Chinese idiom "破釜沉舟" (pò fǔ chén zhōu) translates to "break the cauldrons and sink the boats" in English. It means to commit oneself to a course of action by removing any possibility of retreat, often used to describe someone making a determined and irreversible decision. The phrase originates from a historical event where a general ordered his troops to destroy their cooking pots and boats to force them to fight to the end, knowing there was no way back.

Translate the Chinese idiom ""破釜沉舟" into a corresponding English idiom

The corresponding English idiom for "破釜沉舟" (pò fǔ chén zhōu) would be "burning one's bridges." Both idioms convey the idea of making a decision that eliminates the possibility of retreat, thereby committing fully to the chosen course of action.

Chinese idiom "破釜沉舟"

Ontology Analysis

Ontology analysis involves looking at the concept and its relationships with other concepts. The literal translation of "破釜沉舟" is "break the pots and sink the boats." This idiom originates from a historical event during the Qin Dynasty when a general named Xiang Yu ordered his troops to destroy their cooking pots and boats after crossing a river into enemy territory. This was done to eliminate any possibility of retreat, thereby motivating his troops to fight forward against the enemy as their only option for survival.

Key Concepts and Relationships:

Action: Destruction (of the boats and pots)
Purpose: Eliminate means of retreat
Result: Commitment to a single course of action, i.e., to fight forward
Context: Military strategy, determination, and resolve

Chinese idiom "破釜沉舟"

FrameNet is a project that catalogs how words and phrases fit into different frames (or scenarios) and describes the roles and relationships within these frames.

For "破釜沉舟," the relevant frames might include:

Destruction: This frame involves an agent (the subject carrying out the destruction) and the items being destroyed (pots and boats in this case). It involves intentional action aimed at rendering something unusable or ineffective.

Commitment: This frame would involve committing to a plan or action with determination, where the commitment is demonstrated through some significant act (in this case, the destruction of retreat options).

Resolve: A subframe of Commitment, which deals specifically with a firm decision to act in a particular way, often in the face of obstacles.

Elements of FrameNet Analysis:

Agent: General Xiang Yu and his troops

Theme: The pots and boats

Purpose: To ensure no possibility of retreat

Means: Destruction

Setting: Military encampment during a military campaign

Through these analyses, "破釜沉舟" conveys a broader, metaphorical meaning that extends beyond its literal sense. It symbolizes making a decisive and irreversible decision with a clear focus on achieving a goal or objective, often used in contexts where abandoning all alternative options or potential escape routes underscores the seriousness and determination of the commitment.

Chinese idiom "破釜沉舟"

Here are the top 5 candidates for an English idiom that closely match the meaning of the Chinese idiom "破釜沉舟“ based on the frame and ontology analyses:

- Burn one's boats
- Burn one's bridges
- Cross the Rubicon
- No turning back
- Go all in

Human Expert's Translation

Reference: Strategies for Translating Chengyu (Chinese Idioms), Jim Jones, https://www.ata-divisions.org/CLD/strategies-for-translating-chengyu/)

- Burning one's boats
- Burning the bridges
- Point of no return
- crossing the Rubicon

Chinese idiom "刀山火海“ direct output from GPT-40

Translate the Chinese idiom "刀山火海" into English

The Chinese idiom "刀山火海" can be translated into English as "a mountain of swords and a sea of flames." This phrase metaphorically describes a situation filled with extreme danger or severe challenges, indicating that someone is willing to go through the most dangerous and difficult situations to achieve a goal or demonstrate loyalty.

Translate the Chinese idiom ""刀山火海"" into a corresponding English idiom

The Chinese idiom "刀山火海" (dāo shān huǒ hǎi) literally translates to "mountain of knives and sea of fire." It metaphorically describes a situation that is extremely dangerous, difficult, or filled with challenges. A corresponding English idiom would be "going through hell and high water" or "facing insurmountable obstacles."

Chinese idiom "刀山火海"

Ontology Analysis

Literal Translation

"刀山火海" translates literally to "mountain of knives and sea of fire."

Ontology analysis involves breaking down the components of the idiom and understanding its semantic relationships. Here's a breakdown:

刀 (Dāo) - Knife: Represents danger, sharpness, and potential harm.

山 (Shān) - Mountain: Implies something large, difficult to overcome, or insurmountable.

火 (Huǒ) - Fire: Symbolizes danger, intensity, and destruction.

海 (Hǎi) - Sea: Represents something vast, difficult to navigate, and possibly overwhelming.

These elements combine to create a vivid metaphor for a situation that is both perilous and challenging, where the person is metaphorically climbing a mountain of knives and crossing a sea of fire. This idiom conveys the idea of extreme hardship and adversity.

Chinese idiom "刀山火海"

FrameNet is a theory that focuses on the semantic frames, or conceptual structures, that words and phrases evoke. Let's apply this to "刀山火海":

Frame: Danger

Core Elements:

Dangerous Object (Knives/Fire): The "刀" (knife) and "火" (fire) are central elements that evoke the concept of danger.

Environment (Mountain/Sea): The "山" (mountain) and "海" (sea) provide a setting that amplifies the sense of peril.

Peripheral Elements:

Experiencer: The implied person or entity facing the danger.

Outcome: The potential for harm or disaster if the challenge is not overcome.

Frame: Challenge/Adversity

Core Elements:

Obstacle (Mountain/Sea): The mountain of knives and sea of fire represent significant obstacles or challenges.

Effort: The need for extraordinary effort to overcome these challenges.

Peripheral Elements:

Motivation: The reason why the person is facing such dangers, which could be inferred from context.

Resolution: The possible overcoming of the challenges, though the idiom focuses more on the existence of the challenge than the resolution.

Summary

The idiom "刀山火海" evokes a frame of extreme danger and challenge, combining elements of peril and adversity. The ontology and FrameNet analysis reveal that the idiom encapsulates the essence of facing overwhelming difficulties, where success is uncertain, but the stakes are high.

Chinese idiom "刀山火海"

Here are the top 5 candidates for an English idiom that closely match the meaning of the Chinese idiom "刀山火海 “ based on the frame and ontology analyses:

1. **Run the gauntlet**
   - This idiom means to go through a series of difficulties or dangers to reach a goal, similar to facing a "mountain of knives and sea of fire."
2. **Walk through fire**
   - This idiom conveys the idea of enduring extreme challenges and difficulties, akin to navigating through a perilous situation.
3. **Face the music**
   - While this idiom primarily means to confront the consequences of one's actions, it can also imply facing difficult situations head-on with courage.
4. **Go through hell and high water**
   - This idiom means to endure severe trials and tribulations, reflecting the idea of facing extreme danger and difficulty.
5. **Into the lion's den**
   - This idiom means to enter a very dangerous or hostile situation, similar to confronting a mountain of knives and a sea of fire.

Human Expert's Translation

Reference: Strategies for Translating Chengyu (Chinese Idioms), Jim Jones, https://www.ata-divisions.org/CLD/strategies-for-translating-chengyu/)

- Literally meaning “mountain of knives and sea of fire,”

Chinese idiom “抛砖引玉” direct output from GPT-4O

Translate the Chinese idiom "抛砖引玉" into English

The Chinese idiom "抛砖引玉" literally translates to "throwing a brick to attract jade." It means to offer something of lesser value in the hope of receiving something more valuable in return. It's often used metaphorically to describe someone who presents a simple or modest idea or effort to inspire or prompt others to contribute something better or more refined.

Translate the Chinese idiom ""抛砖引玉"" into a corresponding English idiom

The Chinese idiom "抛砖引玉" can be translated into the English idiom "to break the ice." Both idioms convey the idea of making the first move, often with something modest or simple, to encourage others to contribute something more significant or valuable.

Chinese idiom "抛砖引玉"

Ontology Analysis of the Chinese Idiom "抛砖引玉"

1. Basic Components:

抛 (pāo): To throw or to cast.

砖 (zhuān): Brick, a symbol of something of lesser value or commonness.

引 (yǐn): To attract or lead.

玉 (yù): Jade, a symbol of something valuable, precious, or of higher quality.

2. Ontological Categories:

Entities:

Brick (砖): *Represents something of lesser value, often used metaphorically to denote a modest or insignificant offering.*

Jade (玉): *Represents something of higher value, often used metaphorically to denote a valuable response or outcome.*

Actions:

Throwing (抛): *An action initiating a process or interaction.*

Attracting (引): *An action that results from the initial action, leading to a response.*

3. Relationships:

Causal Relationship: The act of throwing a brick (a simple or humble offering) leads to attracting jade (a valuable or significant return).

Hierarchical Relationship: The brick is ontologically inferior to the jade, which represents the valuable outcome that one hopes to achieve.

4. Metaphorical Mapping:

Source Domain: Throwing a brick (making a modest effort or contribution).

Target Domain: Attracting jade (inspiring or eliciting a valuable response or contribution from others).

Chinese idiom "抛砖引玉"

Frame Analysis Based on FrameNet Theory

Frames Involved:

Giving Frame: The "throwing" of a brick implies an initial act of offering or giving, even though the value of the offering is modest.

Receiving Frame: The "attracting" of jade implies the reception of something valuable, indicating a positive outcome resulting from the initial act.

Value Judgment Frame: The contrast between the brick (less valuable) and the jade (more valuable) involves a judgment of value, highlighting the expectation of a more significant return for a smaller investment.

Frame Elements:

Agent: The person or entity that throws the brick, symbolizing the initiator of the action.

Object: The brick, symbolizing the initial offering or contribution.

Recipient: The person or entity who is expected to respond with the jade, symbolizing the valuable contribution or response.

Result: The acquisition of jade, symbolizing the valuable outcome or reward resulting from the initial action.

Frame Relations:

Inheritance: The "Giving" frame inherits from a broader frame of "Transaction" where an exchange is anticipated.

Subframe: The "Receiving" frame can be seen as a subframe of the broader "Transaction" frame, specifically focusing on the outcome or response.

Perspective: The idiom takes the perspective of the initiator (the one throwing the brick) and anticipates a response from others (attracting jade).

Chinese idiom "抛砖引玉"

Here are the top 5 candidates for an English idiom that closely match the meaning of the Chinese idiom "抛砖引玉" based on the frame and ontology analyses:

"To cast a small stone to attract a gem"

"To plant a seed and harvest a tree"

"To give a penny and get a pound"

"To break the ice for bigger ideas"

"To offer a spark to ignite a flame"

Human Expert's Translation

Reference: Strategies for Translating Chengyu (Chinese Idioms), Jim Jones, https://www.ata-divisions.org/CLD/strategies-for-translating-chengyu/)

"to get the ball rolling by starting with something of average value."

Chinese idiom “不明觉厉” direct output from GPT-40

Translate the Chinese idiom “ " into English

The Chinese idiom "不明觉厉" (bù míng jué lì) can be translated into English as "It’s unclear but impressive" or "I don’t understand it, but it seems awesome."This idiom is often used to describe something that seems profound, complex, or advanced, but the speaker doesn’t fully understand it. Despite the lack of understanding, the speaker can sense its significance or feels that it must be impressive.

Translate the Chinese idiom “不明觉厉" into a corresponding English idiom

A corresponding English idiom for “不明觉厉" (bù míng jué lì) could be "It’s all Greek to me, but it sounds impressive."This idiom captures the idea of something being difficult to understand (like a foreign language) but still appearing significant or impressive.

Chinese idiom “不明觉厉”

FrameNet is a linguistic theory that examines how words evoke certain types of knowledge structures, known as "frames." Frames are conceptual structures that describe various situations, events, or objects and the participants involved.

For the idiom "不明觉厉" (bù míng jué lì), the analysis can be broken down as follows:

1. **Core Frame: Lack of Understanding**
    1. ***Participants:***
        1. **Cognizer**: The individual who is experiencing the lack of understanding.
        2. **Phenomenon**: The subject or content that is not understood.
    2. ***Frame Elements:***
        1. **Lack of Clarity**: The "不明" part of the idiom indicates that the subject is not clearly understood by the cognizer.
2. **Core Frame: Perception and Evaluation**
    1. ***Participants:***
        1. **Evaluator**: The individual who perceives and evaluates the subject.
        2. **Phenomenon**: The subject or content being perceived and evaluated.
    2. ***Frame Elements:***
        1. **Subjective Perception**: The "觉" part of the idiom focuses on the personal feeling or reaction to the unclear subject.
        2. **Positive Evaluation**: The "厉" part of the idiom provides an evaluative judgment that the unclear subject is impressive or awesome.
3. **Integration of Frames:**
    1. *The frames of **Lack of Understanding** and **Perception and Evaluation** are integrated to form the overall meaning of the idiom. The lack of understanding does not hinder the positive evaluation; rather, the positive evaluation emerges precisely because the subject is perceived as complex or profound.*
4. **Cultural Frame:**
    1. *In a broader cultural context, the idiom reflects a value placed on expertise, complexity, and profundity. Even when something is not fully understood, it can still be respected or admired for its apparent depth or significance. This might suggest an underlying cultural appreciation for mystery or complexity.*
5. **Frame Relations:**
    1. ***Causality**: The lack of understanding causes a subjective perception.*
    2. ***Connotation**: The subjective perception leads to a positive connotation (impressive or awesome).*

Chinese idiom "不明觉厉"

Here are the top 5 candidates for an English idiom that closely match the meaning of the Chinese idiom “不明觉厉” based on the frame and ontology analyses:

"I don’t get it, but it’s impressive.“

"It’s over my head, but it’s awesome.”

"Sounds complicated, but it must be brilliant.”

"Looks mysterious, but it’s clearly genius.“

"I’m lost, but it’s obviously genius."

Chinese idiom "男女有别"

Here are the top 5 candidates for an English idiom that closely match the meaning of the Chinese idiom "男女有别" based on the frame and ontology analyses:

"Men are from Mars, women are from Venus."

This idiom emphasizes the inherent differences between men and women, suggesting that they are almost from different worlds in terms of their characteristics, behavior, and thinking."

To each his own.

"While this idiom is more general, it can be applied to suggest that different genders have their own roles, preferences, or behaviors, which should be respected.

"Vive la différence!"

This French phrase, often used in English, celebrates the differences between the sexes, suggesting that these differences are not only natural but also desirable.

"A woman's place is in the home."

Although outdated and controversial, this idiom reflects traditional gender roles, implying that men and women have distinct societal roles.

"Separate spheres."

This phrase historically refers to the idea that men and women occupy different roles or spheres in life—men in public, professional life, and women in private, domestic life.

Conclusion

- The performance was on par with human experts
- By analyzing the semantics, a core aspect of human intelligence, the concepts, properties, and logical rules informing the system's decisions can be understood to enhance translation
- Additionally, semantic reasoning can simulate the LLMs' decision process transparently by applying the same logical inferences over the semantic framework generated by LLMs

Thank you
Ming Qian
919-523-1320
mqian@cra.com
qianmi@gmail.com

Enhancing Localization Workflows

A Deep Dive into Automated Post-Editing with GenAI

Speaker: Maciej Modrzejewski

BIG LANGUAGE SOLUTIONS

NMT Systems: The Industry Standard in MT

- NMT Systems:
  - Leveraging MTPE (Machine Translation Post-Editing) for optimized workflows
  - rawMT
- Addressing Key Challenges in NMT
- Maximizing the Impact of Large Language Models (LLMs)
- Hybrid MT workflows
  - NMT-based workflows augmented by LLMs-based components
  - Use of Quality Estimation (QE) models

BIG LANGUAGE SOLUTIONS

Limitations of Neural Machine Translation Systems

Challenges with Out-of-Domain Scenarios

Handling unfamiliar content & Maintaining quality
Model Robustness

Incorporating Specialized Terminology

Adapting to client-specific terms
Using specialized glossaries

Handling Language Nuances

Idiomatic expressions
Formal vs. informal language

Contextual understanding

LLMs enable paragraph-by-paragraph translations

Addressing Ambiguity and Bias

Managing bias
Cultural nuances

BIG LANGUAGE SOLUTIONS

LLMs address limitations of NMT systems

BIG LANGUAGE SOLUTIONS

Automated Post-Editing (APE)

BIG LANGUAGE SOLUTIONS

"Automated Post-Editing (APE) is the process of refining MT content by sending the source text and the initial NMT output (hypothesis) to a Generative AI engine for linguistic review."

APE Prompt

You will act as an Engine for Automated Post-Edition, specializing in the [domain_name] domain.
You will receive {len(x)} source segments in {source_language} and {len(y)} machine-translated outputs in {target_language} from a custom, domain-adapted NMT engine.

Your task is to:
- Improve the fluency and translation quality of the output.
- Ensure 100% accuracy without introducing any new facts.
- Retain all relevant information.
- Match the capitalization of the source text.

Your final output must be in the target language: {target_language}.

Source: {x}
Custom Model Output: {y} ← MT Hypothesis

Case 1: APE in out-of-domain scenario

- Use APE to post-edit an out-of-domain test set
- Test Data Set:
  - Khresmoi Summary Translation Test Data 2.0
  - Medical domain
  - Language pair: ENG-DEU
  - 500 segments

BIG LANGUAGE SOLUTIONS

Case 1: APE in out-of-domain scenario

- BLEU scores:

	Big Language generic model	Google Translate	DeepL
Regular Translation	32.3	30.8	32.6
After APE with GPT-4o	34.3 (Δ +2.0)	34.2 (Δ +3.4)	33.7 (Δ +1.1)

- Average BLEU improvement: +2.15 BLEU

BIG LANGUAGE SOLUTIONS

Case 1: APE in out-of-domain scenario

- COMET-20 and COMET-22 scores:

	Big Language generic model	Google Translate	DeepL
Regular Translation	COMET-20: 0.6340 COMET-22: 0.8626	COMET-20: 0.6977 COMET-22: 0.8808	COMET-20: 0.6958 COMET-22: 0.8797
After APE (gpt-4o)	COMET-20: 0.6968 COMET-22: 0.8810	COMET-20: 0.7037 COMET-22: 0.8824	COMET-20: 0.7023 COMET-22: 0.8819

BIG LANGUAGE SOLUTIONS

Case 2: APE with a fine-tuned NMT system

- Perform APE on the output from a fine-tuned NMT system
- Training data size: 60k segments
- Test Data Set:
  - True Hold-Out Test set (not used in training)
  - Domain: Healthcare
  - Language pair: ENG-SPA-US
  - 1000 segments

BIG LANGUAGE SOLUTIONS

Case 2: APE with a fine-tuned NMT system

- BLEU and COMET scores:

	Big Language fine-tuned model	Google Translate
Regular Translation	BLEU: 72.8 COMET-20: 0.9675 COMET-22: 0.9119	BLEU: 49.9 COMET-20: 0.8238 COMET-22: 0.8835
After APE (gpt-4o)	BLEU: 63.5 COMET-20: 0.9218 COMET-22: 0.9066	BLEU: 51.5 COMET-20: 0.7961 COMET-22: 0.8730

➢ APE doesn't bring any improvement for fine-tuned NMT systems!

BIG LANGUAGE SOLUTIONS

Case 3: APE with a in-domain ref-free QE model

- Idea: Identify **worst translations** from fine-tuned NMT system with an in-domain, reference-free QE model
- Perform APE only on those segments

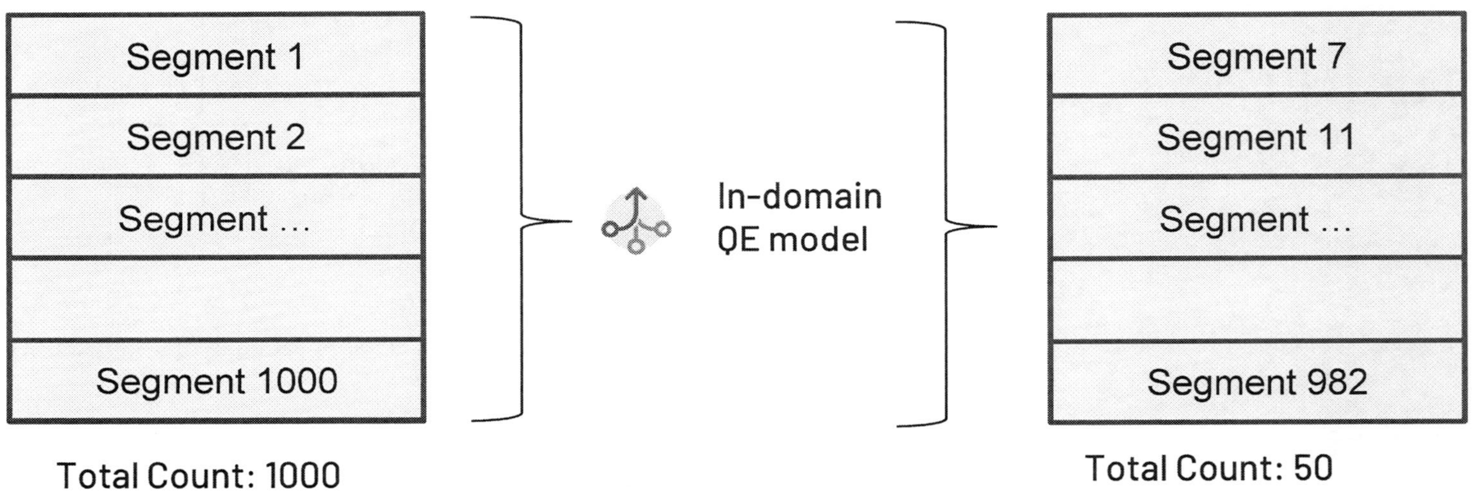

BIG LANGUAGE SOLUTIONS

Case 3: APE with a in-domain ref-free QE model

- Identical test data set as in Case #2
- Evaluation metrics for 50 worst translations (out of 1000 segments):

	Big Language fine-tuned model	Δ
Regular Translation	BLEU: 52.2 COMET-20: 0.5307 COMET-22: 0.8372	BLEU: -1.8 COMET-20: +0.053 COMET-22: +0.024
After APE (gpt-4o)	BLEU: 50.4 COMET-20: 0.5834 COMET-22: 0.8612	

BIG LANGUAGE SOLUTIONS

Case 3: APE with a in-domain ref-free QE model

- Human Evaluation for the 50 worst performing segments
- APE-enhanced translation is preferred:
  - Translation 1: Regular Translation
  - Translation 2: APE-output
  - Linguist's review: *"In my opinion, [Translation 2] was a better translation, because, even though, glossary terms were not translated as per glossary like in Translation 1, there were no missing words, or issues with Spanish style, or inaccurate translations. Additionally, Translation 2 was more natural sounding and clear."*

BIG LANGUAGE SOLUTIONS

Case 3: APE with a in-domain ref-free QE model

- Example for translation improvement:

Source	Division of Neighborhood Health Research	
Reference	División de Investigación Sanitaria del Vecindario	
Fine-tuned NMT model	División de Investigación Médica orientada a los vecindarios	Ref-free QE score: 0.5140
After APE	División de Investigación de Salud en los Vecindarios	Ref-free QE score: 0.5690

BIG LANGUAGE SOLUTIONS

Case 3: APE with a in-domain ref-free QE model

- Edit Distance Report

	Regular Translation	APE-output	Δ
Edited Segments	26/50	20/50	-23%
Absolute Edit Distance	783	655	-16%
Normalized Edit Distance	0.196	0.125	-36%
Total PE Time [in mins]	35	20	-43%
TTE [words/s]	6,84	3,91	

BIG LANGUAGE SOLUTIONS

Conclusions

1. APE Effectiveness
    i. Enhances baseline translation quality in out-of-domain NMT systems.
    ii. Identifies and corrects issues that commonly arise in these systems.
2. In-Domain Scenarios:
    i. APE may not always improve results; potential for performance decline.
    ii. Despite this, APE benefits approximately 5% of the worst translations.
3. Optimization Strategy:
    i. Use in-domain QE model to identify problematic segments.
    ii. Targeted APE application reduces post-editing time by 40% for these segments.
4. Use of GenAI engine interchangeable
    i. Use a fine-tuned LLM for APE for better results

BIG LANGUAGE SOLUTIONS

CantonMT: Cantonese-English Neural Machine Translation Looking into Evaluations

Kung Yin Hong, Lifeng Han *, Riza Batista-Navarro, Goran Nenadic
Department of Computer Science, The University of Manchester
Oxford Rd, Manchester M13 9PL, United Kingdom
kenrick.kung@gmail.com
{lifeng.han, riza.batista, g.nenadic}@manchester.ac.uk
*corresponding author

Abstract

Cantonese-English is a low-resource language pair for machine translation (MT) studies, despite the vast amount of English content publicly available online and the large amount of native Cantonese speakers. Based on our previous work on CantonMT from Hong et al. (2024), where we created the open-source fine-tuned systems for Cantonese-English Neural MT (NMT) using base-models NLLB, OpusMT, and mBART and corpus collections and creation, in this paper, we report our extended experiments on model training and comparisons. In particular, we incorporated human-based evaluations using native Cantonese speakers who are also fluent in the English language. We designed a modified version of the HOPE metric from Gladkoff and Han (2022) for the categorised error analysis and serenity-level statistics (naming **HOPES**). The models selected for human evaluations are NLLB-mBART fine-tuned and two translators from commercial companies: Bing and GPT4. Further analysis of fine-tuned systems and human-evaluation insights can shed some light on Cantonese-English NMT and its future development. The open-source CantonMT toolkit and analytics will be accessible via the GitHub page (at https://github.com/kenrickkung/CantoneseTranslation).

1 Introduction

Cantonese is a Sinitic language spoken in Hong Kong, Macau, and the Guangdong region of southern PRC, it is the second most spoken Sinitic language, after Mandarin Chinese (Wiedenhof, 2015). With a substantial 80 million native speakers (Eberhard et al., 2023), Cantonese is still an under-researched area in the spectrum of Natural Language Processing, as demonstrated in ACL Anthology, where only 47 papers are related to Cantonese, compared with 2355 for (Mandarin) Chinese (Xiang et al., 2022).

Despite having the second most speakers in the family of Sinitic languages, most State-of-the-art commercial translators either do not support Cantonese or have below-par translation quality when translated to English. This leads to scenarios where individuals seeking Cantonese resources face challenges, particularly in casual forums where tones are often very similar to spoken language.

We believe that Cantonese is a unique language that captures the rich cultural history of Hong Kong, Macau, and the Guangdong province of China. Two major challenges when dealing with Cantonese translations are Colloquialism and Multilingualism. Colloquialism, a linguistic style used for informal and casual conversation, often occurs in Cantonese and includes non-standard spelling, slang, and neologisms. As for Multilingualism, Hong Kong was once a British colony and has a rich Chinese cultural influence; code-switching [1] happens often in day-to-day conversation; and words can also be loaned from English through phonetic transliteration (Bauer, 2006).

[1] the act of using multiple languages together

Therefore, following the trend of language diversity and inclusion in NLP, we have set out the aim to develop a translation system that can translate texts from Cantonese to English and reach comparable results against commercial translators, as reported in our CANTONMT1.0 (Hong et al., 2024).

As an extended investigation of our first milestone, regarding the Evaluation Strategy, the models developed are evaluated through a range of metrics, including lexicon-based word surface matching (SacreBLEU and hLEPOR) and those based on embedding spaces (COMET and BERTscore). Following these metrics, the top-performing model is chosen for comparison with the two top-performing commercial translation tools. We designed the HOPES (standing for "Simplified HOPE") human evaluation framework, which we modified based on HOPE, a human-centric post-editing based metric by Gladkoff and Han (2022).

2 Background and Related Works

2.1 Large Language Models

With the rise of LLMs, there are dozens of pre-trained models which are capable on MT tasks with none or few fine-tuning. In our investigation, there are 3 models chosen for further fine-tuning with our dataset, the reason behind choosing these models can be found at CANTONMT1.0. Here is a brief introduction of each model, which could help readers understand the difference with depth.

2.1.1 Opus-MT

Opus-MT (Tiedemann and Thottingal, 2020), developed by Helsinki-NLP, is a Transformer-based NMT, which is using Marian-NMT [2] as the framework for the model training. The model family is trained with a publicly available parallel corpus collected in OPUS[3]. The model is specifically trained for MT task, and should not be classified as a general purpose LLM. Two specific models are used in this project, *Opus-mt-zh-en* and *Opus-mt-en-zh*, which are models that translate Chinese to English and English to Chinese. The forward model (Chinese to English) has around 77M parameters, which is considered quite a small model when compared to LLMs.

[2]https://marian-nmt.github.io/

[3]http://opus.nlpl.eu/

2.1.2 mBART

mBART (Liu et al., 2020), a multilingual Seq2Seq denoising auto-encoder. It is trained with the BART (Lewis et al., 2020) objectives with a multilingual corpus. The pre-training of mBART is trained by corrupting text with a noising function and also learning a model to reconstruct the original text. It uses the CC25 Corpus which contains 25 languages and follows the standard Transformer architecture with 12 layers of encoders and 12 layers of decoders.

In CANTONMT, a specific version of the model is used (*mbart-large-50-many-to-many-mmt*) which supports 50 languages, including (Mandarin) Chinese. However, it does not support Cantonese as a language. The model is also fine-tuned for multilingual translation and is introduced by Tang et al. (2020) which has added 25 additional languages without hurting the performance of the model. The model has a total of 610M parameters, a massive increase compared to the previous Opus model.

2.1.3 NLLB

No Language Left Behind (NLLB) (NLLB-Team et al., 2022), to the best of our knowledge, is the only publicly available LLM which contains the language Cantonese (Lang-Code: yue_Hant). It is trained upon the FLORES-200 dataset which contains 200 languages and serves as a high-quality benchmark dataset. The model architecture is also based on the Transformer encoder-decoder architecture (Vaswani et al., 2017).

In CANTONMT, a distilled version of NLLB (*nllb-200-distilled-600M*) is used since based on our available computation power, there is no chance of fine-tuning a larger model. The model is already fine-tuned on MT task, and the language pair in focus is Cantonese-English.

2.2 Back-Translation

Data Augmentation via Back translation is a technique used by MT researchers when tackling low-resource languages. Typically, since not enough data is available, the model may not be able to learn the translation of the language thoroughly and, thus might harm the performance of MT. This technique has been one of the standards for leveraging monolingual corpora since SMT (Bojar and Tamchyna,

2011), and is still being used with NMT (Sennrich et al., 2016).

The approach uses a model, which translates target language text to the source language (back model), for translating a monolingual corpus in the target language to the source language. This creates a synthetic parallel corpus (Silver Standard), which is different from human annotated parallel corpus (Gold Standard). In theory, with more data, the model can be performing better.

2.3 MT on Cantonese

2.3.1 Commercial Translators

A survey has been conducted on four different commercial MT software, including Google, Bing, Baidu, and DeepL.

For Google[4] and DeepL[5], despite being the most popular software used for translation in daily lives, they do not support Cantonese as an option, but only (Mandarin) Chinese. Therefore, no further investigations are being made on the platforms. For Bing[6] and Baidu[7], there are native Cantonese support in translation and therefore are chosen as a state-of-the-art comparison in the following sections.

With the rise of LLMs, there are also questions on whether or not this kind of model with prompting can give better results when compared with a more traditional approach with fine-tuning on LLMs. In this project, Generative Pre-trained Transformers(GPT)-4 (OpenAI, 2024) are being investigated with specific prompting to compare against our model. The implementation of GPT-4 that we used is Cantonese Companion, which was custom-made for translation to Cantonese by a community builder.[8] However, it should be noted that we do not know how much data was used for this community-trained Cantonese Companion and the training was not transparent, in addition to its dependence on the commercial platform.

2.3.2 Research Models and Toolkits

Research work focusing on Cantonese-English MT has not gained much attention up to date unfortunately. Some typical literature work we found includes example-based MT by Wu et al. (2006); RNN-based model by Wing (2020); BiLSTM model by Liu (2022); Transformer-models by Yi Mak and Lee (2022). In addition, TransCan[9] is a NMT model which translates English to Cantonese and is trained based on bart-base-Chinese and BART with additional linear projection to connect them.

3 Review CANTONMT Methodology

3.1 Datasets and Preprocessing

Since Cantonese-English parallel corpora are not readily available, combinations of different datasets are used for the initial training of baseline models. Furthermore, to aid the back-translation strategy in the latter part of the project, monolingual corpora for both Cantonese and English are required, and therefore, they will be discussed in the following section.

3.1.1 Parallel Corpus

To fine-tune different baseline models, a parallel corpus is required to train the model to translate Cantonese to English at a reasonable level. In the end, three different parallel corpora are found between different timestamps of the investigation. Therefore, the latter two are used for training only, while the former are used for training and evaluation.

Words.hk Corpus Words.hk[10] is an open Cantonese-English dictionary publicly available for people to download. We used the full dataset from their website, which contains different Cantonese words and some example sentences with their English translation. An example of the word "投資/ touzi" in the dictionary is given in Figure 1.

From the data, only the sentence after the tag *eng* has been used in this case, the sentence, "*She invested $1 million in renovating the shop*", has been extracted and also its corresponding Cantonese translation which is the sentence after the tag *yue*. Data pre-processing has also been done, including removing hashtags and space since there is quite a lot in the dataset, potentially affecting data quality. In ad-

[4]https://translate.google.com/
[5]https://www.deepl.com/translator
[6]https://www.bing.com/translator
[7]https://fanyi.baidu.com
[8]https://chat.openai.com/share/7ee588af-dc48-4406-95f4-0471e1fb70a8
[9]https://github.com/ayaka14732/TransCan
[10]https://words.hk

```
85826,投資:tau4 zi1,"(pos:動詞)
<explanation>
yue:付出#資金，以知識去搵#尋租、搵減少市場競爭嘅方法，期望將來有#回報
eng:to invest
<eg>
yue:佢投資咗一百萬去裝修呢間舖頭。 (keoi5 tau4 zi1 zo2 jat1 baak3 maan6 heoi3 zong1 sau1 ni1 gaan1 pou3 tau2)
eng:She invested $1 million in renovating the shop.",,OK,已公開
```

Figure 1: Sample Data Format for Words.hk

dition, there are sentences with multiple translations; in that case, the first translation has been taken. In the end, 44K sentences have been extracted from the dataset. A graph of the frequencies of the length of the Cantonese sentence has been plotted in Figure 2. It is noticed that despite the effort only to keep sentences and no definitions, there are still quite a lot of short sentences in the dataset. Since for short sentences, it could be straightforward for the model to translate and, therefore, may lead to a bias in the evaluation, we have decided to split the dataset into short sentences and long sentences, where short sentences are sentences that have ten characters or less. In the end, there are 19.4K short sentences and 24.6K long sentences. Since data are already very scarce, we have decided not to opt into the standard train-dev-test split of 8/1/1 or 7/2/1 and instead went for the approach of a 3K dev set and 3K test set. The reason behind this is based on that the standard practice for Workshop of Machine Translation (WMT)[11] shared task uses around 3K sentences for test sets when comparing different MT systems.

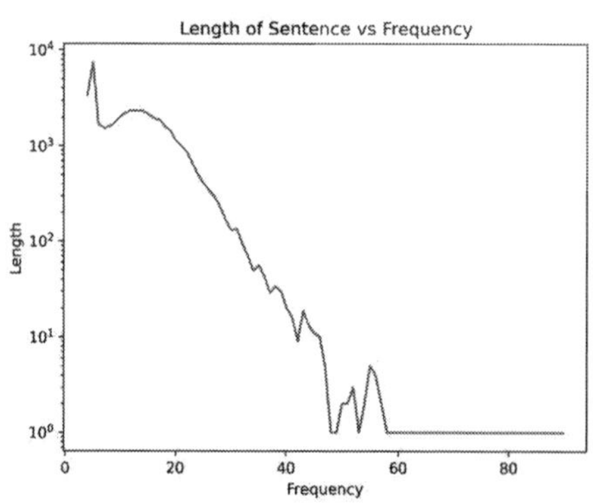

Figure 2: Words.hk - Sentence Length

[11]https://www2.statmt.org/wmt24

[12]https://wenlin.com

[13]https://opus.nlpl.eu/

Wenlin Corpus Wenlin Institute [12] creates software and dictionaries for learning the Chinese language, and there is a dictionary, ABC Cantonese-English Comprehensive Dictionary, which is readily available for registered users to use for research purposes. The process to obtain the dataset, however, is not straightforward. It involves first getting a list of URLs which store the data, and after that, it requires web scraping; at the end, an XML file is obtained, which includes all the sentences and other content.

Extracting is required to convert an XML file to a parallel corpus after obtaining an XML file. Based on initial inspection, the sentence should be inside the tag *WL*; therefore, regular expression techniques are used to extract those sentences. After that, similar pre-processing as Words.hk has been done to obtain the training set and 14.5K parallel sentences are extracted.

Opus Corpora (Tiedemann and Nygaard, 2004) is a collection of translated documents collected from the internet. The corpus is already aligned, and therefore, no pre-processing is required. It can be easily downloaded via their website [13]. An additional 9.6K parallel sentences are added to the final training set.

3.1.2 Monolingual Corpus

To aid the process of back-translation, a monolingual corpus from both the source and target language is required to investigate the *iterative back-translation* approach.

English Corpus - There are many English monolingual corpora available, and in this project, the dataset we have decided to use is from the WMT 2012 News Collection (Callison-Burch et al., 2012). It can be downloaded on the WMT website and contains 434K sentences, which is more than required for the back-translation.

Cantonese Corpus - However, for the Cantonese corpus, it is difficult to find an existing monolingual corpus. There is a Hong Kong Cantonese Corpus (HKCanCor) available (Lee et al., 2022). However, this is based on spontaneous speech and radio programs from the late 1990s and, therefore, might be outdated and there is the language evolution factors with time passing by. Another reason for not choosing the data is that it only consists of 10K sentences, which is insufficient for back-translation purposes.

Based on findings from Liang et al. (2021), there should be abundant data on social media, including Facebook, YouTube, Instagram and different local forums. Since it will be hard to filter out Hong Kong users who use Cantonese in their social media comments, we have decided to turn to local forums. There are few mainstream ones which have an abundance of data, including Baby-Kingdom[14], DiscussHK[15], and LIHKG[16].

In the end, based on tools available online, we have decided to collect data from LIHKG. It is an online forum platform that was launched in 2016 and has multiple categories, including sports, entertainment, hot topics, gossip, current affairs, etc. There is a scraper readily available online from Ho and Or (2020), which we have used to scrape the data from LIHKG. Data is scraped in CSV format, where an example can be seen in Figure 3 (profile ID masked).

Overall, 29K posts have been scraped, and only the text part has been used as the monolingual data. Some more **pre-processing** has been done to the data, including stripping all the links in the data and filtering out all the sentences shorter than 10 Chinese characters. In the end, 1.1M sentences have been scraped, which is more than enough for our investigation. We **shuffled** the dataset so that it can be used by the research community for free, as long as they sign a user agreement form for non-commercial usage.

3.2 Model Trainings

The model fine-tuning methodology of CANTONMT is presented in Figure 4, which includes the following steps:

1. DataPrep: data collection and pre-processing
2. ModelFineTunePhase1: model selection for initial translator fine-tuning (ft, v1)
3. SynDataGenerate: synthetic data generation using the initial translator and cleaned data
4. ModelFineTunePhase2: second step MT fine-tuning using real and synthetic data (ft-syn)
5. ModelEval: model evaluation using both embedding-based metrics (BERTscore and COMET) and lexical metrics (SacreBLEU and hLEPOR)

Detailed techniques on each step was explained in CANTONMT1.0 by Hong et al. (2024). We also report comparisons with commerically available translation engines such as the Baidu Translator, Bing Translator and GPT4. The implementation of GPT-4 that we used is Cantonese Companion, which was custom-made for translation to Cantonese by a community builder.[17]

3.3 Automatic Evaluations

We used a range of different evaluation metrics including the lexical-based SacreBLEU (Post, 2018) and hLEPOR (Han et al., 2013a, 2021), and the embedding-based BERTscore (Zhang et al., 2020) and COMET (Rei et al., 2020). hLEPOR has reported much higher correlation scores to the human evaluation than BLEU and other lexical-based metrics on the WMT shared task data (Han et al., 2013b). However, recent WMT metrics task findings have demonstrated the advantages of neural metrics based on embedding space similarities (Freitag et al., 2022).

The automatic evaluation scores from CANTONMT models and other commercial engines are listed in Table 1. From the automatic evaluation metrics, the results demonstrated that the model-switch fine-tuned NLLB-mBART using 1:1 ratio of synthetic and real data achieved relatively higher scores than other fine-tuning models. Thus, we selected this model into the human evaluation loop, together with Bing and GPT4-ft.

[14] https://www.baby-kingdom.com/forum.php

[15] https://www.discuss.com.hk/

[16] https://lihkg.com

[17] https://chat.openai.com/share/7ee588af-dc48-4406-95f4-0471e1fb70a8

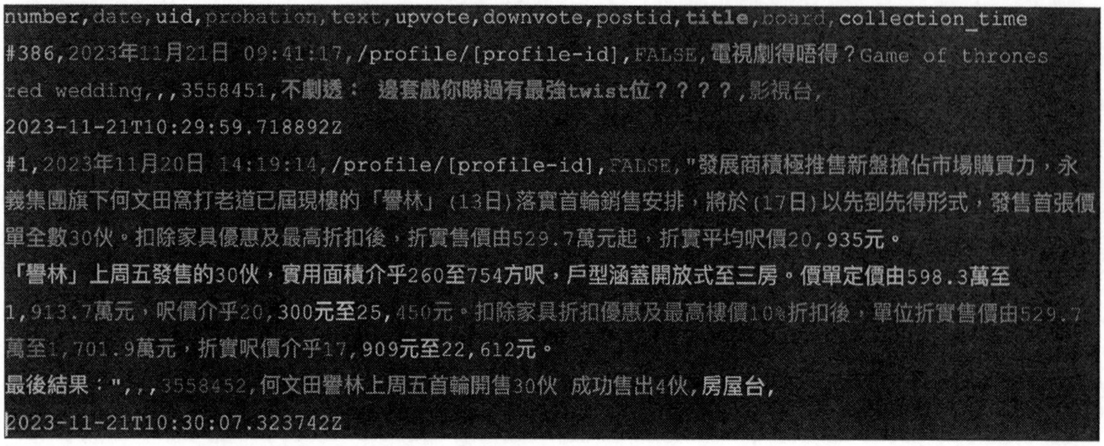

Figure 3: LIHKG Data Example

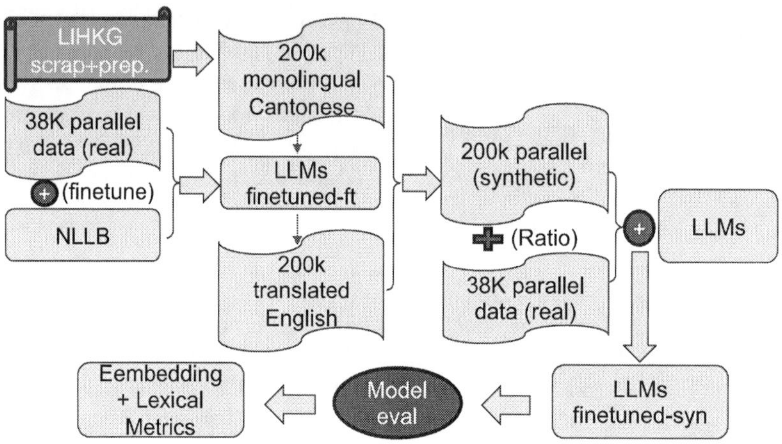

Figure 4: CANTONMT Pipeline: data collection and preprocessing, synthetic data generation, model fine-tuning, model evaluation Hong et al. (2024)

4 Human Evaluations

Even with four different automatic metrics, it is still hard to judge the model's performance based on those chosen metrics. Therefore, human evaluations are conducted to understand better the comparison with state-of-the-art models and the *different types* of errors that the trained models or deployed translators tend to make.

4.1 HOPES framework

With that in mind, we have borrowed the HOPE framework (Gladkoff and Han, 2022). The original HOPE framework includes eight detailed error types from industrial practice, already much simpler than MQM (Lommel et al., 2024). However, upon our review, some error types can be merged to make the human evaluation task more efficient and better match our data, where a modified framework, HOPE-Simplified (HOPES), is proposed. The merging procedure is shown in the below list.

1. **Merge Impact(IMP) and Mistranslation(MIS) as MIS**:
   The definitions of IMP and MIS are "The translation fails to convert main thoughts clearly" and "Translation distorts the meaning of the source and presents mistranslation or accuracy error" respectively. They overlap in accuracy and meaning preservation from the source sen-

Model Name	SacreBLEU	hLEPOR	BERTscore	COMET
nllb-forward-bl	16.5117	0.5651	0.9248	0.7376
nllb-forward-syn-h:h	15.7751	0.5616	0.9235	0.7342
nllb-forward-syn-1:1	**16.5901**	0.5686	**0.925**	**0.7409**
nllb-forward-syn-1:1-10E	16.5203	**0.5689**	0.9247	0.738
nllb-forward-syn-1:3	15.9175	0.5626	0.924	0.7376
nllb-forward-syn-1:5	15.8074	0.562	0.9237	0.7386
nllb-forward-syn-1:1-mbart	**16.8077**	**0.571**	**0.9256**	**0.7425**
nllb-forward-syn-1:3-mbart	15.8621	0.5617	0.9246	0.7384
nllb-forward-syn-1:1-opus	16.5537	0.5704	0.9254	0.7416
nllb-forward-syn-1:3-opus	15.9348	0.5651	0.9242	0.7374
mbart-forward-bl	15.7513	0.5623	0.9227	0.7314
mbart-forward-syn-1:1-nllb	**16.0358**	**0.5681**	**0.9241**	**0.738**
mbart-forward-syn-1:3-nllb	15.326	0.5584	0.9225	0.7319
opus-forward-bl-10E	**15.0602**	**0.5581**	**0.9219**	**0.7193**
opus-forward-syn-1:1-10E-nllb	13.0623	0.5409	0.9164	0.6897
opus-forward-syn-1:3-10E-nllb	13.3666	0.5442	0.9167	0.6957
baidu	16.5669	0.5654	0.9243	0.7401
bing	17.1098	0.5735	0.9258	0.7474
gpt4-ft(CantoneseCompanion)	**19.1622**	**0.5917**	**0.936**	**0.805**
nllb-forward-bl-plus-wenlin14.5k	*16.6662*	*0.5828*	*0.926*	0.7496
mbart-forward-bl-plus-wenlin14.5k	15.2404	0.5734	0.9238	0.7411
opus-forward-bl-plus-wenlin14.5k	13.0172	0.5473	0.9157	0.6882
nllb-200-deploy-no-finetune	11.1827	0.4925	0.9129	0.6863
opus-deploy-no-finetune	10.4035	0.4773	0.9082	0.6584
mbart-deploy-no-finetune	8.3157	0.4387	0.9005	0.6273
nllb-forward-all3corpus	*16.9986*	*0.583*	*0.927*	*0.7549*
nllb-forward-all3corpus-10E	16.1749	0.5728	0.9254	0.7508
mbart-forward-all3corpus	16.3204	0.5766	0.9253	0.7482
opus-forward-all3corpus-10E	14.4699	0.5621	0.9191	0.7074

Table 1: Automatic Evaluation Scores from Different Models in CANTONMT. bl: bilingual real data; syn: synthetic data; h:h - half and half; 1:1/3/5 - 100% real + 100/300/500% synthetic; 10E: 10 epochs (default: 3); top-down second slot: model switch: model type using NLLB but synthetic data from other models (mBART and OpusMT); top-down third slot: including model switch for mBART fine-tuning using synthetic data generated from NLLB; similarly top-down forth slot: including model switch for OpusMT fine-tuning using synthetic data from NLLB. Bottom slot of Cluster 1: Bing/Baidu Translator and GPT4-finetuned Cantonese Companion; **bold** case is the best score of the same slot among the same model categories. Cluster 2: bilingual fine-tuned models using 38K words.hk data plus 14.5k Wenlin data; *italic* indicates the number outperforms the same model fine-tuned with less data 38K. Cluster 3: Deployed Model without fine-tuning Cluster 4: Finetuned with the previous 2 corpora and an additional 10K data from OPUS Corpora we managed to find in the end - it shows the evaluation improvement continues Hong et al. (2024)

tence, which both reflect the semantics error. Therefore, it is merged as Mistranslation(MIS), where the new definition is given as "perceived meaning differs from the actual meaning". Furthermore, the original data does not define the scoring mechanism in a specific way. For example, when the translation mistranslates a critical word, should it be given as a critical error since it distorts the meaning, or a minor error since there is only one mistake in the translation? With the newly defined MIS, the first case could be covered by that, and therefore, a minor error should be given.

2. **Merge Terminology(TRM) and Proper Name (PRN) as Terms(TRM)**:
The original definitions of TRM and PRN are "incorrect terminology, inconsistency on the translation of entities" and "a proper name is translated incorrectly" respectively. In our experimental data, the name is not popular, and proper names can be entity types if they appear in the test set. Therefore, the error types are merged as TRM, with the new definition of "Incorrect terminology", including proper names or inconsistency of translation of entities, where a higher score means there are more incorrect terms".

3. **Merge Style (STL), Proofreading (PRF), Required Adaptation Missing (RAM) into Style(STL).**
The original definitions of these three are "translation has poor style but is not necessarily ungrammatical or formally incorrect", "linguistic error which does not affect accuracy or meaning transfer but needs to be fixed", and "source contains error that has to be corrected or target market requires substantial adaptation of the source, which translator failed to make; impact on the end user suffers". These errors are all related to localisation and adaptation. We *summarise* the merged error type Style as "Translation has poor style, but is not necessarily ungrammatically or formally incorrect. It may also include linguistic error which does not affect meaning, but potentially makes the end user suffer".

Based on literature from Gladkoff et al. (2022) regarding evaluation uncertainty, less than 200 human evaluation sentences are insufficient to make a statistical significance. Therefore, 200 sentences from the test set are randomly sampled from the test set and used for human evaluation. Three different translation systems are chosen, including the best model from our training (NLLB-mBART), one of the commercial translators (Bing) and community-finetuned GPT4.

There were a total of 4 annotators who are fluent English speakers and native Cantonese users annotated the translations for the 200 x 3 translations. Each translation is then evaluated by two annotators to measure the agreement level between them, and therefore, the results should be more accurate and reflect the performance of each system. It should also be noted that the results can also help us understand the general error types the models are making, which may be useful for future work.

4.2 Human Evaluation Outcomes

4.2.1 Text Degeneration

Upon first glance at the synthetic data and test set translations, some interesting phenomena are happening, described as *neural text degeneration* (Holtzman et al., 2020). Examples of text degeneration can be seen in Table 2. From the example, "handwritten" has been repeated multiple times, indicating the models generate repetitive and dull loops. This could be another point of future work to adopt some methods for minimising these situations.

4.2.2 Results

The results are then used to calculate inter-annotator agreement (IAA), via a quadratic-weighted Cohen's Kappa metric (Cohen, 1968), where the ratings are grouped into two individual raters. The results are shown in Table 3.

The results show that the annotators have a substantial agreement level in the category of mistranslation (Landis and Koch, 1977) and the overall rating, which is calculated by adding all 4 metrics together. For the other metrics, terminology and grammar have shown a moderate agreement between annotators. However, there seems to be a low agreement level for style, which suggests that the guidelines might need more refinement and detailed explanations, or more likely, translation style is very personal and should not be a major contributing factor to whether or not the translation is good or not.

Since the annotators have shown some kind of agreement, the results shown in Table 4 should have some indication of whether or not the translation is up-to-standard and can provide a better understanding of the models' performance. Another table can be seen in Table 5 for errors in individual models, where a major error is defined as a total score higher than 15 and a minor error is defined as lower than 15

Source Sentence	佢踢住對人字拖嗽行出。
Model Translation	He walked out with a pair of handwritten handwritten handwritten.

Table 2: Example of Text Degeneration

Metric	NLLB	Bing	GPT4
MIS	0.6671	0.6102	0.5700
TERM	0.5700	0.4775	0.3874
STYLE	0.1123	0.3490	0.0348
GRAM	0.4212	0.2899	0.2850
Overall	0.6230	0.6136	0.4935

Table 3: Cohen's Kappa for Different Models and Metrics

but excluding 0. Translations with no errors in all 4 categories are defined as No error.

The results have shown that fine-tuned GPT4 "CantoneseCompanion" is by far the best model for translation, where over half of the translations have shown no errors, and only 3% of translations have major errors according to the metric. Also, for the different metrics, GPT4 has shown similar performance except for **grammar**, which indicates that *error types are quite diverse for GPT4.*

Moreover, Bing performs better than the best model from NLLB, which is in line with the automatic metric. Nevertheless, both models have only around 25% translation, which is error-free. In the evaluation, it can be seen that there are quite a few cases for both models to translate the sentence literally, which leads to some slang not being correctly translated and, therefore, affects the quality of translation.

For our system, most errors stem from either *mistranslation* or *terminology*, which is often correlated since when a term is not correctly translated, it often causes meaning loss in the sentence. It can also be noticed that most of the sentences are often grammatically correct, which should be expected since the decoder part of the Transformers is trained with large amounts of English data and, therefore, should be well-versed in grammar knowledge.

The result here shows that additional effort will be needed to surpass one of the commercial translators, where there should be more effort put into improving the model's knowledge of *terminology and slang*. For example, having a knowledge graph and knowledge base to represent different terminology and slang (Zhao et al., 2020; Han et al., 2020) could potentially allow the model to understand more terminology in Cantonese. Further pre-training in Cantonese can potentially improve performance too.

5 Discussion and Conclusion

In this paper, we further investigated the system performances from CANTONMT, an open-sourced platform for Cantonese⇔English translation. We designed HOPES metric for human evaluation purposes, which is a simplified version of the HOPE framework by Gladkoff and Han (2022). The simplified HOPES metric has only four error types including mistranslation (MIS), term errors (TERM), style (STYLE), and grammatical errors (GRAM), while keeping the original error severity features from HOPE. The human evaluation result shows that NLLP-mBART fine-tuned model has average error score 12.58, vesus 8.3475 and 2.3575 from Bing and GPT4-ft. Regarding error severity levels, NLLB-mBART has fewer minor-errors than Bing, though more major-errors at this stage.

As we mentioned in CantonMT (Hong et al., 2024), in terms of concerns of **data privacy** such as handling of sensitive data (e.g., in clinical applications related to health analytics of patient data (Han et al., 2024)), CANTONMT can be fully controlled by users without interference from any third parties. We believe the performance of CantonMT models can be continuously improved with more high-quality real and synthetic data integrated for fine-tuning.

Metric	NLLB	Bing	GPT4
MIS	4.8025	2.9875	0.7025
TERM	3.62	2.1425	0.655
STYLE	3.01	2.3975	0.8425
GRAM	1.1475	0.82	0.1575
Overall	12.58	8.3475	2.3575

Table 4: Average Score for Different Models and Metrics on Error Types

Errors	NLLB	Bing	GPT4
No Error	81	119	242
Minor Error	183	206	144
Major Error	136	75	14

Table 5: Error Severity for different models (200 sentences x 2 annotators for each model)

Acknowledgements

We thank the reviewers for their valuable comments and feedback on our work. LH and GN are grateful for the grant "Integrating hospital outpatient letters into the healthcare data space" (EP/V047949/1; funder: UKRI/EPSRC).

References

Bauer, R. S. (2006). The stratification of English loanwords in Cantonese. *Journal of Chinese Linguistics*, 34(2):172–191.

Bojar, O. and Tamchyna, A. (2011). Improving translation model by monolingual data. In Callison-Burch, C., Koehn, P., Monz, C., and Zaidan, O. F., editors, *Proceedings of the Sixth Workshop on Statistical Machine Translation*, pages 330–336, Edinburgh, Scotland. Association for Computational Linguistics.

Callison-Burch, C., Koehn, P., Monz, C., Post, M., Soricut, R., and Specia, L. (2012). Findings of the 2012 workshop on statistical machine translation. In *Proceedings of the Seventh Workshop on Statistical Machine Translation*, pages 10–51, Montréal, Canada. Association for Computational Linguistics.

Cohen, J. (1968). Weighted kappa - nominal scale agreement with provision for scaled disagreement or partial credit. *Psychological bulletin*, 70:213–20.

Eberhard, D. M., Simons, G. F., and Fennig, C. D. (2023). *Ethnologue: Languages of the World*. SIL International, 26th edition.

Freitag, M., Rei, R., Mathur, N., Lo, C.-k., Stewart, C., Avramidis, E., Kocmi, T., Foster, G., Lavie, A., and Martins, A. F. T. (2022). Results of WMT22 metrics shared task: Stop using BLEU – neural metrics are better and more robust. In *Proceedings of the Seventh Conference on Machine Translation (WMT)*, pages 46–68, Abu Dhabi, United Arab Emirates (Hybrid). Association for Computational Linguistics.

Gladkoff, S. and Han, L. (2022). HOPE: A task-oriented and human-centric evaluation framework using professional post-editing towards more effective MT evaluation. In *Proceedings of the Thirteenth Language Resources and Evaluation Conference*, pages 13–21, Marseille, France. European Language Resources Association.

Gladkoff, S., Sorokina, I., Han, L., and Alekseeva, A. (2022). Measuring uncertainty in translation quality evaluation (TQE). In Calzolari, N., Béchet, F., Blache, P., Choukri, K., Cieri, C., Declerck, T., Goggi, S., Isahara, H., Maegaard, B., Mariani, J., Mazo, H., Odijk, J., and Piperidis, S., editors, *Proceedings of the Thirteenth Language Resources and Evaluation Conference*, pages 1454–1461, Marseille, France. European Language Resources Association.

Han, A. L.-F., Wong, D. F., Chao, L. S., He, L., Lu, Y., Xing, J., and Zeng, X. (2013a). Language-independent model for machine translation evaluation with reinforced factors. In *Proceedings of Machine Translation Summit XIV: Posters*, Nice, France.

Han, A. L.-F., Wong, D. F., Chao, L. S., Lu, Y., He, L., Wang, Y., and Zhou, J. (2013b). A description of tunable machine translation evaluation systems in WMT13 metrics task. In *Proceedings of the Eighth Workshop on Statistical Machine Translation*, pages 414–421, Sofia, Bulgaria. Association for Computational Linguistics.

Han, L., Gladkoff, S., Erofeev, G., Sorokina, I., Galiano, B., and Nenadic, G. (2024). Neural machine translation of clinical text: an empirical investigation into multilingual pre-trained language models and transfer-learning. *Frontiers in Digital Health*, 6:1211564.

Han, L., Jones, G., and Smeaton, A. (2020). AlphaMWE: Construction of multilingual parallel corpora with MWE annotations. In *Proceedings of the Joint Workshop on Multiword Expressions and Electronic Lexicons*, pages 44–57, online. Association for Computational Linguistics.

Han, L., Sorokina, I., Erofeev, G., and Gladkoff, S. (2021). cushLEPOR: customising hLEPOR metric using optuna for higher agreement with human judgments or pre-trained language model LaBSE. In *Proceedings of the Sixth Conference on Machine Translation*, pages 1014–1023, Online. Association for Computational Linguistics.

Ho, J. C. T. and Or, N. H. K. (2020). Lihkgr. `https://github.com/justinchuntingho/LIHKGr`. An application for scraping LIHKG.

Holtzman, A., Buys, J., Du, L., Forbes, M., and Choi, Y. (2020). The curious case of neural text degeneration. In *International Conference on Learning Representations*.

Hong, K. Y., Han, L., Batista-Navarro, R., and Nenadic, G. (2024). Cantonmt: Cantonese to english nmt platform with fine-tuned models using synthetic back-translation data. In *EAMT 2024*.

Landis, J. R. and Koch, G. G. (1977). The measurement of observer agreement for categorical data. *Biometrics*, 33 1:159–74.

Lee, J. L., Chen, L., Lam, C., Lau, C. M., and Tsui, T.-H. (2022). Pycantonese: Cantonese linguistics and nlp in python. In *Proceedings of The 13th Language Resources and Evaluation Conference*. European Language Resources Association.

Lewis, M., Liu, Y., Goyal, N., Ghazvininejad, M., Mohamed, A., Levy, O., Stoyanov, V., and Zettlemoyer, L. (2020). BART: Denoising sequence-to-sequence pre-training for natural language generation, translation, and comprehension. In Jurafsky, D., Chai, J., Schluter, N., and Tetreault, J., editors, *Proceedings of the 58th Annual Meeting of the Association for Computational Linguistics*, pages 7871–7880, Online. Association for Computational Linguistics.

Liang, G., Zhao, J., Lau, H. Y. P., and Leung, C. W.-K. (2021). Using social media to analyze public concerns and policy responses to covid-19 in hong kong. *ACM Trans. Manage. Inf. Syst.*, 12(4).

Liu, E. K.-Y. (2022). Low-resource neural machine translation: A case study of Cantonese. In *Proceedings of the Ninth Workshop on NLP for Similar Languages, Varieties and Dialects*, pages 28–40, Gyeongju, Republic of Korea. Association for Computational Linguistics.

Liu, Y., Gu, J., Goyal, N., Li, X., Edunov, S., Ghazvininejad, M., Lewis, M., and Zettlemoyer, L. (2020). Multilingual denoising pre-training for neural machine translation. *Transactions of the Association for Computational Linguistics*, 8:726–742.

Lommel, A., Gladkoff, S., Melby, A., Wright, S. E., Strandvik, I., Gasova, K., Vaasa, A., Benzo, A., Sparano, R. M., Foresi, M., Innis, J., Han, L., and Nenadic, G. (2024). The multi-range theory of translation quality measurement: MQM scoring models and statistical quality control.

NLLB-Team, Costa-jussà, M. R., Cross, J., Çelebi, O., Elbayad, M., Heafield, K., Heffernan, K., Kalbassi, E., Lam, J., Licht, D., Maillard, J., Sun, A., Wang, S., Wenzek, G., Youngblood, A., Akula, B., Barrault, L., Gonzalez, G. M., Hansanti, P., Hoffman, J., Jarrett, S., Sadagopan, K. R., Rowe, D., Spruit, S., Tran, C., Andrews, P., Ayan, N. F., Bhosale, S., Edunov, S., Fan, A., Gao, C., Goswami, V., Guzmán, F., Koehn, P., Mourachko, A., Ropers, C., Saleem, S., Schwenk, H., and Wang, J. (2022). No language left behind: Scaling human-centered machine translation.

OpenAI (2024). Gpt-4 technical report.

Post, M. (2018). A call for clarity in reporting BLEU scores. In *Proceedings of the Third Conference on Machine Translation: Research Papers*, pages 186–191, Brussels, Belgium. Association for Computational Linguistics.

Rei, R., Stewart, C., Farinha, A. C., and Lavie, A. (2020). COMET: A neural framework for MT evaluation. In *Proceedings of the 2020 Conference on Empirical Methods in Natural Language Processing (EMNLP)*, pages 2685–2702, Online. Association for Computational Linguistics.

Sennrich, R., Haddow, B., and Birch, A. (2016). Improving neural machine translation models with monolingual data. In Erk, K. and Smith, N. A., editors, *Proceedings of the 54th Annual Meeting of the Association for Computational Linguistics (Volume 1: Long Papers)*, pages 86–96, Berlin, Germany. Association for Computational Linguistics.

Tang, Y., Tran, C., Li, X., Chen, P.-J., Goyal, N., Chaudhary, V., Gu, J., and Fan, A. (2020). Multilingual translation with extensible multilingual pretraining and finetuning.

Tiedemann, J. and Nygaard, L. (2004). The OPUS corpus - parallel and free: `http://logos.uio.no/opus`. In Lino, M. T., Xavier, M. F., Ferreira, F., Costa, R., and Silva, R., editors, *Proceedings of the Fourth International Conference on Language Resources and Evaluation (LREC'04)*, Lisbon, Portugal. European Language Resources Association (ELRA).

Tiedemann, J. and Thottingal, S. (2020). OPUS-MT — Building open translation services for the World. In *Proceedings of the 22nd Annual Conferenec of the European Association for Machine Translation (EAMT)*, Lisbon, Portugal.

Vaswani, A., Shazeer, N., Parmar, N., Uszkoreit, J., Jones, L., Gomez, A. N., Kaiser, L., and Polosukhin, I. (2017). Attention is all you need.

Wiedenhof, J. (2015). *A Grammar of Mandarin*. John Benjamins, Amsterdam.

Wing, L. H. (2020). Machine translation models for cantonese-english translation project plan.

Wu, Y., Li, X., and Lun, C. (2006). A structural-based approach to Cantonese-English machine translation. In *International Journal of Computational Linguistics & Chinese Language Processing, Volume 11, Number 2, June 2006*, pages 137–158.

Xiang, R., Tan, H., Li, J., Wan, M., and Wong, K.-F. (2022). When Cantonese NLP Meets Pre-training: Progress and Challenges. In Alonso, M. A. and Wei, Z., editors, *Proceedings of the 2nd Conference of the Asia-Pacific Chapter of the Association for Computational Linguistics and the 12th International Joint Conference on Natural Language Processing: Tutorial Abstracts*, pages 16–21. Association for Computational Linguistics.

Yi Mak, H. and Lee, T. (2022). Low-resource nmt: A case study on the written and spoken languages in hong kong. In *Proceedings of the 2021 5th International Conference on Natural Language Processing and Information Retrieval*, NLPIR '21, page 81–87, New York, NY, USA. Association for Computing Machinery.

Zhang, T., Kishore, V., Wu, F., Weinberger, K. Q., and Artzi, Y. (2020). Bertscore: Evaluating text generation with bert.

Zhao, Y., Xiang, L., Zhu, J., Zhang, J., Zhou, Y., and Zong, C. (2020). Knowledge graph enhanced neural machine translation via multi-task learning on sub-entity granularity. In *Proceedings of the 28th International Conference on Computational Linguistics*, pages 4495–4505, Barcelona, Spain (Online). International Committee on Computational Linguistics.

Leveraging AI Technologies for Enhanced Multimedia Localization

Ashley Mondello amondello@languagescientific.com
Sahil Rasane srasane@languagescientific.com
Language Scientific, Boston, MA, USA

Alina Karakanta a.karakanta@hum.leidenuniv.nl
Leiden University Centre for Linguistics, Leiden University, the Netherlands

Laura Casanellas Laura@lcmt.solutions
LCTM Solutions, Dublin, Ireland

Abstract

As demand for multilingual video content rises, multimedia localization is becoming crucial for Language Service Providers (LSPs), offering revenue growth and new business opportunities. To cope with labor-intensive multimedia workflows and the rise in client demand for cheaper and faster multimedia localization services, LSPs are starting to leverage advanced AI applications to streamline the localization process. However, workflows and tools adopted by media service providers may not be suitable for LSPs, while the plethora of available solutions makes it hard for LSPs to choose the ones that most effectively optimize their workflows. In this presentation, we assess AI technologies that offer efficiency and cost reduction in the traditionally human-driven workflows of transcription, translation, voice-over (VO), and subtitling with the goal to offer insights into how an LSP can evaluate which tools work best for their processes.

1 Introduction

With the growing demand for multilingual video content as a tool for companies to enhance their global communication and engagement, multimedia localization is becoming an important growth vector for Language Service Providers (LSPs), presenting opportunities to boost revenues and expand to new business cases (Slator, 2024). There are clear challenges faced by LSPs in multimedia localization currently; the most significant are lengthy timelines, high execution costs, as well as difficulty sourcing and managing voice talent and video engineering resources. To cope with labor-intensive multimedia workflows and the rise in client demand for cheaper and faster multimedia localization services, LSPs are starting to leverage advanced AI applications to streamline the localization process. However, LSPs are often not prepared to adopt workflows and tools used by media service providers, while choosing tools that most effectively optimize their workflows is challenging due to the plethora of available solutions.

In this presentation, we assess AI solutions that offer efficiency and cost reduction in the traditionally human-driven workflows of transcription, translation, voice-over (VO), and subtitling with the goal of guiding LSPs in selecting the tools that work best for their processes. We investigate three categories of AI solutions for video localization workflows: open-source tools, commercial AI services and APIs, and dedicated video localisation platforms. Our evaluation examines tools for automatic transcription, machine translation, synthetic voices, and automatic subtitling in two high-demand language pairs: English to Chinese (Simplified) and English to Spanish (Latin American). We assess the tools based on criteria such as ease of use, cost, language availability and quality. Our analysis suggests that out-of-the-box solutions that offer easy integration into existing workflows are a good transition step towards adopting AI, especially for low/medium project volumes. The existence of an in-house development team and higher volumes may justify investing in tailored solutions. Still, the availability of languages is the most decisive factor in tool selection. We also show preliminary productivity gains when AI tools are applied in existing manual workflows. We conclude with recommendations for LSPs in selecting AI tools based on key aspects like price, volume of multimedia projects, language pairs and the existence or not of an internal development team.

2 Background

2.1 Traditional Multimedia workflows

Multimedia localization involves the adaptation of audiovisual content, such as videos, to make it accessible and relevant to different linguistic and cultural audiences. Traditionally, this process has been heavily reliant on human labor, encompassing various stages including transcription, translation, voice-over, and subtitling. Each stage requires specific skills and significant time investment, making the overall process labor-intensive and costly.

Subtitling Workflow The traditional subtitling workflow encompasses multiple stages. Initially, the process begins with transcription and time-coding of the video content to generate a script for translation. This script undergoes a thorough quality assurance review to ensure accuracy before advancing to the translation phase. Following translation, the content is carefully edited. Subsequent steps involve video engineering to format the subtitle lengths and burn the subtitles to the video. Finally, several rounds of video QA and verification are performed, culminating in the finalization of the video.

Voice-Over Workflow The voice-over workflow is equally rigorous, beginning with transcription, time-coding, and a quality assurance review to produce the final script. This is followed by translation and editing of the script. Once translated, the script proceeds to voice-over recording, accompanied by additional QA and necessary revisions. The process continues with video engineering to sync the individual audio segments to the video to ensure the audio and video are aligned. Finally, multiple stages of video QA and verification are performed, leading to the finalization of the video.

2.2 Challenges for LSPs

The traditional manual workflows present several challenges for Language Service Providers (LSPs). Firstly, the labor-intensive nature of these workflows results in high operational costs. Each stage requires specialized human resources, which increases the overall expense of the localization process. Second, due to the sequential and manual nature of the tasks, the localization process is time-consuming. Meeting tight deadlines becomes challenging, especially when handling large volumes of content or multiple language pairs simultaneously. Another challenge is resource management. Managing and coordinating the different stages of the workflow requires meticulous planning and resource allocation. The availability of skilled translators, editors, subtitlers, voice-over artists, and video engineers is critical, and any delays in one stage can impact the entire timeline. Last comes quality control, which entails ensuring consistent quality across all stages. Each step involves human intervention, which can introduce variability in the output quality. Maintaining high standards requires rigorous QA processes, further adding to the time and cost.

2.3 The Role of AI in Enhancing Efficiency

To address these challenges, the adoption of AI technologies in multimedia localization is becoming increasingly essential. AI offers several advantages that can enhance efficiency and reduce costs, first of all the automation of repetitive tasks. Tools like automatic speech recognition (ASR), automatic time-coding and machine translation (MT) can significantly reduce the time required for these tasks. In addition, AI solutions can handle large volumes of content and multiple language pairs simultaneously. This scalability is crucial for LSPs dealing with high-demand projects and tight deadlines. Consequently, by automating labor-intensive tasks, AI can significantly reduce operational costs. The reduced reliance on human resources for certain stages of the workflow allows LSPs to allocate their resources more efficiently. AI tools can also process content much faster than humans. This speed is particularly beneficial for projects with quick turnaround times, allowing LSPs to deliver localized content more rapidly.

3 Methodology

This section presents the settings to test AI tools and solutions for multimedia localisation, using workflows adopted by the company Language Scientific (LS) as a case study.

3.1 Data

To test the quality of the tools, we used previously completed multimedia projects in the life sciences domain from LS for the language pairs English to Chinese (Simplified) and English to Spanish (Latin American). These amount to several hours of content and contain videos focusing on medical topics, such as e-learning, presentations, webinars and doctor-patient discussions. Thus they contain both scripted and unscripted content, single- and multi-speaker videos and speakers with different accents. The human outputs serve as references for computing automatic quality metrics.

3.2 Tools and systems

We investigate three categories of AI solutions for video localization workflows: open-source tools (e.g. Whisper), commercial AI services and APIs (e.g. Amazon Transcribe, Google text-to-speech) and dedicated video localisation platforms (e.g. Matesub, Speechify). Our evaluation examines tools for automatic transcription with timestamp prediction, machine translation, synthetic voices, and automatic subtitling. Specifically, we assess the following tools:

- Transcription: Whisper (Radford et al., 2023), Amazon Transcribe and Matesub[1]
- Translation: Amazon Translate, ChatGPT (OpenAI, 2023), Google Translate
- Subtitling: Amazon subtitling pipeline[2], Matesub
- Voice-over: Amazon Polly[3], Google text-to-speech, Speechify[4]

3.3 Evaluation criteria

The evaluation contains the following criteria:

- Ease of use (EoU): User interface, learning curve, integration capabilities. Since ease of use is different depending on the profile and technical skills of the person operating the tool, we report ease of use for project managers and developers separately. Two project managers and two developers at LS assessed the usability of the tools as 'low', 'medium' or 'high'.
- Cost: Pricing models, total cost of ownership. Assessed as 'low', 'medium', 'high', with low pricing being most suitable for LSPs with up to 50% of revenue comprised by multimedia, medium pricing being most suitable for LSPs with between 50%-75% of revenue comprised of multimedia and high pricing being most suitable for LSPs with over 75% of revenue comprised by multimedia.
- Language coverage: Number of supported languages, dialects, and regional varieties.
- Quality: The evaluation is performed with automatic metrics and, when possible, using human ratings. The accuracy of transcription is evaluated with Word Error Rate and the translation quality using COMET (Rei et al., 2020). For voice-over, we collect human ratings from 5 native speakers on the naturalness and clarity of the generated speech. Subtitle quality, synchronization and readability is evaluated using SubER (Wilken et al., 2022), an edit-based metric which considers edits in the text, timestamps and segmentation, while we also report subtitle conformity to the formal constraints of length (42 characters per line [CPL] for Es and 16 for Zh) and reading speed (21 characters per second [CPS] for Es and 9 for Zh) (Papi et al., 2023).

4 Results

4.1 Transcription

For transcription, the tools we compared are Whisper, Amazon Transcribe and Matesub. We only tested tools that output timestamps, since these are vital for synchronization both in subtitling and

[1]https://matesub.com/

[2]https://aws.amazon.com/transcribe/subtitling/

[3]https://aws.amazon.com/polly/

[4]https://speechify.com/

	Whisper	Amazon	Matesub
EoU - Dev	High	Med	High
EoU - PM	Low	Med	High
Cost	Low	Low	Med
Lang. cov.	99	102	85
Quality			
WER ↓	**7.32**	8.38	7.80
CPL↑	63.0%	32.4%	**100%**
CPS↑	62.8%	**86.3%**	73.8%

Table 1: Evaluation of transcription tools. Ease of Use (EoU) for the developer and project manager, language coverage (Lang. cov.) in number of languages and quality scores: Word error rate (WER), percentage of subtitles conforming to the maximum length of 42 CPL and maximum reading speed of 21 CPS. Best scores in bold.

	Google	Amazon	ChatGPT
EoU - Dev	High	High	Med
EoU - PM	High	High	Low
Cost	Low	Low	Med
Lang. cov.	134	75	99
Quality			
COMET Es	**89.5**	88.3	88.6
COMET Zh	**80.3**	79.7	80.0

Table 2: Evaluation of translation tools. Ease of Use (EoU) for the developer and project manager, language coverage (Lang. cov.) in number of languages and quality scores: COMET for Spanish (Es) and Chinese (Zh). Best scores in bold.

voice-over. The evaluation is shown in Table 1. In terms of ease of use, Whisper scores high for the developer, but low for the PM. Even though it is straightforward to use by persons with programming skills, the majority of PMs may not be familiar with operating a computer terminal. Amazon and Matesub offer a friendly user interface and thus their EoU for the PM is higher. Whisper has a low cost, since it only requires a computer with some computational power to run on and no subscription. Amazon comes next, with a pay-as-you-go model, while Matesub requires a subscription with a dedicated number of minutes available per month.

When it comes to quality, Whisper has the lowest WER on LS projects (7.32), followed by Matesub (7.8) and Amazon (8.38). It is worth mentioning that the Matesub timed transcription is different than that of Amazon and Whisper in terms of form, as shown by the conformity to length (CPL) and reading speed (CPS). Matesub, being a subtitle tool, generates short segments, conforming 100% to the length constraint of 42 CPL, while the mean line length for Amazon and Whisper is 57 and 49 respectively. Generating short subtitles comes at the expense of reading speed, with Amazon having a better conformity of reading speed than Matesub (86.3% vs 73.8%). To conclude, the timed transcriptions of Matesub are more suitable for subtitling projects, while Amazon and Whisper generate longer segments, which make them ideal for voice-over projects, which need to maintain longer units to improve prosody of synthetic outputs.

4.2 Translation

Translation for transcribed video content poses challenges compared to text translation, such as oral style and partial inputs (subtitles or incomplete sentences). The evaluation for Google Translate, Amazon Translate and ChatGPT for translation is shown in Table 2. Google and Amazon score similarly in terms of EoU and cost, since they are both well integrated in most CAT tools and offer APIs or UI to obtain the translations. ChatGPT has a lower ease of use both for developer and PM, and a higher cost. It should also be noted that it is a general purpose LLM and not a dedicated translation system. While most providers are expanding their language support in MT, language availability is still higher for Google. Translation quality for the content commonly translated in LS multimedia projects, as shown by COMET, is higher for Google, followed by ChatGPT and Amazon. While all three tools produced similar quality, our evaluation determined that, currently, Google and Amazon are the most suitable options for LSPs based on their high EoU and low pricing compared to ChatGPT.

	Amazon	Matesub
EoU - Dev	High	Med
EoU - PM	Med	High
Cost	Low	Med
Lang. cov.	75	85
Quality		
SubER Es	**55.9**	59.01
CPL↑	33.5%	**97.8%**
CPS↑	66.5%	**78.5%**
SubER Zh	**82.6**	198.1
CPL↑	62.6%	**100%**
CPS↑	**98.3%**	95.3%

Table 3: Evaluation of subtitling tools. Ease of Use (EoU) for the developer and project manager, language coverage (Lang. cov.) in number of languages and quality scores: Subtitle edit rate (SubER), percentage of subtitles conforming to the maximum length of 42 CPL for Es and 16 for Zh and maximum reading speed of 21 CPS for Es and 9 for Zh. Best scores in bold.

	Google	Amazon	Speechify
EoU - Dev	Med	Med	Med
EoU - PM	Low	Med	High
Cost	Low	Low	Med
Lang. cov.	58	38	130
Quality (Naturalness & clarity)			
Es-fem	3.25	3.5	**3.63**
Es-male	**4**	3.25	3.63
Zh-fem	3.25	4.5	**5**
Zh-male	3.25	-	**5**

Table 4: Evaluation of synthetic voice tools for voice-over. Ease of Use (EoU) for the developer and project manager, language coverage (Lang. cov.) in number of languages and quality scores: Averaged naturalness and clarity scores from 5 native speakers of Zh and Es for female and male voices. Best scores in bold.

4.3 Subtitling

The evaluation of the Amazon subtitling pipeline and Matesub is shown in Table 3. In Amazon, subtitles are generated in a two step process, combining two services; transcription with timestamps (see Sec. 4.1) and machine translation (see Sec. 4.2). They can be performed by uploading and downloading input/output files in a user interface. In Matesub, the video is uploaded in the platform and the subtitling guidelines and target languages are selected, making it easier to use by PMs who are familiar with the requirements of subtitling, but not as straightforward for developers.

In terms of subtitling quality on LS projects, Amazon has a better SubER than Matesub. The high SubER for Zh is due to the fact that LS subtitling projects allow a higher CPL than 16, which is the maximum subtitle length Matesub models are trained to produce. However, Amazon has a very low CPL conformity (33.5 vs 97.8 for Es and 62.6 vs 100 for Zh). As also noted in the results for transcription, Matesub subtitles have better conformity to the constraints of length and reading speed, and therefore the tool is more suitable for subtitling projects.

4.4 Voice-over

The evaluation of Amazon, Google and Speechify synthetic voices for voice-over generation is shown in Table 4. Google and Amazon have a medium to low EoU. Voice generation is performed through an API or user interface where text is pasted. Because voice-over has to be synchronized with the video, it has to be generated sentence by sentence and not as a large chunk of text, which is time consuming for the PM. For this reason, PM's EoU is lower for Google and Amazon. Google had a demanding set up process for the API because of the modular structure of Google cloud, but once set up, it was relatively easy to use, hence the medium rating. Speechify allows for uploading a timed .srt file, which performs synchronization automatically. Speechify has also an integrated voice editor, which allows a PM to adjust the speed, prosody and synchronization of the generated voice samples.

Language coverage is an issue in voice-over, since both Google and Amazon support a limited number of languages and language varieties. In addition, very few languages have models for both female and male voices, which is often a requirement for voice-over when the persons are on screen. Such is the case with the Chinese male voice for Amazon. Chinese voices were not available in Google's GUI but could be used through the API. Another issue is that the language may be available but at a low model quality. For example, Google offers different model types: standard, neural, wavenet, studio, in an ascending order of quality.

In terms of naturalness and clarity of speech, Google scores higher for the Spanish male voice (4), while Speechify for the female (3.63). It is worth noting that this rating is higher than the rating for the human female voice from the reference project, which scored an average of 3.25. For Chinese, all participants rated the Speechify voices with the highest score in terms of naturalness and clarity (5), showing that, for some languages and project types, synthetic voices may be a feasible alternative. To conclude, for voice-over projects, language/model type availability is the most decisive factor when selecting provider. Speechify has high quality of synthetic voices and an integrated editor, while Amazon and Google can be good for occasional projects, but require video synchronization as an extra step.

5 Preliminary productivity evaluation

To evaluate productivity gains of using AI in the multimedia localization process, we conducted a series of real-life scenario tests using various AI tools. Our initial test, covered in this paper, involved subtitling and voice-over of an 11-minute video with two speakers (male, female), replacing specific steps in traditional workflows with AI tools without the integration of workflow automation. The primary goal was to assess the productivity impact of low-level AI integration for LSPs beginning their AI adoption journey.

5.1 Testing process

The tests involved replacing human-driven steps with AI tools while maintaining all quality assurance steps with human resources to ensure the highest level of quality. The replacements included:

Subtitling Workflow: 1) Replacing human transcription with Amazon Transcribe, 2) Replacing human translation with Amazon Translate.

Voice-over Workflow: 1) Replacing human transcription with Amazon Transcribe, 2) Replacing human translation with Amazon Translate, 3) Replacing voice-over recording with Amazon Polly for Spanish and Google Text-to-Speech for Chinese.

The workflows were evaluated by comparing the time and effort required for both traditional and AI-assisted processes.

5.2 Findings

The integration of AI tools resulted in significant time savings and efficiency improvements. In the **Subtitling Workflow**, the Traditional Workflow required **19** hours of human labor per language for the 11-minute video, while the AI-Assisted Workflow was reduced to **8** hours of human labor, saving 11 hours per project. Time gains were recorded in transcription, from 4 to 2 hours, in translation from 10 hours to 2 hours, while a gain from 5 hours to 4 hours was also reported in video engineering.

In the **Voice-over Workflow**, the Traditional Workflow required **24** hours of human labor per language, while the AI-Assisted Workflow was reduced to **12** hours, saving 12 hours per project. Time gains were recorded in transcription, from 4 to 2 hours, in translation from 10 hours to 2 hours, and voice-over engineering from 9 hours to 7 hours.

The evaluation revealed that AI-assisted workflows can reduce the required labor hours by over 50% in both subtitling and voice-over processes. The quality and availability of AI tools, however, vary depending on the language pair, underscoring the importance of selecting appropriate tools based on specific project requirements.

6 Recommendations for LSPs regarding AI tool selection

When deciding which AI tools to integrate into their workflows, LSPs should follow a systematic approach that takes into account the following aspects of their own production workflows: the volume of multimedia projects per year, the availability of a research and implementation budget, whether there is time to test different solutions beforehand, the main language pairs, whether there are engineers in the team who can work with open source solutions and, finally, whether the linguists assigned to multimedia projects are familiar with the tools or whether they need to be trained.

Our exploration of AI solutions for multimedia projects revealed that commercial AI services, which offer an all-in-one solution by the same provider and require medium technical skills, can be a good starting point in integrating AI and more suitable for low/medium project volumes. For high volumes, open source tools such as Whisper can prove a worthy investment, but require staff with technical skills, as well as equipment with some computational power. Tailored solutions also suit higher volumes. Multimedia platforms, such as Matesub for subtitling and Speechify for voice-over, offer high quality and low management effort, but the cost is slightly higher and linguists need to be trained in using the tools.

When selecting AI tools, LSPs should not only consider the factors previously mentioned but also assess whether their multimedia projects are suitable for AI integration. The efficiency gains from using AI in multimedia projects can be significantly influenced by the complexity of the source material. For example, videos featuring multiple speakers, extensive on-screen text, or embedded PowerPoint presentations present synchronization challenges when processed with AI tools. Furthermore, the target audience of these videos must be taken into account, especially in VO projects. Despite considerable advancements in synthetic voice technology, AI-generated voices remain distinguishable from human voices. LSPs must carefully evaluate how the intended audience might react to synthetic voices when considering AI's role in their projects.

7 Conclusion

The integration of AI technologies into traditional multimedia localization workflows offers significant advantages in terms of efficiency and cost reduction, all while maintaining high-quality standards. LSPs can harness these tools to optimize their processes and effectively meet growing client demands. However, it is important to consider the initial effort required to incorporate AI solutions into existing workflows. Depending on the chosen tools, this integration may demand varying levels of resource training, technical support, and budget allocation before realizing the anticipated time and cost savings. Ongoing research should explore a broader spectrum of AI tools and refine evaluation criteria to support comprehensive tool selection strategies for LSPs. We hope this presentation equips LSPs to navigate the evolving landscape of multimedia localization, enabling them to meet client demands with efficiency and effectiveness, while upholding high-quality standards.

References

OpenAI (2023). ChatGPT (Mar 14 version) [large language model].

Papi, S., Gaido, M., Karakanta, A., Cettolo, M., Negri, M., and Turchi, M. (2023). Direct speech translation for automatic subtitling. *Transactions of the Association for Computational Linguistics*, 11:1355–1376.

Radford, A., Kim, J. W., Xu, T., Brockman, G., McLeavey, C., and Sutskever, I. (2023). Robust speech recognition via large-scale weak supervision. In *Proceedings of the 40th International Conference on Machine Learning*, ICML'23. JMLR.org.

Rei, R., Stewart, C., Farinha, A. C., and Lavie, A. (2020). COMET: A neural framework for MT evaluation. In Webber, B., Cohn, T., He, Y., and Liu, Y., editors, *Proceedings of the 2020 Conference on Empirical Methods in Natural Language Processing (EMNLP)*, pages 2685–2702, Online. Association for Computational Linguistics.

Slator (2024). 2024 Language Industry Market Report — Language AI Edition.

Wilken, P., Georgakopoulou, P., and Matusov, E. (2022). SubER - a metric for automatic evaluation of subtitle quality. In Salesky, E., Federico, M., and Costa-jussà, M., editors, *Proceedings of the 19th International Conference on Spoken Language Translation (IWSLT 2022)*, pages 1–10, Dublin, Ireland (in-person and online). Association for Computational Linguistics.

Open-Source LLMs vs. NMT Systems: Translating Spatial Language in EN-PT-br Subtitles

Rafael Fernandes rafael.macario@usp.br
Marcos Lopes marcoslopes@usp.br
Department of Linguistics, University of São Paulo, São Paulo, 05508-220, BR

Abstract

This work, originating as part of a master's thesis, investigates the challenges of translating spatial language using open-source Large Language Models (LLMs) compared to traditional Neural Machine Translation (NMT) systems. It focuses on the accurate translation of two preposition pair – ACROSS and THROUGH, and INTO and ONTO – which present overlapping meanings when translating from English to Brazilian Portuguese (EN-PT-br). Correctly translating these prepositions is crucial for maintaining the source text's semantic integrity while ensuring fluency and adherence to the target language's lexicalization patterns (House, 2014, 2018; Talmy, 2000a,b; Slobin, 2005). The research contextualizes the challenges of spatial language translation, highlighting NMT limitations and potential LLM advantages. A comprehensive literature review traces the evolution of translation theories, NMT development, and the rise of LLMs, while also discussing the limitations of these approaches. The methodology involves a corpus-based analysis using a bilingual dataset centered on spatial prepositions from TED Talks subtitles sourced from the OPUS platform. This dataset was meticulously pre-processed for automated metrics calculation and manual error analysis. The evaluation metrics used include BLEU, METEOR, BERTScore, COMET, and TER, while the manual analysis identifies and categorizes specific types of mistranslation errors. The findings reveal that moderate-sized LLMs, such as LLaMa-3-8B and Mixtral-8x7B, achieve accuracy comparable to NMT systems like DeepL. However, this relationship between architecture and performance might not always linear; for instance, Gemma-7B, despite being heavily penalized by automatic metrics, performed similarly to more robust models in human reviews. LLMs generally exhibited serious translation issues, including interlanguage/code-switching (in) and anglicism (an), often failing to convey fluency in the target language. DeepL, on the other hand, demonstrated better accuracy and precision in this domain. Nevertheless, manual error analysis highlights ongoing challenges in translating spatial language, with both LLMs and NMT systems consistently making errors related to polysemy (po) and syntactic projection (sp), where they either fail to translate a preposition's meaning accurately or replicate the source language's lexicalization patterns (Fernandes et al., 2024; Oliveira and Fernandes, 2022), accounting for 27.84% of preposition-related errors. The study concludes that despite advancements, significant challenges remain in translating spatial language for this language pair. It suggests that future research should focus on enhancing and curating training datasets, refining model architectures, and developing more sophisticated evaluation metrics that better capture the subtleties of spatial language. This study contributes to the field by providing a detailed comparison of model performance in spatial language translation from EN-PT-br and proposing directions for future improvements.

Keywords

Natural Language Processing (NLP), Open-source Large Language Models (LLMs), Neural Machine Translation (NMT), Machine Translation (MT) Evaluation, Spatial Semantics, Polysemy, Language Typology

References

Fernandes, R., Souza, R., Lopes, M., Santos, P., and Finbow, T. (2024). Spatial information challenges in English to Portuguese machine translation. In Gamallo, P., Claro, D., Teixeira, A., Real, L., Garcia, M., Oliveira, H. G., and Amaro, R., editors, *Proceedings of the 16th International Conference on Computational Processing of Portuguese*, pages 620–626, Santiago de Compostela, Galicia/Spain. Association for Computational Lingustics.

House, J. (2014). Translation quality assessment: Past and present. In *Translation: A multidisciplinary approach*, pages 241–264. Springer.

House, J. (2018). *Translation: The Basics*. Routledge.

Oliveira, A. and Fernandes, R. (2022). *Expressing complex paths of motion in Brazilian Portuguese: a closer look at frog stories*, pages 21–35. In: Chiappara, Juan Pablo and Siqueira, Joelma Santana and Oliveira, Aparecida de Araújo and Gediel, Ana Luisa.

Slobin, D. (2005). Relating narrative events in translation. In Ravid, D. and Shyldkrot, H., editors, *Perspectives on language and language development: Essays in honor of Ruth A. Berman*, pages 115–129. Springer, Dordrecht.

Talmy, L. (2000a). *Toward a cognitive semantics: Concept structuring systems*, volume 1. MIT Press.

Talmy, L. (2000b). *Toward a cognitive semantics: Typology and process in concept structuring*, volume 2. MIT Press.

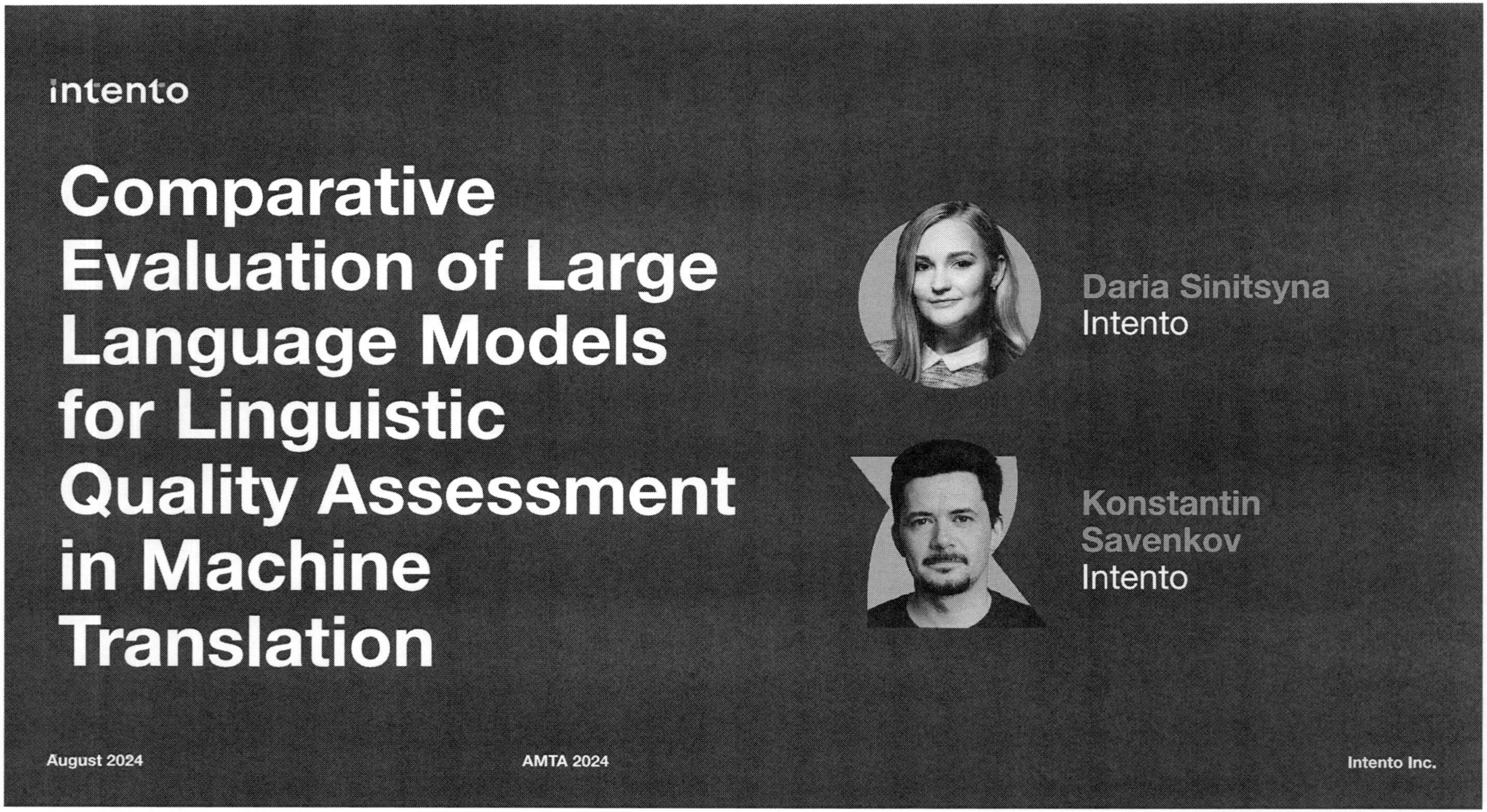

intento
Comparative Evaluation of Large Language Models for Linguistic Quality Assessment in Machine Translation
Daria Sinitsyna
Intento
Konstantin Savenkov
Intento
August 2024
AMTA 2024
Intento Inc.

Summary

Goals

Research goals

1. How well can LLMs perform Linguistic Quality Assessment (LQA)?
2. What is the **best LLM solution design** for automatic LQA (zero-shot, CoT, multi-agent)?
3. **Which LLM is the best today** for identifying and classifying translation errors?
4. How do they compare cost-wise?

Background

intento

Complexity of MT post-editing largely depends on quality requirements.

Reaching perfect automatic translation (no edits) requires a way to automatically assess and improve translation quality.

intento

AMTA 2024

This research is dedicated to finding the best design and building blocks for such solution.

For that, we evaluate design choices and LLMs on a simple and well-defined task - automatic LQA based on the MQM error typology.

intento AMTA 2024

Last year we have assessed GPT-4 capabilities for Linguistic Quality Assessment using DQF-MQM error typology*

German	**78%** accuracy**
	76% agreement with linguists
Spanish	**80%** accuracy**
	82% agreement with linguists

* review was done on samples of 50 segments from Annual State of MT Report 2023 and presented at TAUS 2023

** precision

Methodology

The Approach

1. Choose a quality estimation agent design for the multi-agent LQA (with GPT-4o as the baseline & Reviewer Agent) with the MQM error typology.
    a. Zero-shot LLM agent for all MQM dimensions
    b. A system of one agent per MQM dimension
    c. Zero-shot Chain of Thought agent
2. Compare 6 LLMs as a model for the QE agent of quality estimation agent combined with a reviewer agent (based on Claude 3.5 Sonnet)
3. Check correlation of different multi-agent systems with each other to understand whether they have similar biases and limitations
4. Analyze all issues found by all multi-agent LQA systems with human linguists
5. Compare LLMs in terms of false alarms and found issues

In a nutshell

Models:

- OpenAI GPT-4o
- OpenAI GPT-4o mini
- Anthropic Claude 3.5 Sonnet
- Gemini 1.5 Flash
- Gemini 1.5 Pro
- Llama 3.1 405B

Prompting techniques:

- Zero-shot LLM agent for all MQM dimensions
- A system of one agent per MQM dimension
- Zero-shot Chain of Thought agent

Language pairs:

- English-Spanish
- English-German
- English-Chinese

Data

intento

AMTA 2024

Notes on Data Preparation

- 500 longest, or contextually rich, segments taken from our Annual State of MT Report with no reference translations
- Chosen using stratified sampling based on COMET score
- Larger proportion of segments with lower score where issues are more prominent
    - 250 low-scoring segments
    - 150 segments with middle scores
    - 100 high-scoring segments

Choosing the approach

intento

AMTA 2024

We use MQM dimensions that LLMs can work around without additional contextual knowledge

- Terminology
- Mistranslation
- Over-translation
- Under-translation
- Addition
- Omission
- Untranslated text
- Culture-specific reference
- Markup

- Awkward style
- Unidiomatic style
- Inconsistent style
- Formatting
- Grammar
- Spelling
- Punctuation
- Character encoding

Choosing the approach

Zero-shot LLM agent for all MQM dimensions
+
Reviewer agent

A system of one agent per MQM dimension
+
Reviewer agent

Zero-shot Chain of Thought agent
+
Reviewer agent

When choosing the multi-agent solution architecture, we assess the differences in judgment, not the absolute LQA accuracy

- We focus on segments where LLM solutions with different architecture disagree about the translation quality
- For each solution, we select segments where there's a disagreement (one setup finds much less issues/less critical issues than another)
- A human assessor determines:
  - Which approach led to a more accurate analysis
  - Whether both, neither, or only one of the analyses is correct

Reviewer has assessed CoT as the more correct when it comes to approach disagreement but states CoT and zero-shot LLM agent are of nearly the same quality

- Zero-shot LLM agent
- A system of one agent per MQM dimension
- Zero-shot CoT agent
- Both approaches are correct
- Neither approach is correct

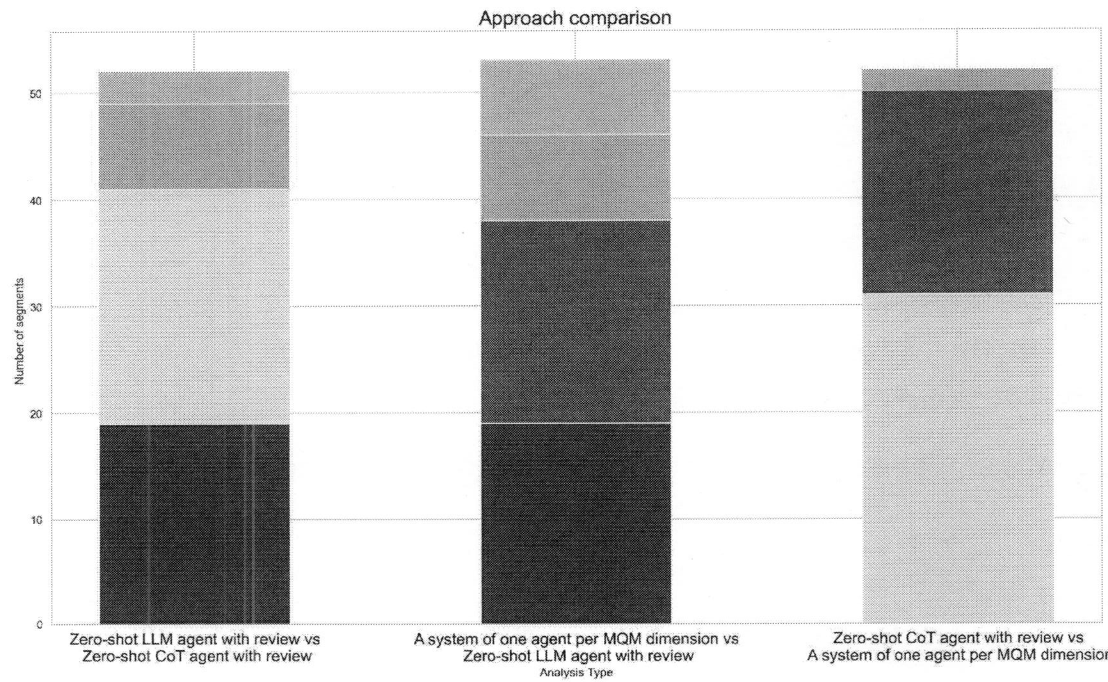

intento

AMTA 2024

We proceed with one prompt MQM with a reviewer model

- Between the compared models, zero-shot LLM agent is the fastest:
  - Zero-shot LLM agent takes ~20 minutes per 500 segments
  - Zero-shot CoT takes ~30 minutes per 500 segments
  - A system of one agent per MQM dimension takes ~150 minutes per 500 segments
- It is also the least expensive due to having the least tokens in the system message
- Quality-wise, zero-shot LLM agent and CoT have nearly identical results however, since one-prompt LLM agent is first by other parameters, we use it in the final setup
- We proceed with zero-shot LLM agent with the same reviewer model for all models - Claude 3.5 Sonnet

Model Analysis

intento

AMTA 2024

There is high degree of agreement and consistency between different LLMs

Chinese

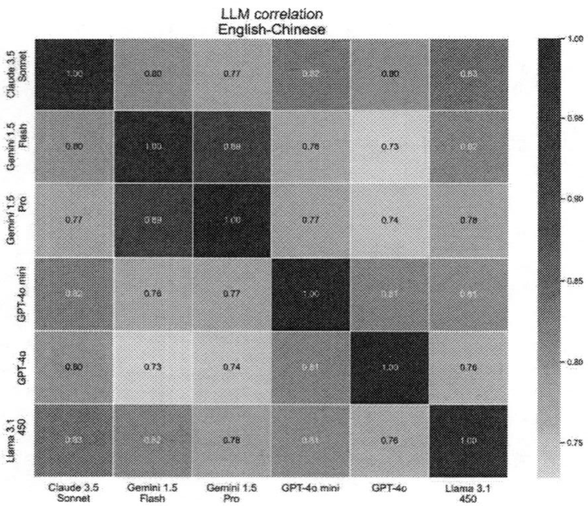

German

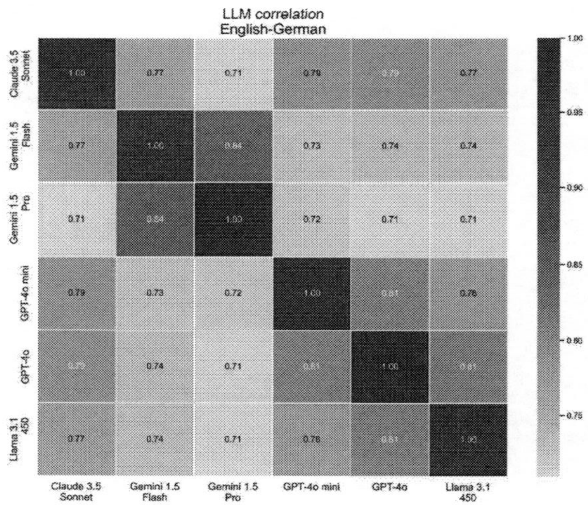

Spanish

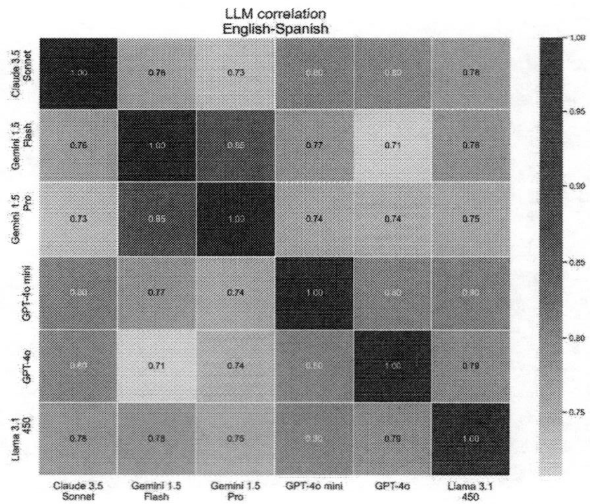

The correlation is shown between multi-agents: systems where the LQA agent is one of the 6 LLMs and reviewer agent is Claude 3.5 Sonnet

While Gemini models produce the least false alarms, GPT-4o tends to find the most major and critical relevant issues

False alarms　　Missed issues

Chinese

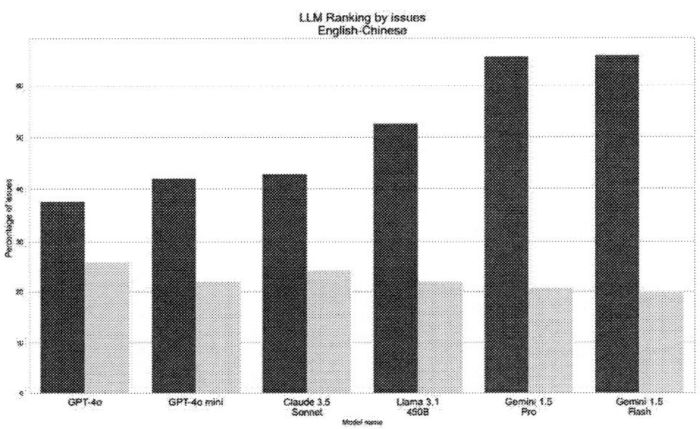

German

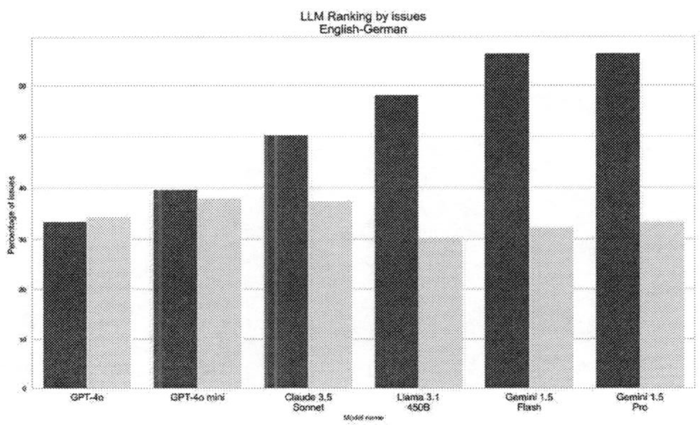

Spanish

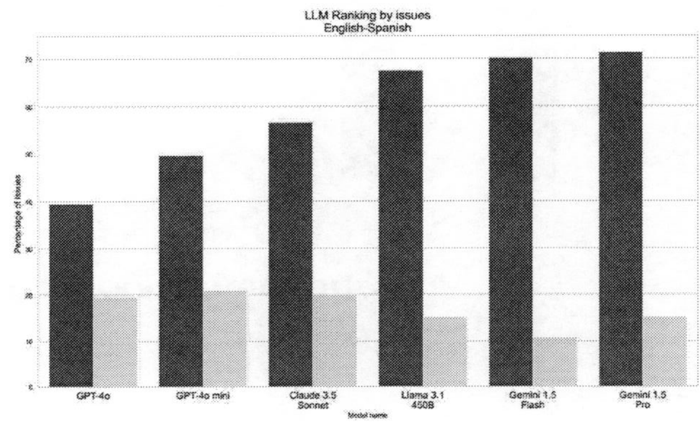

Different LLMs excel in detection of different issues, and higher results could be achieved with model ensembling

False alarms   Missed issues

Mistranslation detection

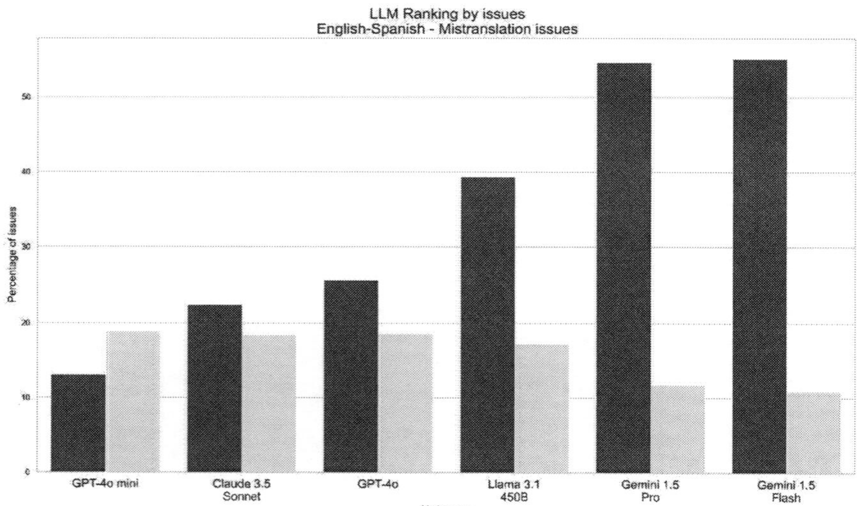

Terminology detection

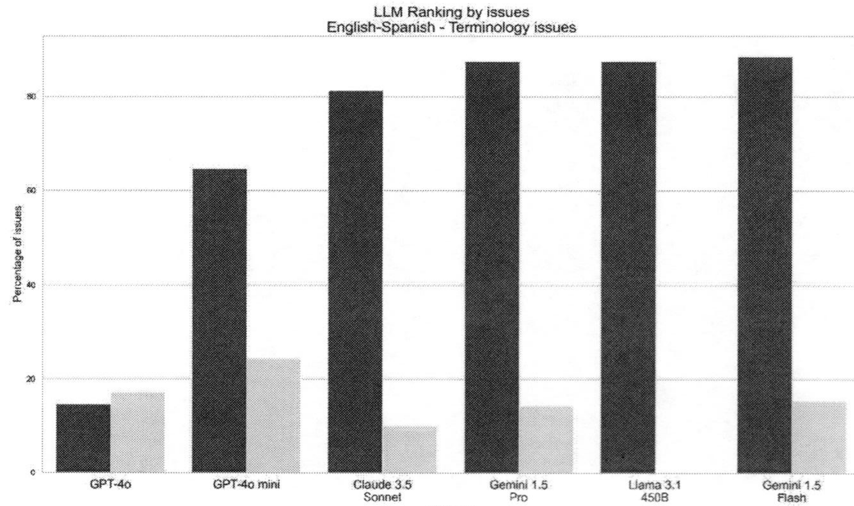

GPT-4o mini has the lowest number of missed terminology errors while GPT-4o nearly excels in domain terminology issue detection in Spanish

intento   AMTA 2024

GPT-4o shows the best results in terms of identified major and critical issues

- GPT-4o perform the best in all language pairs, showing the best harmony between the number of false alarms and identifying correct issues
- Gemini models produce the least false alarms in all languages, as on average, only 18% of all issues Gemini models identified were false alarms
- GPT4o and GPT-4o mini models find the most issues compared to the rest of LLMs, as between all languages pairs, they identify nearly major and critical 70% issues
- The latest Llama 3.1 with 450B parameters shows comparable results to commercially available models
- The highest rate of identified issues can be achieved with model ensembling due to different LLMs excelling in different issues' detection

Cost analysis

intento

AMTA 2024

Cost analysis

- Since we used Llama-3.1 model through OctaAI, costs for this model were calculated using pricing on the official website:
- https://octo.ai/docs/getting-started/pricing-and-billing.

LQA pricing

Prices for each model and language pair per 1 million characters with Claude 3.5 Sonnet as the reviewer model

Language pair	GPT-4o	GPT-4o mini	Gemini 1.5 Pro	Gemini 1.5 Flash	Claude 3.5 Sonnet	Llama 3.1 450B
English-German	19.00	9.38	16.08	9.13	18.00	15.00
English-Spanish	13.42	6.62	11.36	6.45	6.36	10.06
English-Chinese	25.33	12.50	21.43	12.18	24.00	20.01

Conclusion

intento

AMTA 2024

Conclusion

1. Between several approaches, zero-shot LLM agent is the fastest, least expensive prompting method, comparable in quality with Chain of Thought only, with Reviewer agent being the key to achieving higher quality results.
2. GPT-4o showcases the best harmony between the comparatively low number of false alarms and identifying correct issues, proving to be the best at Linguistic Quality Assessment among all language pairs.
3. Cost-wise, GPT-4o mini and Gemini 1.5 Flash are the cheapest, although all models are comparable in price.
4. We generally see even better results when it comes to client data LQA due to the possibility of adding more information and shots to the LQA and reviewer agents.

Thank you!

ks@inten.to

daria.sinitsyna@inten.to

An independent multi-domain
evaluation of MT engines

Commercially available
pre-trained MT models

2261 Market St, #4273
San Francisco, CA 94114

inten.to

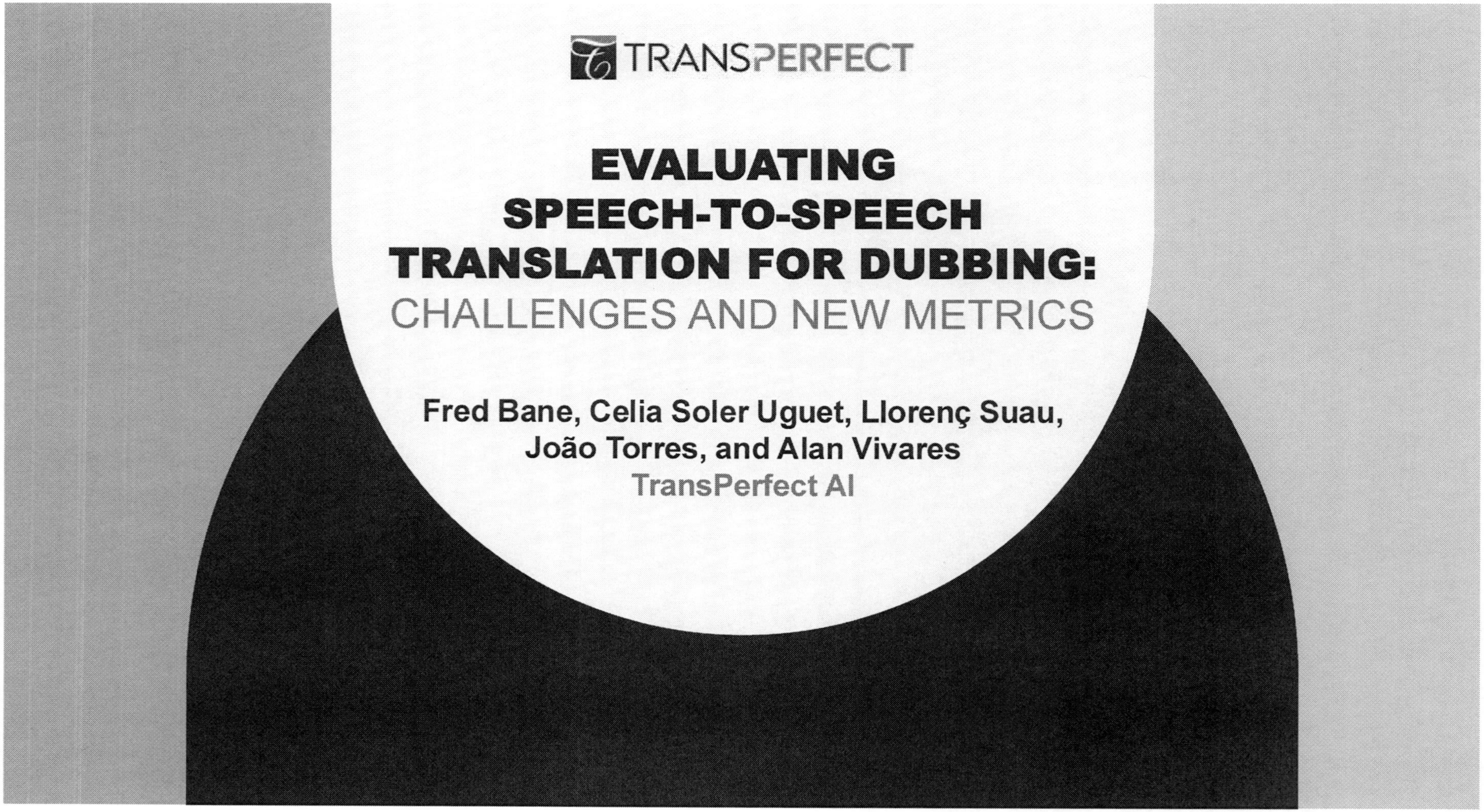
TRANSPERFECT
EVALUATING
SPEECH-TO-SPEECH
TRANSLATION FOR DUBBING:
CHALLENGES AND NEW METRICS
Fred Bane, Celia Soler Uguet, Llorenç Suau,
João Torres, and Alan Vivares
TransPerfect AI

AGENDA

Translation of speech vs. text

Dubbing and Voice Over (V.O.)

New developments in speech translation

Existing evaluation methods

What *should* we be evaluating?

Pilot evaluation results

TEXT VS SPEECH TRANSLATION

Differences in the translation of text and speech.

WORKING WITH SPEECH VS. TEXT

Text	Speech
Discrete input	Continuous input
Singular signal	Mixed signals
Time-independent	Time-dependent
Linguistic evaluation	Linguistic + Voice evaluation
Less information overall	More information overall
Compact representation	Larger representation

DUBBING AND VOICE-OVER

Key differences with other applications of speech translation

- **Timing:** Must fit in the same time span as the original
- **Synchronization:** In dubbing, synchronization of the voice with the lip movements is critical
- **Emotional expressivity:** In dubbing, matching the emotional content of the voice to the situation is critical
- **Fidelity:** Natural speech content that does not break immersivity is more important than maintaining fidelity
- **Character appropriateness:** The voice, speech content, and expressivity must be appropriate for the character

SPEECH-SPEECH TRANSLATION IS ENTERING A NEW ERA

THE DEVELOPMENT OF AI-DRIVEN TRANSLATION

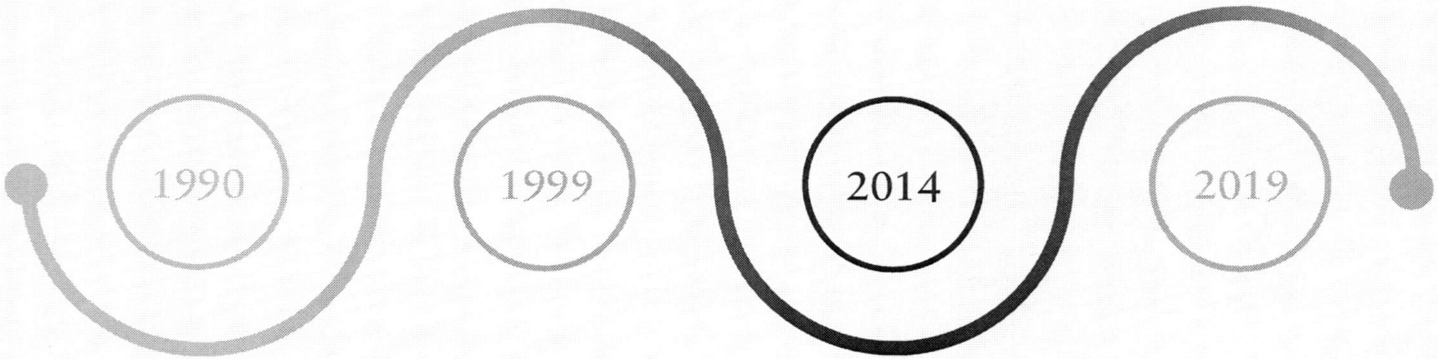

EARLY DEVELOPMENT

1990s: The concept of machine translation (MT) began to gain traction, with early models focusing primarily on text-based translations.

1999: Early S2S translation system introduced by the C-STAR-2 Consortium. By 2003, similar systems were developed for handheld devices.

THE RISE OF NEURAL NETWORKS

2014: Microsoft introduced (cascade-based) speech translation in Skype. Around the same time, Google launched Neural Machine Translation (NMT),

2019: Google introduced Translatotron, the first end-to-end model that directly translated speech from one language to another, bypassing text altogether.

THE DEVELOPMENT OF AI-DRIVEN TRANSLATION

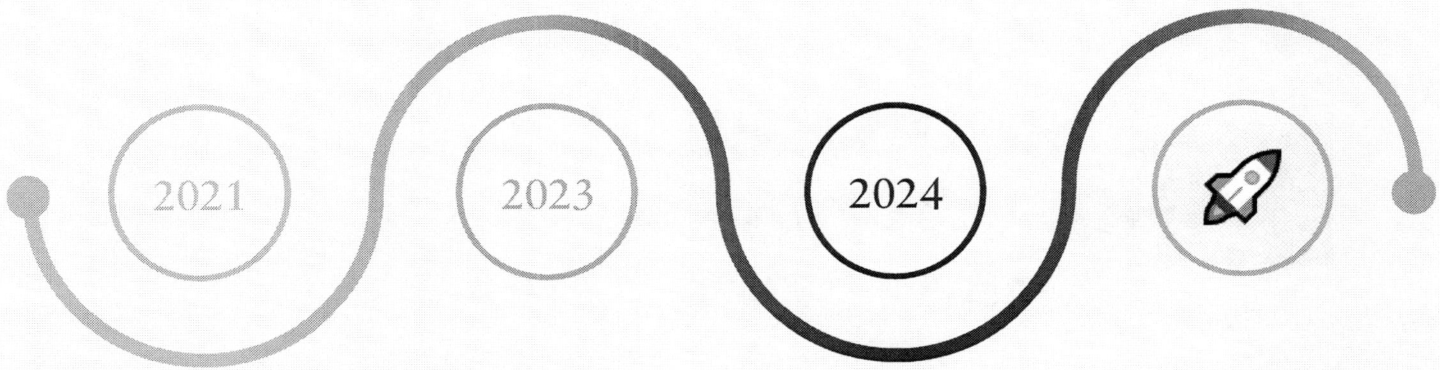

RECENT ADVANCEMENTS

2021: Meta introduced SeamlessM4T, a multilingual and multimodal model capable of both text-to-text and speech-to-speech translation.

2023: Translatotron, Meta's SeamlessM4T and others continued to evolve, covering more languages, and improving emotional expressivity

FUTURE TRENDS

The future of AI in translation is expected to see further advancements in real-time translation capabilities across multiple modalities, particularly in enhancing the translation of low resource languages and incorporating non-verbal communication cues. LLMs have started to roll out voice capabilities, but audio is still separate from visual input.

EXISTING EVALUATION METHODS

TRANSLATION EVALUATION IS STILL TEXT-BASED

ASR-BLEU: Transcribing the speech using ASR and calculating BLEU, a text-based measure of similarity

- Dependent on the quality of the ASR system
- Not robust to dialectal variations or non-standardized orthographies
- Falls short in low-resource languages

BLEU has long been considered a poor metric for text translation, it is even less adequate for speech

VOICE QUALITY IS EVALUATED MANUALLY

Most major papers use Mean Opinion Score (MOS) as the only way of measuring voice quality.

The Seamless Expressive paper is a welcome exception: automated tools for sentence-level prosody similarity, and a rhythm evaluation toolkit

ALTERNATIVE EVALUATION METHODS

What *should* we be evaluating?

VOICE

- **Intelligibility**
- **Voice quality**
  - Articulation, fluency, projection
- **Appropriateness**
  - Suitability for character, cultural appropriateness
- **Expressivity**
  - Emotional content, consistency with context
- **Timing** ***(task specific)***
  - Duration, lip synchronization

LINGUISTIC

- **Accuracy**
  - Mistranslation, over/under-translation, addition, omission, untranslated
- **Style**
  - Organizational, language register, consistency
- **Terminology**
  - Wrong term, consistency
- **Linguistic Conventions**
  - Grammar, word form, part of speech, tense, agreement, word order
- **Locale Conventions**

VOICE - QUALITY

❖ Articulation

Phoneme Error Rate (PER):

- Quantifies the accuracy of phoneme production by comparing expected vs. actual phonemes. This is useful for identifying pronunciation issues.

Mel cepstral distortion

Formant Analysis:

- Analyzes the resonant frequencies (formants) of the vocal tract, particularly crucial for vowel sounds. Deviations from expected formant values can indicate articulation issues.

❖ Projection

Similarity of amplitude envelope features (inspired by Cummings et al. 1999)

VOICE - QUALITY

❖ Fluency

Perplexity of vocal path through frequency-time space

- Transform the voice into frequency-time space, fit Bezier curves to the resulting path, calculate perplexity compared with a dataset of natural speech

Rhythmic analysis

- Speech rate (Librosa, AutoPCP), pauses (Praat, pydub, Rhtyhm Toolkit)

F0 contour and amplitude envelope (Cummins et al., 1999)

VOICE - INTELLIGIBILITY

Perplexity of audio -> phoneme decoder

VOICE - APPROPRIATENESS

Mel frequency cepstral coefficient similarity

Cosine distance embedding vectors (x-vectors, PnG NAT TTS model in Nobuyuki et al., 2022)

Automated MOS prediction (MOSnet in Lo et al. 2019)

Classifier trained to predict if the voice is the same

VOICE - EXPRESSIVITY

Prosody similarity (AutoPCP)

Emotion detection systems

LINGUISTIC – ACCURACY

Encoder embedding similarity (BLASER - Bilingual and Language-Agnostic Speech Evaluation by Retrieval)

Round-trip phoneme F1

- Back-translating the output translation into the source language and comparing the two audios represented as sequences of phonemes

Round-trip BLASER

- BLASER may capture semantic features, in a way that COMET can augment chrF1/BLEU scores for text translation

LINGUISTIC – STYLE

???

LINGUISTIC – TERMINOLOGY

???????

LINGUISTIC/LOCALE CONVENTIONS

???????????

There is still a long way to go ☺

PILOT EVALUATION RESULTS

Results from a small-scale pilot, reviewed manually with the error taxonomy shown previously

PILOT SETUP

- Short clips from movies, web series, and documentaries, showcasing a variety of expressive conditions;
- We first separated speech signals from background noise in the audio track;
- Then we translated each vocal track into FR and ES using Seamless Expressive and a cascade approach (whisper → internally trained MT models → internally developed TTS models);
- Next, translated audio was reinserted into the background noise at the corresponding time using the time codes of the speech signals;
- Reviewers worked on the DataForce platform to annotate errors, indicating the type, severity, start time, and end time of each error.

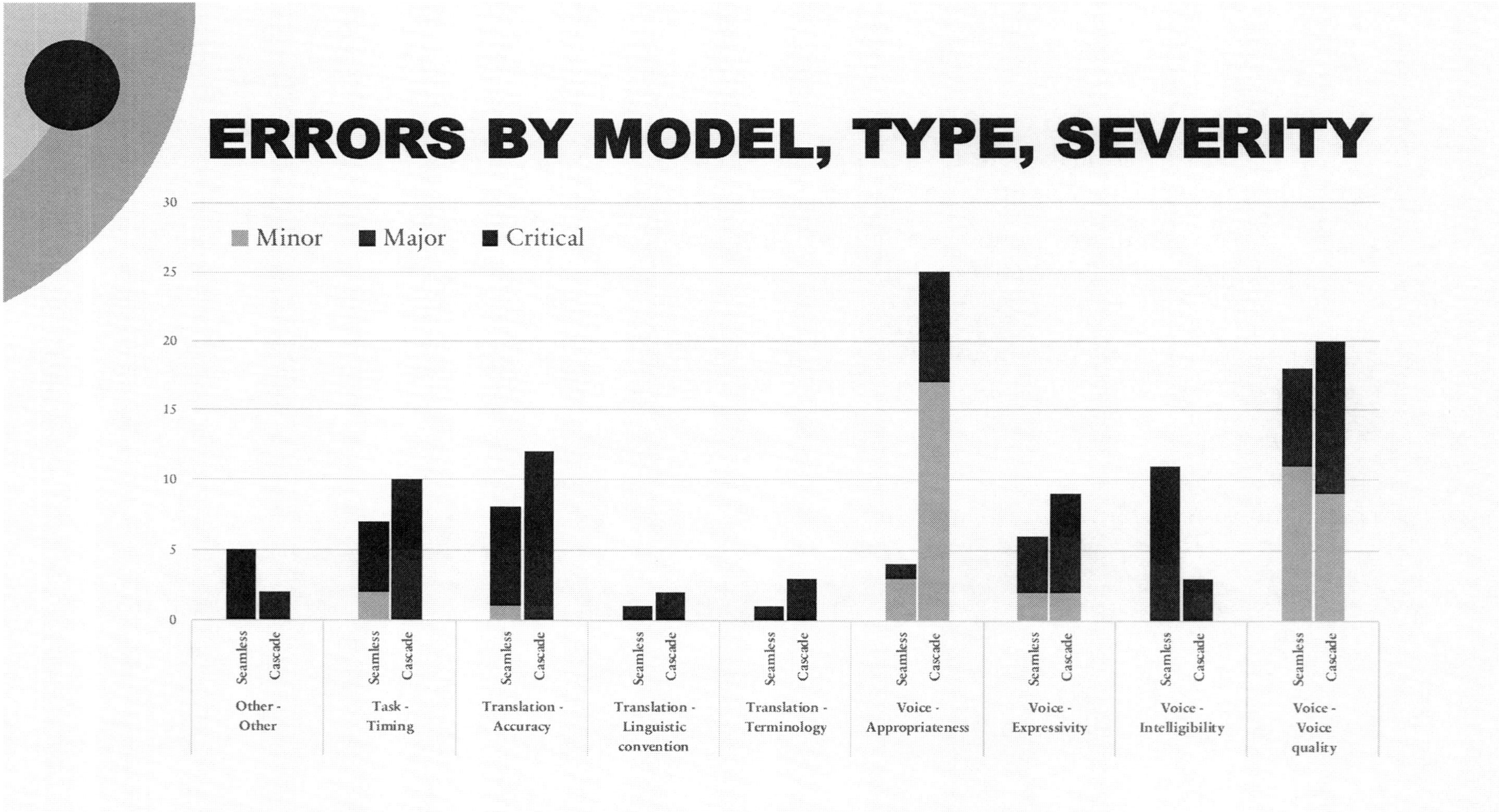
ERRORS BY MODEL, TYPE, SEVERITY
Minor
Major
Critical
0
5
10
15
20
25
30
Seamless
Cascade
Other - Other
Task - Timing
Translation - Accuracy
Translation - Linguistic convention
Translation - Terminology
Voice - Appropriateness
Voice - Expressivity
Voice - Intelligibility
Voice - Voice quality

PILOT RESULTS VS BLASER

- Round-Trip Phoneme F1 scores exhibit a similar trend to BLASER. However, French translations using the Cascade model received much lower BLASER scores, possibly due to differences in vocal rather than linguistic characteristics of the translations

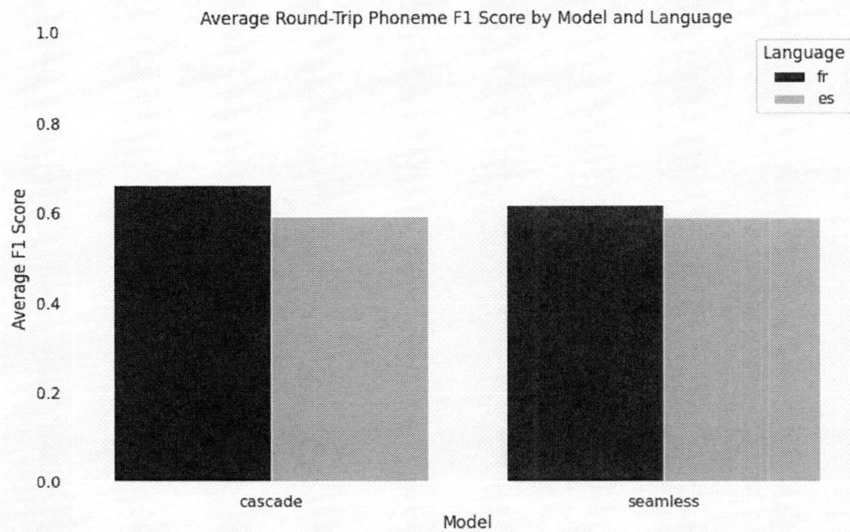

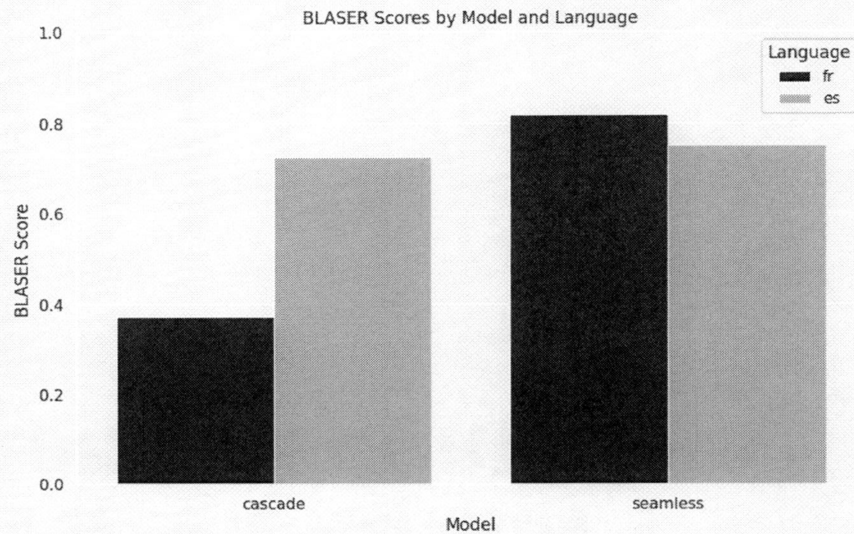

CORRELATION BETWEEN HUMAN EVALUATION AND PILOT SCORES

- We normalized the Human Evaluation Scores to a scale between 0 and 1, with 1 representing a perfect, error-free translation. This normalization allowed us to benchmark the Round-Trip Phoneme F1 Score against human judgment;
- Although the positive slope indicates that higher human scores generally align with better F1 scores, the correlation is not statistically significant.

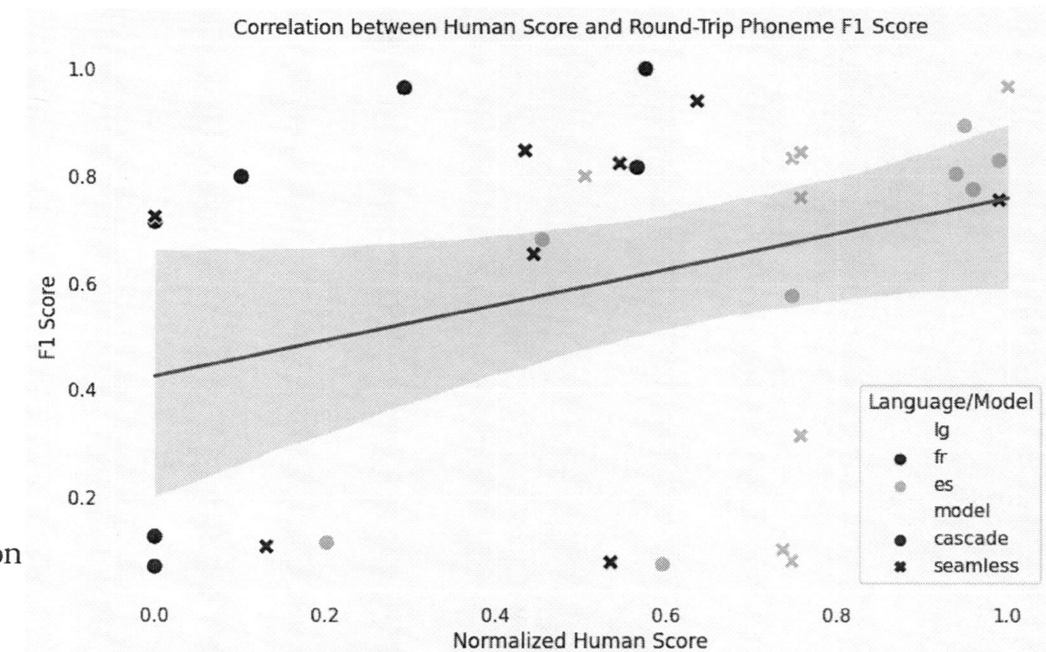

THANK YOU
Fred Bane
fbane@translations.com
github.com/TransperfectAI/amta2024_S2SEvaluation
TRANSPERFECT

AMTA 20
CHICAGO24
Enhancing Consistency
Through Prompt-Tuning
for Style Guide Adaptation
By Zidian(Rosetta) Guo, Ming Qian, 2024

Research Background

Main difficulties in crafting prompts as style guides

- Complexity of Language Rules
- Amount of tokens
- Limitation of LLM's Implementation
- Scalability Issues

Differences in info delivery for human v.s. LLM

- File Format
- Learning and Adaptation Pattern
    - Contextual Understanding
    - Rule Adherence

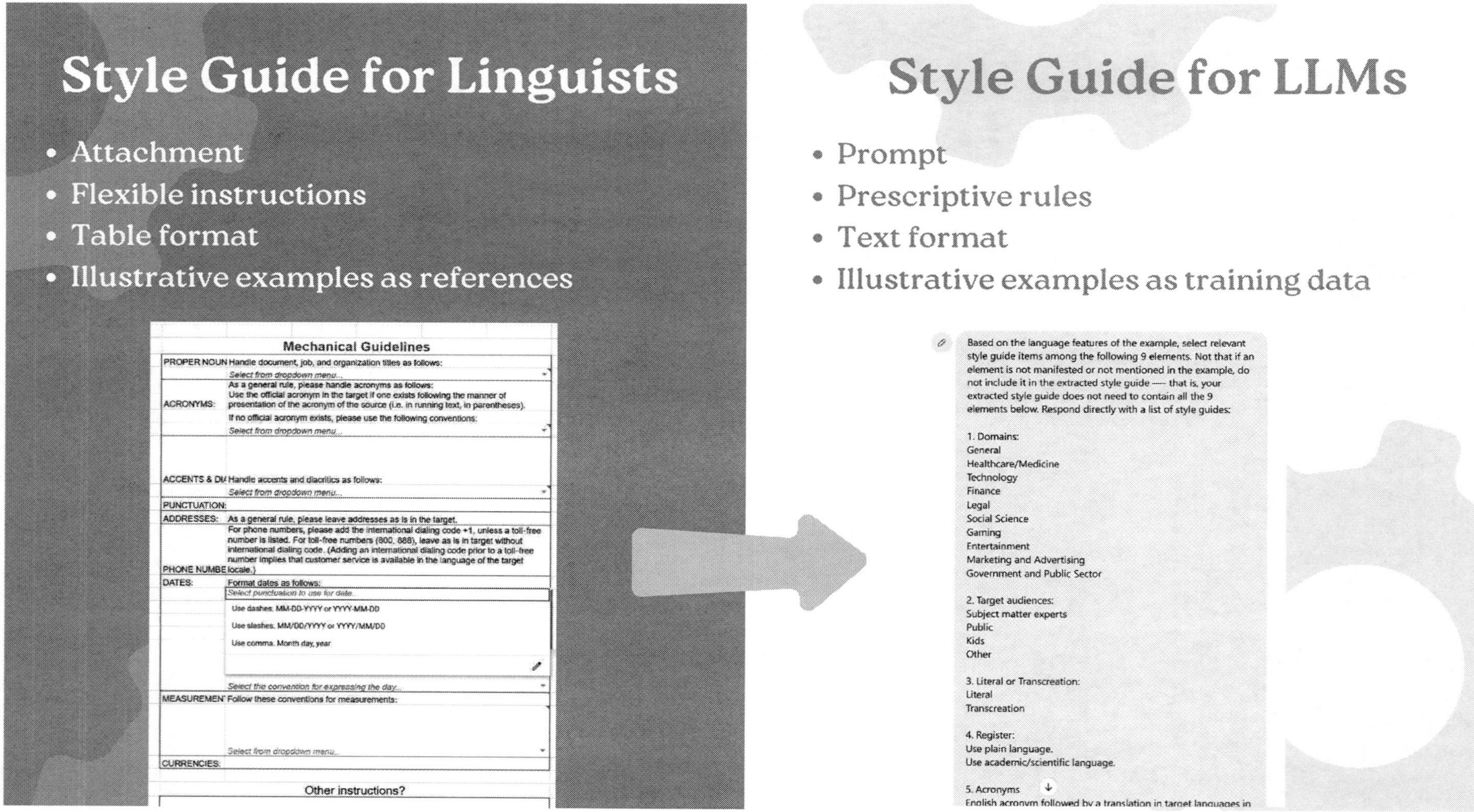
Style Guide for Linguists
Attachment
Flexible instructions
Table format
Illustrative examples as references
Mechanical Guidelines
PROPER NOUN Handle document, job, and organization titles as follows:
Select from dropdown menu...
ACRONYMS: As a general rule, please handle acronyms as follows:
Use the official acronym in the target if one exists following the manner of presentation of the acronym of the source (i.e. in running text, in parentheses).
If no official acronym exists, please use the following conventions:
Select from dropdown menu...
ACCENTS & DI/ Handle accents and diacritics as follows:
Select from dropdown menu...
PUNCTUATION:
ADDRESSES: As a general rule, please leave addresses as is in the target.
PHONE NUMBE For phone numbers, please add the international dialing code +1, unless a toll-free number is listed. For toll-free numbers (800, 888), leave as is in target without international dialing code. (Adding an international dialing code prior to a toll-free number implies that customer service is available in the language of the target locale.)
DATES: Format dates as follows:
Select punctuation to use for date...
Use dashes: MM-DD-YYYY or YYYY-MM-DD
Use slashes: MM/DD/YYYY or YYYY/MM/DD
Use comma: Month day, year
Select the convention for expressing the day...
MEASUREMEN Follow these conventions for measurements:
Select from dropdown menu...
CURRENCIES:
Other instructions?
Style Guide for LLMs
Prompt
Prescriptive rules
Text format
Illustrative examples as training data
Based on the language features of the example, select relevant style guide items among the following 9 elements. Not that if an element is not manifested or not mentioned in the example, do not include it in the extracted style guide — that is, your extracted style guide does not need to contain all the 9 elements below. Respond directly with a list of style guides:
1. Domains:
General
Healthcare/Medicine
Technology
Finance
Legal
Social Science
Gaming
Entertainment
Marketing and Advertising
Government and Public Sector
2. Target audiences:
Subject matter experts
Public
Kids
Other
3. Literal or Transcreation:
Literal
Transcreation
4. Register:
Use plain language.
Use academic/scientific language.
5. Acronyms

Prompt Engineering V.S. Prompt Tuning

- Crafting specific input instructions
- Widely used for one-off tasks
- Relies on the skill of the user to manually adjust and refine prompts, which can be time-consuming and may not always produce consistent results across different tasks.

- Systematically adjusted prompts over time
- Leveraging an initial prompt to create an extended prompt
- Used for tasks that require consistent results across multiple instances
- More suitable for dynamic problems, where the context or requirements may change over time.

Research Scope

Project Focus:

- Individual User Experience:
  - This research focuses on the application of Prompt Tuning (PT) within the UI of ChatGPT rather than through the API.
  - The goal is to explore how individual linguists can leverage PT directly to enhance style guide adaptation.

Models Tested:

- ChatGPT-3.5, -4, and -4 omni

The PT - Style Guide Adaptation Process

Basic Process

Rule for Prompt Tuning

1. Select from 9 elements

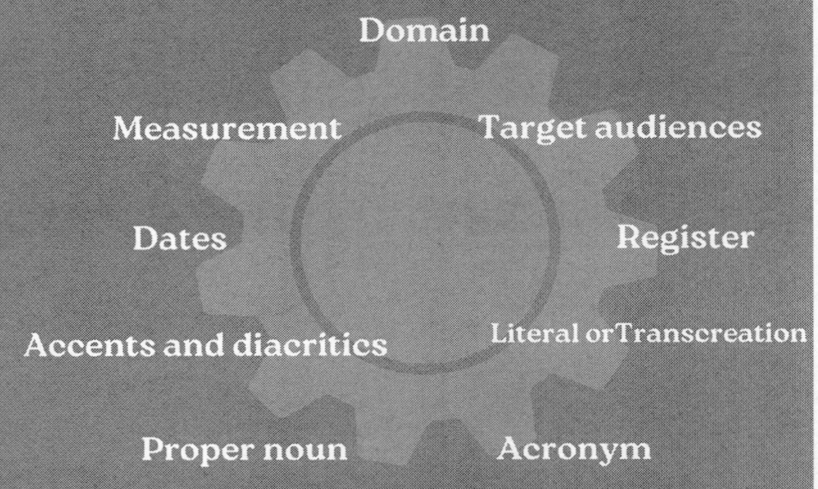

2. Remove irrelevant element(s)

Based on the language features of the example, select relevant style guide items among the following 9 elements. Note that if an element is not manifested or not mentioned in the example, do not include it in the extracted style guide —- that is, only contain necessary elements in your extracted style guide. Respond directly with a list of style guides:

1. **Domains:**
   - General
   - Healthcare/Medicine
   - Technology
   - Finance
   - Legal
   - Social Science
   - Gaming
   - Entertainment
   - Marketing and Advertising
   - Government and Public Sector

2. Target audiences:
- Subject matter experts
- Public
- Kids
- Other

3. Literal or Transcreation:
- Literal
- Transcreation

4. Register:
- Use plain language.
- Use academic/scientific language.

5. Acronyms
- English acronym followed by a translation in target languages in parentheses for the first instance of an acronym in the section. For all subsequent instances of an acronym in the section use the English acronym only.
- e.g. ISO (International Organization for Standardization)
- Translate the acronym into full words and indicate the English acronym in parentheses for the first instance of an acronym in the section. For all subsequent instances of an acronym in the section use the English acronym only.
- e.g. International Organization for Standardization (ISO)

6. Proper nouns
- Capitalize all major words in the title.
- e.g. International Organization for Standardization
- Capitalize only the first word in the title.
- e.g. International organization for standardization

7. Accents & Diacritics:
- Use accents and diacritics on CAPITAL letters.
- Do not use accents and diacritics on CAPITAL letters.

8. DATES (Remember to manage the order)
- Use dashes： MM-DD-YYYY
- Use slashes： MM/DD/YYYY
- Use comma： Month, day, year

9. MEASUREMENTS
- Convert All Measurements to Local Units
- Keep Original Measurements
- Provide Dual Measurements

Style Guide Extracted

1. Domains:
   - Healthcare/Medicine
   - Technology
2. Target audiences:
   - Subject matter experts
   - Public
3. Literal or Transcreation:
   - Literal
4. Register:
   - Use academic/scientific language.
5. Acronyms
   - Translate the acronym into full words and indicate the English acronym in parentheses for the first instance of an acronym in the section. For all subsequent instances of an acronym in the section use the English acronym only.
   - e.g. International Organization for Standardization (ISO)
6. Proper nouns
   - Capitalize all major words in the title.
   - e.g. International Organization for Standardization
7. DATES
   - Use comma.
   - Month, day, year

Style Guide Implemented

I am going to assign you a translation/LQA task from ZH to EN, adhering to the extracted style guides above. Begin your response directly with the information requested.
硝酸甘油是一种血管舒张药物，在临床应用于心绞痛、劳力型心力衰竭和急性心肌梗死等疾病的治疗已达百余年。
硝酸甘油主要通过扩张外周血管降低心脏前后负荷，扩张冠状动脉减少心肌耗氧而发挥作用。
然而临床中发现，硝酸甘油长期应用会导致其扩血管作用减弱甚至消失，即形成所谓的硝酸甘油耐受。
关于耐受的形成机制，近年来国内外在硝酸甘油生物转化、活性氧作用及环鸟苷酸-环鸟苷酸依赖的蛋白激酶信号通路障碍等方面有很多重要认识，发现硝酸甘油长期应用可以影响其生物活化途径的各个环节，以及引起血管内皮功能障碍，从而导致硝酸甘油耐受的形成。

Nitroglycerin as a Vasodilator Drug: Over a Century of Clinical Use and Tolerance Issues

Nitroglycerin is a vasodilator drug that has been used clinically for over a century to treat conditions such as angina, effort-induced heart failure, and acute myocardial infarction. The primary mechanism of nitroglycerin involves dilating peripheral blood vessels to reduce both preload and afterload on the heart, and dilating coronary arteries to decrease myocardial oxygen consumption.

However, it has been observed in clinical settings that long-term use of nitroglycerin can lead to a reduction or even disappearance of its vasodilatory effects, a phenomenon known as nitroglycerin tolerance. Recent domestic and international research has significantly advanced our understanding of the mechanisms behind this tolerance. Studies have highlighted the role of nitroglycerin's biotransformation, reactive oxygen species, and disruptions in the cyclic guanosine monophosphate (cGMP)-dependent protein kinase signaling pathway. It has been found that prolonged use of nitroglycerin can affect various aspects of its bioactivation pathways, as well as cause endothelial dysfunction, leading to the development of nitroglycerin tolerance.

Looking Forward

- Hierarchy in Prompt Tuning
- Locale Variations
- Performance Evaluation of Prompt Tuning
- Rule-Based Structures

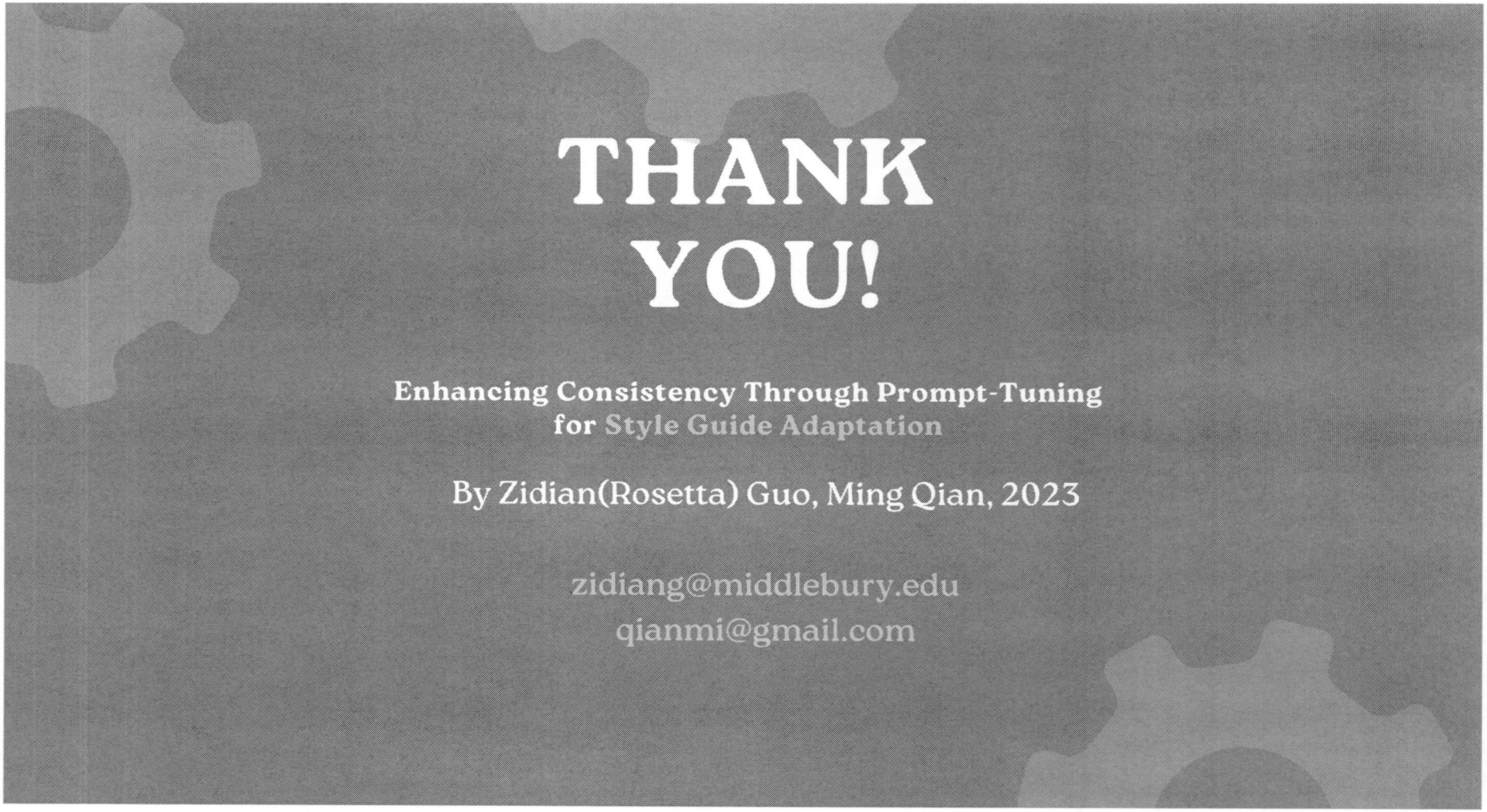
THANK
YOU!
Enhancing Consistency Through Prompt-Tuning
for Style Guide Adaptation
By Zidian(Rosetta) Guo, Ming Qian, 2023
zidiang@middlebury.edu
qianmi@gmail.com

This page intentionally left blank.

An Evaluation of English to Spanish Medical Translation by Large Language Models: A Quantitative and Qualitative Analysis

Nicholas Riina* nicholas.riina@icahn.mssm.edu
Likhitha Patlolla* likhitha.patlolla@icahn.mssm.edu
Camilo Hernandez Joya camilo.hernandezjoya@icahn.mssm.edu
Roger Bautista roger.bautista@icahn.mssm.edu
Melissa Olivar-Villanueva melissa.olivar-villanueva@icahn.mssm.edu
Anish Kumar anish.kumar@icahn.mssm.edu
Icahn School of Medicine, Mount Sinai Hospital, New York, 10029, USA

*Both authors contributed equally

Abstract

Medical translation is a critical tool for overcoming the barriers of discordant cultural backgrounds and languages within the healthcare field. Large Language Models (LLMs) that advertise translation and multilingual capabilities, like ChatGPT, pose a newfound solution that could include unique abilities that a typical machine translation (MT) system does not exhibit (e.g. catering a translation for a specific patient, such as a child). This work compares the English to Spanish translation of three LLMs: ChatGPT3.5 Turbo, ChatGPT4o, and Aguila with the performance of Google Translate. Medical Translations were provided by MedlinePlus, a parallel dataset developed by the National Library of Medicine that consists of four categories of information for patients in English and Spanish: health topics, patient instructions, lab tests, and drug information. Each model translated 15,816 sentences which were scored by three automated metrics: BLEU, BERTscore, and METEOR. 100 sentences were also graded by three Spanish interpreters using metrics defined in this paper: Fluency (is the translation correct Spanish), Adequacy (does the translation convey the original meaning), and Patient-friendliness (is the translation written in language that a patient can easily understand). The human evaluated translations were then subject to qualitative analysis that examined frequent errors and word choice. Automated results indicated that Chat-GPT4o performed equivalently to Google Translate, with ChatGPT3.5 not far behind. Human rated scores found both Chat-GPT models to perform statistically similar to Google Translate in all three metrics. Aguila, the only model intended for primarily Spanish and Catalan use, surprisingly performed much worse than the other models. However, qualitative analysis of Aguila's translations reveal the use of terms that may reach a broader audience, rendering the Spanish used more accessible than the other models. It is important, as MT systems are applied to the medical field, that the translations provided by these models are not only factually correct and patient safe, but accessible by vulnerable populations. This work provides an evaluation of the most recent ChatGPT model's medical translations with a comparison to a well-researched system, Google Translate, using verified metrics. Our work also highlights small, yet important disparities between the Spanish use of LLMs with English as a primary language and other LLMs that are intended for Spanish use.

1 Introduction

It is well-understood that in today's increasingly diverse America, the healthcare field must overcome barriers of discordant races, ethnicities, cultures, and languages to deliver high-quality care to all patients. According to the 2020 census, approximately 8.3% of American residents speak English less than "very well" (US Census Bureau, 2020). Metropolitan areas are disproportionately home to a large number of immigrants (29% in New York City), many of them not proficient in English (Profile of the Foreign-Born Population in New York, New York, 2023). Urban settings experience amplified disparities in care for underserved populations, including immigrants, refugees and limited-English proficiency, or LEP, patients. LEP status has been linked to greater health disparities (e.g. via poorer preventative screening) and worse health outcomes (Cheng et al., 2007; Ponce et al., 2006; Shi et al., 2009). In such cities, medical education institutes and academic health centers are a crucial form of advocacy and social justice that address disparities through service-learning mechanisms (Rupert et al., 2022). For instance, several medical schools operate student-run free clinics (SRFC) for uninsured patients in their communities. However, language and medical literacy barriers in these patients present a challenge for trainees to ensure their patients, who often have many chronic conditions, understand their diagnosis, medication regime, necessary lifestyle changes, specialist referrals, etc. (Rupert et al., 2022). For SRFCs and other healthcare settings that deal with a large number of LEP patients, artificial-intelligence (AI) or machine translation (MT)-based solutions present a potential low-cost, convenient, and efficient tool to address language barriers in patients. However, maintaining accurate, patient-friendly translations without compromising medical accuracy is a limiting factor of such translation services. Thus, phone interpretation services such as CyraCom and Pacific Interpreters remain the standard practice for communicating with LEP patients. Unfortunately, phone interpretation itself is limited by potentially poor acoustics, lack of visual cues, and lack of context provided to the interpreter (Cho, 2023).

Large language models (LLMs) are deep-learning algorithms that are trained to accomplish various natural language processing tasks like text classification and text generation, among others. A chatbot, like ChatGPT, is a system which has been optimized for conversation with a user. ChatGPT, along with other LLMs, is reported to able to use multiple languages, and has anecdotally been reported as an effective translator between languages (Achiam et al., 2023). However, there has not been a formal study looking at the medical translation capabilities of LLM chatbots that were not formally trained for translation versus dedicated machine translation algorithms, like Google Translate (GT).

The goal of this research was to quantify the effectiveness of various chatbot LLMs for translating health information from English to Spanish in a patient-friendly manner. At a preliminary stage, we are evaluating the potential of four models with multilingual capabilities to provide translations of English take-home instructions and clinical information into Spanish.

2 Related Work

Automated medical translation has benefited from research in the fields of both machine translation and LLMs.

2.1 LLM Translation

Over the last 5 years, LLMs have been researched as translators and compared with other neural MTs like DeepL and GT (Jiao et al., 2023). Several popular LLMs have been used for research without any fine tuning. Yao et al. compares GPT-3.5-turbo-1106 with LLaMA2-7B alongside GT and NLLB on translating between English and four other languages. For English to Spanish translations, as in this paper, Yao et al. (2023) found GT to have a BLEU score of 42.9, GPT3.5 Turbo to have 47.9, LLaMA2 to have 44.6, and NLLB to show 48.8. Yao interestingly found GPT3.5 to out-perform GT. Hendy et al. (2023) found that GPT3.5, on zero-shot translation, performed slightly worse than Microsoft Translator for a variety of languages, with GPT3.5's BLEU scores ranging from 25.9 (ZH>EN) to 41.0 (RU>EN).

This literature shows that LLMs are competitive translators without any fine tuning or training examples. Brown et al. (2020) also found that GPT model architectures improve in performance with exposure to correct examples from zero-shot, one-shot, and multi-shot learning.

2.2 Machine Medical Translation

The medical field is especially challenging for translation due to an abundance of medical jargon. Thus, a MT system is tasked with either translating the medical jargon into medical jargon in the target language or explaining the medical term in the target language's common terms. Skianis et al. (2020) shows that BLEU and METEOR scores both improve dramatically for English to French translations by statistical MT and neural MT systems when finetuned with medical terminology datasets. In their study, the medical terminology datasets were constructed from 5 datasets of English and French medical jargon. Pretrained Neural MTs (a pretrained Convolutional Neural Network from fairseq) had an improvement of BLEU score from 42.93 to 53.40 after pretraining with the medical terminology. However, this is unhelpful for low-health literacy patients.

Electronic health records of patients are commonly studied with MT systems as they are a rich source of clinical data (Johnsi Rani et al., 2019; Liu & Cai, 2015; Weng et al., 2019; Zeng-Treitler et al., 2010). Again, linguistics properties of health records are often vastly different from those of conversations between clinicians and patients, which are often the use case for medical translation. Other studies therefore have focused on MT translation of public health education texts (Almahasees et al., 2021; Chen et al., 2017; Das et al., 2019; Dew et al., 2015; Khanna et al., 2011; Kirchhoff et al., 2011; Turner et al., 2015), patient instructions (Lester et al., 2021; Miller et al., 2018; Taira et al., 2021) and general patient-provider communication (Kapoor et al., 2022; Patil & Davies, 2014; Turner et al., 2019). Automatic evaluation was used less often than human evaluation. Results from these studies demonstrate that MTs like GT are somewhat successful at medical translation, though some errors, especially with longer sentences, may relay dangerously inaccurate information.

3 Novel Contributions

To our knowledge, this is the first work that examines the most recent ChatGPT model, GPT4o, on medical translation from English to Spanish. This work also contributes to the literature by comparing neural MTs with translation by LLMs using commonly used automated scoring metrics, and newly applies these metrics to evaluate patient-provider communication. Finally, our study looks at LLMs developed with primarily English usage compared with one LLM that is intended for Spanish chat. Our qualitative analysis finds small yet important differences in the Spanish word choice among different models and highlights areas where medical MTs fall short.

4 Methods

In this section we will discuss the selection and cleaning of the dataset, methods applied for automated scoring and human evaluation, and the models tested and corresponding prompts.

4.1 Dataset

The MedlinePlus English-Spanish corpus encompasses 7,033 articles with information in four categories--health topics (e.g. strokes, diabetes, etc.), patient instructions, lab tests, and drug information--provided by the US National Library of Medicine. The dataset contains free health information for patients in both English and Spanish written in a patient-friendly manner. This corpus is representative of the types of conversations that a clinical Spanish interpreter may encounter. The Spanish articles are exact translations of the English articles and used as reference translations for human and automatic evaluation of all LLM translations.

4.2 Data Preparation

The articles were chosen from each category at random, to

Category	Sentences Translated
Patient instructions	3,014
Health topics	3,289
Lab tests	3,259
Drug information	6,254
Total	15,816

Table 1: Sentences translated for each category of information in the MedlinePlus dataset.

translate a minimum of 3000 lines per category. The total amount of lines translated was proportional to the size of each category. After a file was selected for translation, each sentence was separated and paired with its Spanish counterpart. Files that did not have the same number of sentences between English and Spanish were not used. After the file was parsed into sentences, formatting symbols and speaker designations were stripped.

4.3 Models

Three LLMs models were used. GPT3.5 turbo version gpt-3.5-turbo-0125 and GPT4o version gpt-4o-2024-05-13 (Achiam et al. 2023) These GPT models were selected since they did not require a paid OpenAI subscription and were more accessible to patients and providers. GPT4o is also reported to have translation capabilities. These models were both accessed through the OpenAI API. The prompt used mirrored that in He (2024) and is shown below:

messages= [

{"role": "system", "content": "You are a medical translator. Translate the following into Spanish while preserving the file format"},

{"role": "user", "content": SENTENCE TO TRANSLATE}]

The third LLM is Aguila, an LLM finetuned with 26 billion tokens of Spanish and Catalan data that was designed for chat in Spanish and Catalan. Aguila was developed by the Barcelona Supercomputing center by finetuning Falcon-7B with a dataset that was approximately 40% Spanish, 40% Catalan, and 20% English (mapama247 2023). 455 million words in the dataset were medical terms. The prompt used for translations is shown below:

'The sentence "SENTENCE TO TRANSLATE" translated into Spanish is'

The final MT used was GT, a neural MT system based on a transformer architecture. GT is a common benchmark for translation tasks and has been shown to be effective with translating medical Spanish (Khoong et al. 2019). GT was accessed through the Google Translate API and no prompt was used (Googletrans).

4.4 Scoring metrics

Three automated scoring metrics and three human evaluation metrics were used for this paper. The automated scoring metrics used in this paper include BLEU, METEOR, and BERTscore (Papineni et al., 2002; Banerjee & Lavie, 2005; Zhang et al; 2020). The METEOR metric is an n-gram based metric that is proven to correlate better than BLEU with human judgements on sentence-level translations, as it also better accounts for synonyms and morphological variants. BERTscore, a more recently developed metric, uses a pretrained BERT model to assess the cosine similarity between model embeddings of the translation and the reference, better accounting for paraphrases and distant clause dependencies. These three-scoring metrics have been used often when evaluating MTs as evidenced by the metareviews by Zappatore & Ruggeiri (2024) and Dew et. al. (2018).

Human evaluation metrics are still considered best practice despite being subjective and labor-intensive, as it allows application of cultural and contextual knowledge that reference-based methods lack. The human rated metrics we used were adapted from metrics used in the Workshop on Machine Translation. These metrics include Adequacy and Fluency scoring (WMT06-07), relative ranking (WMT07-16), and average score and z score (WMT17). Adequacy and Fluency are scores of translation accuracy and language accuracy, respectively. A high Adequacy score reflects a translation that contains all the semantic meaning of the reference text. A high Fluency score reflects a translation that is grammatically correct. Average and z score are the Fluency and Adequacy rankings after being normalized within each scorer (Harison, 2023).

These metrics were all ordinal and scored on a scale of 1-5. The definitions provided to human scorers are below:

Fluency score: Is it fluent Spanish? 5 is completely fluent, 1 is not fluent at all.

Adequacy score: Does it convey the original meaning? 5 is conveys original meaning perfectly, 1 is doesn't convey original meaning at all.

Patient-friendliness score: Is it written in language that a patient can easily understand? 5 is completely patient-friendly, 1 is not patient-friendly at all.

All the human scorers are interpreters at a student run free clinic associated with the Icahn School of Medicine. Scorers were provided with all translations from one model at a time. After completing all the evaluations, the scorers reported patterns and observations of frequent errors and model differences, which are discussed in the qualitative analysis.

5 Results

The results of MT translation will be presented first as automated metrics, human evaluation metrics, and qualitative analysis respectively. Following will be an analysis of human evaluation quality. Patient-friendliness was a new metric defined in this paper to capture how understandable a medical translation is for the general patient population. This metric is especially important for medical translation where medical terminology provides a unique challenge and patient understanding is especially critical.

5.1 Automated Evaluation Scores

The number of sentences translated per category of information is presented in Table 1. Score distributions from all three metrics were tested for normalcy and equal variance with the Shapiro Wilk Test and Levene's Test respectively. All the data

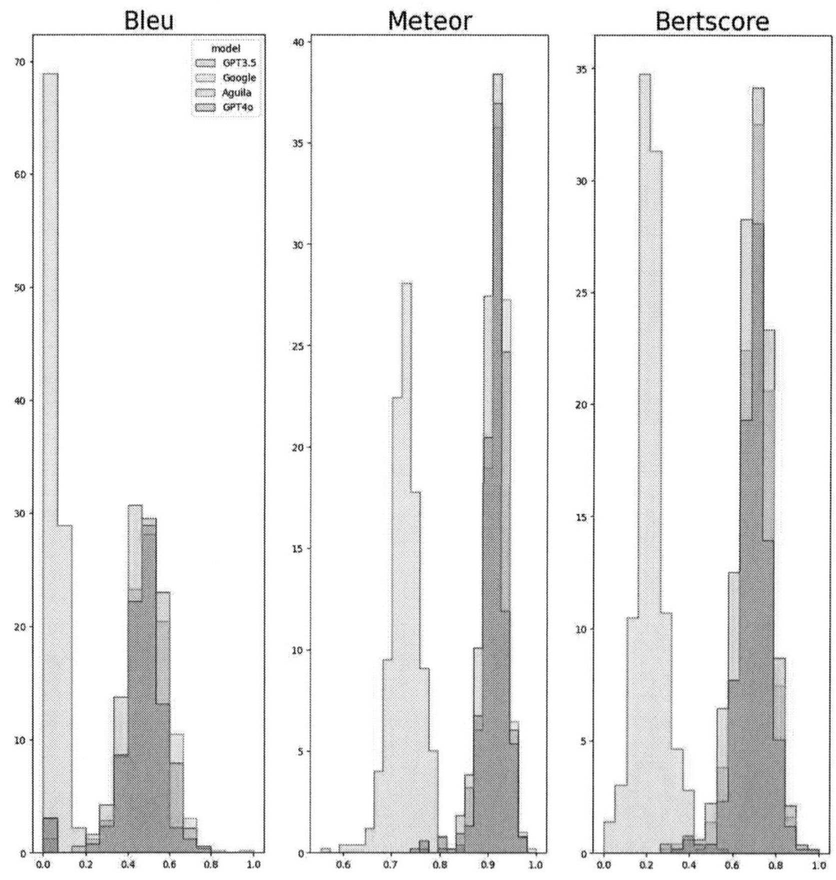

Figure 1: Distribution of Automated Scores by model. Scores for Aguila (green) are significantly lower while the other three models are almost identical. Google Translate is orange, GPT3.5 is blue and GPT4o is red.

Automated Scores		BLEU			METEOR			BERTscore		
Model A	Model B	Mean of Model A	Mean of Model B	P value	Mean of Model A	Mean of Model B	P value	Mean of Model A	Mean of Model B	P value
Aguila	Google Translate	0.0564 +/- 0.029	0.493 +/- 0.111	3.82 e-14	0.215 +/- 0.069	0.697 +/- 0.0828	0.00	0.729 +/- 0.031	0.915 +/- 0.0249	0.00
Aguila	ChatGPT3.5	0.0564 +/- 0.029	0.449 +/- 0.118	9.13 e-14	0.215 +/- 0.069	0.678 +/- 0.084	0.00	0.729 +/- 0.031	0.908 +/- 0.026	3.28 e-13
Aguila	GPT4o	0.0564 +/- 0.029	0.482 +/- 0.120	1.69 e-13	0.215 +/- 0.069	0.709 +/- 0.076	2.18 e-13	0.729 +/- 0.031	0.914 +/- 0.024	5.62 e-13
Google Translate	ChatGPT3.5	0.493 +/- 0.111	0.449 +/- 0.118	9.58 e-09	0.697 +/- 0.0828	0.678 +/- 0.084	1.67 e-03	0.915 +/- 0.0249	0.908 +/- 0.026	2.91 e-05
Google Translate	GPT4o	0.493 +/- 0.111	0.482 +/- 0.120	4.06 e-01	0.697 +/- 0.0828	0.709 +/- 0.076	5.86 e-02	0.915 +/- 0.0249	0.914 +/- 0.024	9.24 e-01
ChatGPT3.5	GPT4o	0.449 +/- 0.118	0.482 +/- 0.120	6.85 e-05	0.678 +/- 0.084	0.709 +/- 0.076	2.39 e-09	0.908 +/- 0.026	0.914 +/- 0.024	2.30 e-04

Table 2: Automated score means, standard deviations, and P values from the Games Howel Post Hoc Significance Test. BERTscore reported as F1 score. The only non-significant difference (p=0.05) is between Google Translate and ChatGPT4o and highlighted in green. The maximum scores are highlighted yellow.

was found to be significantly non-normal and to have significantly non-equal variance with p = 0.05. The score distribution is shown in a set of histograms in Figure 1. The means of each score and significant difference are reported in Table 2. All models were significantly different from each other except GPT4o and GT, the two top performing models. Interestingly, GPT3.5 Turbo and GPT4o are significantly different. Aguila performed much worse than the other models in all scoring metrics.

5.2 Human Evaluation Scores

Due to a strong right-skew in the human scored data (Appendix B), analysis assumed non-normal distributions. The Kruskal-Wallis Test, a non-parametric test for significance between multiple, non-normally distributed distributions of ordinal data, was used. The test was performed for the Fluency, Adequacy, and Patient-friendliness scores to assess differences between the models. These are all less than the alpha (p = 0.05) indicating that there are significant differences between models, which was individually assessed with a Games-Howell post hoc test (Table 3). GPT3.5 Turbo, GPT4o, and GT all scored similarly, with GPT4o scoring slightly better than the other two. Aguila again scored the worst in all metrics.

Human Evaluation Scores		Fluency			Patient-friendliness			Adequacy		
Model A	Model B	Mean of Model A	Mean of Model B	P value	Mean of Model A	Mean of Model B	P value	Mean of Model A	Mean of Model B	P value
Aguila	Google Translate	3.38 +/- 1.43	4.89 +/- 0.37	0.0	2.91 +/- 1.40	4.90 +/- 0.37	8.25 e-14	3.64 +/- 1.45	4.72 +/- 0.59	0.0
Aguila	ChatGPT3.5	3.38 +/- 1.43	4.81 +/- 0.52	4.39 e-14	2.91 +/- 1.40	4.92 +/- 0.31	1.57 e-13	3.64 +/- 1.45	4.76 +/- 0.54	2.02 e-14
Aguila	ChatGPT4o	3.38 +/- 1.43	4.95 +/- 0.25	9.33 e-15	2.91 +/- 1.40	4.97 +/- 0.21	7.92 e-14	3.64 +/- 1.45	4.79 +/- 0.47	0.0
Google Translate	ChatGPT3.5	4.89 +/- 0.37	4.81 +/- 0.52	1.41 e-01	4.90 +/- 0.37	4.92 +/- 0.31	8.13 e-01	4.72 +/- 0.59	4.76 +/- 0.54	8.88 e-01
Google Translate	ChatGPT4o	4.89 +/- 0.37	4.95 +/- 0.25	9.31 e-02	4.90 +/- 0.37	4.97 +/- 0.21	4.66 e-01	4.72 +/- 0.59	4.79 +/- 0.47	2.60 e-02
ChatGPT3.5	ChatGPT4o	4.81 +/- 0.52	4.95 +/- 0.25	2.09 e-04	4.92 +/- 0.31	4.97 +/- 0.21	9.48 e-01	4.76 +/- 0.54	4.79 +/- 0.47	1.02 e-01

Table 3. Human evaluated score means, standard deviation, and P values from the Games Howel Post Hoc Significance Test. The only non-significant differences (p = 0.05) are between Google Translate and both ChatGPT4o and ChatGPT3.5 and is highlighted in green. The maximum scores are highlighted in yellow.

5.3 Human Evaluation Qualitative Analysis

Qualitative feedback from scorers reported that GT, GPT3.5, and GPT4o produce very similar translations, and both GPTs capture and translate meaning as well as GT. All three were also very good at providing patient-friendly translations, provided that the input itself is patient-friendly. One scorer noted that any drop in Patient-friendliness score would be due to the input itself containing some jargon (this may be due to the random selection of individual sentences without their surrounding context). Another scorer noted that the only consistent error made by all three of these models is the dropping of articles in front of certain words, i.e. *glucosa en sangre o azúcar en sangre instead of la glucosa en sangre o el azúcar en sangre.* Aguila would make errors quite frequently, including adding inaccurate information, conjugating incorrectly, including Catalan words, and altering crucial semantic relationships within sentences. Table 3 provides a list of common errors with examples. However, two scorers noted that amongst its few successful translations, Aguila's word choice was more accessible and patient-friendly compared to the other models. For instance, the GPTs and GT used *revestimiento del estómago* in contrast to Aguila's usage of *mucosa estomacal* to translate stomach

Type of Error	Example
Added additional information not present in original sentence	funciona cambiando el nivel de ciertos neurotransmisores en el cerebro", **que se traduce a "cambiando el nivel de neurotransmisores en el cerebro"; es decir no es literal, sino más bien metafórico, ya que el cerebro es una red neuronal y no una "cantidad" de sustancias sino de conexiones y neurotransmisores.**
Added irrelevant commentary in English	"LASIK is unable to permanently change the shape of the cornea. **The translator was not perfect, but his translation is very good.**"
Inaccurate translation	""tu puedes prevenir la **gastroenteritis** bebiendo liquido" *should have been* "tu puedes prevenir la **enfermedad por calor** bebiendo liquido"
Conjugation errors	"si se los **ingiera**" *should have been* "si se los **ingiere**"
Formality errors	"**Toma** moxifloxacino" *should have been* "**Tome** moxifloxacino"
Incorrect use of articles	"**la** chance" *should have been* "**el** chance"
Impaired semantic relationships	"**No** se absorbe bien en el estómago vacío y lleno" *should have been* "se absorbe bien en el estómago vacío y lleno"

Table 3. Frequent errors made by Aguila.

lining. *Mucosa* is more descriptive and can be understood even if a person does not know what the stomach lining is, while understanding *revestimiento* is dependent on whether the patient knows this less frequently used term.

GPT3.5 and GPT4o also sometimes used the more patient-friendly term with Aguila, whereas GT consistently used less accessible, more formal terms. For instance, Aguila and GPT3.5 used *la parte inferior de la espalda* and *la parte baja de la espalda*, respectively, instead of *zona lumbar*, which GT used, to translate lower back. GT's word choice is dependent on understanding the names of the zones of the back, which many patients likely do not. Finally, while GT and GPT3.5 use the word *afección* to translate condition, Aguila and GPT4o use *condición*. While *afección* can be used, it has another meaning that means attachment, so the use of this word can be slightly confusing. A more widely understood translation, and the actual direct translation of the word condition, is *condición.*

5.4 Human Evaluation Metrics Validation

To gain insight into the consistency of each scoring metric across judges to judge each metric's validity, we evaluated each scoring metric across judges with intraclass correlation (Appendix A) and visually (Appendix B).

In Appendix A, the ICC was calculated for Random Fixed rates and was reported as a single ICC where each rater is evaluated compared to their own mean, and an average where each rater is evaluated compared to the group mean. The highest ICCs were found with the Adequacy score and with the set containing all the scores. The ICC was recalculated after normalizing each scorer's responses with z-score normalization and all the ICCs increased. The final ICCs were all above 0.7 and were significant with p value = 0.05. Patient-friendliness had the lowest ICC.

6 Discussion

The automated evaluation results demonstrate that GPT3.5 and GPT4o perform similarly to GT for medical translation accuracy across all scoring metrics: BLEU, METEOR, and BERTscore (Table 2). Analysis with the Games-Howell non-parametric post hoc test highlights that all three automated scoring metrics were not significantly different between GT and GPT4o (P = 0.05). GPT3.5 scored slightly, but significantly lower on all three metrics. Aguila performed worse than the other models for all scoring metrics.

Human evaluation also corroborated the pattern discerned by automated metrics. GPT4o was the top performing model for all categories. Notably, GPT4o scored significantly higher than GT for Adequacy and significantly higher than GPT3.5 in Fluency (Table 3). Otherwise, there were no significant differences in the scores for GT, GPT4o, and GPT3.5. Once again, Aguila performed worse than the other models in all categories. However, out of all metrics, it scored best in patient-friendliness.

Aguila was notably inconsistent with its translation accuracy. Despite some successful translations, the qualitative analysis found that the Spanish model made grammatical errors as well as translation errors. For instance, Aguila often added new information to the sentence and often incorrectly translated semantic relationships (e.g. *This medication can be taken vs This medication cannot be taken*) (Table 3). Both types of errors pose dangers to patients if the information transmitted to the patient is distorted. However, two scorers reported that Aguila occasionally utilized the most patient-friendly lexicon of the three models (e.g. *mucosa estomacal* instead of *revestimiento del estómago*). The lexicon of Aguila in these instances were described as 'more conversational language' and words that are suited for a larger audience. We hypothesize this may result from Aguila's development as a LLM fine-tuned with mostly Spanish/Catalan as opposed to an LLM used predominantly in English that is able to translate into other secondary languages like ChatGPT. More research is required to identify why the existences between the word choice of Aguila and the other two models differed. These results highlight the need for medical MT systems to be evaluated for the accessibility in terms of word choice in addition to the quality of their translations. GPT4o also used more patient-friendly and conversational terms, such as *condición* instead of *afección*, when compared to GT and GPT3.5.

Overall, despite some miniscule grammatical errors GT, GPT3.5, and GPT4o translated effectively without dangerously changing the original meaning of the sentence. One limitation of this study is that the translations were not graded by patients or bilingual physicians, but by medical students who interpret for the free clinic associated with the Icahn School of Medicine. Clinical research with patients and/or physicians is needed to determine if the ChatGPTs and GT are effective medical translators.

The human evaluation metrics were verified using ICC scores. High ICC scores above 0.7 for Fluency, Adequacy, Patient-friendliness demonstrate a strong similarity between scorers for each metric. While Fluency and Adequacy were human evaluation metrics adapted from the Workshop on Machine Translation in 2006, the Patient-friendliness metric was created in this study for the purpose of discerning differences in word choice. However, Patient-friendliness was not significantly higher for the ChatGPTs compared to GT as hypothesized.

Our results were limited by using only one prompt for each model without an exhaustive search for the optimal prompt. Additionally, as human scorers evaluated translations from one model at a time, they could have developed a bias for a certain score for each model. Still, this method of scoring was chosen so that scorers could discern patterns in the translations of each model. Finally, noting that Patient-friendliness had the lowest ICC score, it is possible that a clearer description of this measurement could better standardize evaluator interpretations, a suggestion that was also reflected by testimonies from human scorers. One scorer interpreted Patient-friendliness as primarily accounting for word choice, while another scorer mentioned they gave higher Patient-friendliness scores when a model explained a medical term instead of just translating to the corresponding Spanish medical term. These two views differ yet both can be interpreted as patient-friendliness.

7 Conclusion

This study sought to quantify the translation capabilities of LLM chatbots like GPT3.5, GPT4o, and Aguila for use in healthcare contexts. These models are not specifically designed for translation, but have capabilities that typical MTs lack, such being tasked with translating for a particular target audience. To our knowledge, this is the first study to employ automated evaluation metrics to translate a large test set representing clinical patient-provider communication. This is also the first to evaluate the newest ChatGPT model, GPT4o, in this manner and context. This work's findings confirm that the widely accessible LLM chatbots GPT3.5 Turbo and GPT4o indeed have medical MT capabilities on par with GT to translate clinical communication from English to Spanish. They hold promise for use in a variety of healthcare settings, from creating public health education texts to explaining physical examinations and inquiring about symptoms to providing take-home patient instructions. The Spanish chatbot Aguila was less successful at translating from English to Spanish, although when successful, its Spanish lexicon was much more conversational and accessible than the other models. Further studies should seek to evaluate LLM chatbots' performances at completing various clinical translation tasks in a real clinical setting, as well as explore more translation prompts.

8 Acknowledgements

This work was guided by Dr. Eric Oermann and Xujin Chris Liu with the OLAB at New York University. The work was also guided by Dr. Yasmin Meah and the East Harlem Health Outreach Partnership, the free clinic associated with the Icahn School of Medicine at Mount Sinai.

References

Achiam, J., Adler, S., Agarwal, S., Ahmad, L., Akkaya, I., Aleman, F. L., ... & McGrew, B. (2023). Gpt-4 technical report. arXiv preprint arXiv:2303.08774.

Almahasees, Z., Meqdadi, S., & Albudairi, Y. (2021). Evaluation of google translate in rendering English COVID-19 texts into Arabic. 17(4), 2065–2080. https://doi.org/10.3316/informit.228360028176817

Banerjee, S., & Lavie, A. (2005). METEOR: An Automatic Metric for MT Evaluation with Improved Correlation with Human Judgments. *Meeting of the Association for Computational Linguistics*, 65–72.

Brown, T., Mann, B., Ryder, N., Subbiah, M., Kaplan, J. D., Dhariwal, P., ... & Amodei, D. (2020). Language models are few-shot learners. Advances in neural information processing systems, 33, 1877-1901.

Chen, X., Acosta, S., & Barry, A. E. (2017). Machine or Human? Evaluating the Quality of a Language Translation Mobile App for Diabetes Education Material. *JMIR Diabetes*, *2*(1), e7446. https://doi.org/10.2196/diabetes.7446

Cheng, E. M., Chen, A., & Cunningham, W. (2007). Primary Language and Receipt of Recommended Health Care Among Hispanics in the United States. *Journal of General Internal Medicine*, *22*(2), 283–288. https://doi.org/10.1007/s11606-007-0346-6

Cho, J. (2023). Interpreters as Translation Machines: Telephone Interpreting Challenges as Awareness Problems. *Qualitative Health Research*, *33*(12), 1037–1048. https://doi.org/10.1177/10497323231191712

Das, P., Kuznetsova, A., Zhu, M., & Milanaik, R. (2019). Dangers of Machine Translation: The Need for Professionally Translated Anticipatory Guidance Resources for Limited English

Proficiency Caregivers. *Clinical Pediatrics*, *58*(2), 247–249. https://doi.org/10.1177/0009922818809494

Dew, K., Turner, A. M., Desai, L., Martin, N., Laurenzi, A., & Kirchhoff, K. (2015). PHAST: A Collaborative Machine Translation and Post-Editing Tool for Public Health. *AMIA Annual Symposium Proceedings*, *2015*, 492–501. https://www.ncbi.nlm.nih.gov/pmc/articles/PMC4765627/

Dew, K. N., Turner, A. M., Choi, Y. K., Bosold, A., & Kirchhoff, K. (2018). Development of machine translation technology for assisting health communication: A systematic review. *Journal of Biomedical Informatics*, *85*, 56–67. https://doi.org/10.1016/j.jbi.2018.07.018

Googletrans. Free and unlimited google translate API for python¶. (n.d.-a). https://py-googletrans.readthedocs.io/en/latest/

Google Cloud. (2024, June 6). *Evaluating models | AutoML Translation Documentation*. Google Cloud. https://cloud.google.com/translate/automl/docs/evaluate

Hakami, H., & Bollegala, D. (2017). A classification approach for detecting cross-lingual biomedical term translations. *Natural Language Engineering*, *23*(1), 31–51. https://doi.org/10.1017/S1351324915000431

Harison, T. (2023, October). *Human evaluation metrics*. Machine Translate. https://machinetranslate.org/human-evaluation-metrics

He, S. (2024). Prompting ChatGPT for Translation: A Comparative Analysis of Translation Brief and Persona Prompts. arXiv preprint arXiv:2403.00127.

Hendy, A., Abdelrehim, M., Sharaf, A., Raunak, V., Gabr, M., Matsushita, H., ... & Awadalla, H. H. (2023). How good are gpt models at machine translation? a comprehensive evaluation. arXiv preprint arXiv:2302.09210.

Jiao, W., Wang, W., Huang, J. T., Wang, X., & Tu, Z. (2023). Is ChatGPT a good translator? A preliminary study. arXiv preprint arXiv:2301.08745, 1(10).

Jimeno Yepes, A., Prieur-Gaston, É., & Névéol, A. (2013). Combining MEDLINE and publisher data to create parallel corpora for the automatic translation of biomedical text. *BMC Bioinformatics*, *14*, 146. https://doi.org/10.1186/1471-2105-14-146

Johnsi Rani, J., Gladis, D., & Mammen, J. (2019). Regional Language Support for Patient-inclusive Decision Making in Breast Cancer Pathology Domain. *International Journal of Recent Technology and Engineering (IJRTE)*, *8*, 8392–8399. https://doi.org/10.35940/ijrte.C6518.098319

Kapoor, R., Corrales, G., Flores, M. P., Feng, L., & Cata, J. P. (2022). Use of Neural Machine Translation Software for Patients With Limited English Proficiency to Assess Postoperative Pain and Nausea. *JAMA Network Open*, *5*(3), e221485. https://doi.org/10.1001/jamanetworkopen.2022.1485

Khanna, R. R., Karliner, L. S., Eck, M., Vittinghoff, E., Koenig, C. J., & Fang, M. C. (2011). Performance of an online translation tool when applied to patient educational material. *Journal of Hospital Medicine*, *6*(9), 519–525. https://doi.org/10.1002/jhm.898

Khoong, E. C., Steinbrook, E., Brown, C., & Fernandez, A. (2019). Assessing the use of Google Translate for Spanish and Chinese translations of emergency department discharge instructions. JAMA internal medicine, 179(4), 580-582.

Kirchhoff, K., Turner, A. M., Axelrod, A., & Saavedra, F. (2011). Application of statistical machine translation to public health information:

A feasibility study. *Journal of the American Medical Informatics Association: JAMIA, 18*(4), 473–478. https://doi.org/10.1136/amiajnl-2011-000176

Lankford, S., Afli, H., Ní Loinsigh, Ó., & Way, A. (2022). gaHealth: An English–Irish Bilingual Corpus of Health Data. In N. Calzolari, F. Béchet, P. Blache, K. Choukri, C. Cieri, T. Declerck, S. Goggi, H. Isahara, B. Maegaard, J. Mariani, H. Mazo, J. Odijk, & S. Piperidis (Eds.), *Proceedings of the Thirteenth Language Resources and Evaluation Conference* (pp. 6753–6758). European Language Resources Association. https://aclanthology.org/2022.lrec-1.727

Lester, C. A., Ding, Y., Li, J., Jiang, Y., Rowell, B., & Vydiswaran, V. G. V. (2021). Human versus machine editing of electronic prescription directions. *Journal of the American Pharmacists Association, 61*(4), 484-491.e1. https://doi.org/10.1016/j.japh.2021.02.006

Liu, B., & Huang, L. (2021). ParaMed: A parallel corpus for English–Chinese translation in the biomedical domain. *BMC Medical Informatics and Decision Making, 21*(1), 258. https://doi.org/10.1186/s12911-021-01621-8

Liu, W., & Cai, S. (2015). Translating Electronic Health Record Notes from English to Spanish: A Preliminary Study. In K. B. Cohen, D. Demner-Fushman, S. Ananiadou, & J. Tsujii (Eds.), *Proceedings of BioNLP 15* (pp. 134–140). Association for Computational Linguistics. https://doi.org/10.18653/v1/W15-3816

mapama247. (2023, July 19). Introducing Ǎguila, a new open-source LLM for Spanish and Catalan. Medium. https://medium.com/@mpamies247/introducing-a%CC%8Cguila-a-new-open-source-llm-for-spanish-and-catalan-ee1ebc70bc79

Manzini, E., Garrido-Aguirre, J., Fonollosa, J., & Perera-Lluna, A. (2022). Mapping layperson medical terminology into the Human Phenotype Ontology using neural machine translation models. *Expert Systems with Applications, 204*, 117446. https://doi.org/10.1016/j.eswa.2022.117446

Mauser, A., Hasan, S., & Ney, H. (n.d.). *Automatic evaluation measures for statistical machine translation—System optimization.*

Miller, J. M., Harvey, E. M., Bedrick, S., Mohan, P., & Calhoun, E. (2018). Simple Patient Care Instructions Translate Best: Safety Guidelines for Physician Use of Google Translate. *Journal of Clinical Outcomes Medicine, 25*(1), 18–27.

Papineni, K., Roukos, S., Ward, T., & Zhu, W. (2002). BLEU: A method for Automatic Evaluation of Machine Translation. *Proceedings of the 40th Annual Meeting of the Association for Computational Linguistics*, 311–318. https://doi.org/10.3115/1073083.1073135

Patil, S., & Davies, P. (2014). Use of Google Translate in medical communication: Evaluation of accuracy. *BMJ, 349*, g7392. https://doi.org/10.1136/bmj.g7392

Ponce, N. A., Hays, R. D., & Cunningham, W. E. (2006). Linguistic Disparities in Health Care Access and Health Status Among Older Adults. *Journal of General Internal Medicine, 21*(7), 786–791. https://doi.org/10.1111/j.1525-1497.2006.00491.x

Profile of the foreign-born population in New York, New York. (2023). Vera Institute of Justice. https://www.vera.org/downloads/publications/profile-of-foreign-born-population-new-york-city.pdf

Renato, A., Castaño, J., Ávila, P., Berinsky, H., Gambarte, L., Park, H., Pérez, D., Otero, C., & Luna, D. (2024). *A Machine Translation Approach for Medical Terms*. 369–378. https://www.scitepress.org/Link.aspx?doi=10.5220/0006555003690378

Rupert, D. D., Alvarez, G. V., Burdge, E. J., Nahvi, R. J., Schell, S. M., & Faustino, F. L. (2022). Student-Run Free Clinics Stand at a Critical Junction Between Undergraduate Medical Education, Clinical Care, and Advocacy. *Academic Medicine : Journal of the Association of American Medical Colleges, 97*(6), 824–831. https://doi.org/10.1097/ACM.0000000000004542

Shi, L., Lebrun, L. A., & Tsai, J. (2009). The influence of English proficiency on access to care. *Ethnicity & Health, 14*(6), 625–642. https://doi.org/10.1080/13557850903248639

Skianis, K., Briand, Y., & Desgrippes, F. (2020). Evaluation of Machine Translation Methods applied to Medical Terminologies. In E. Holderness, A. Jimeno Yepes, A. Lavelli, A.-L. Minard, J. Pustejovsky, & F. Rinaldi (Eds.), *Proceedings of the 11th International Workshop on Health Text Mining and Information Analysis* (pp. 59–69). Association for Computational Linguistics. https://doi.org/10.18653/v1/2020.louhi-1.7

Taira, B. R., Kreger, V., Orue, A., & Diamond, L. C. (2021). A Pragmatic Assessment of Google Translate for Emergency Department Instructions. *Journal of General Internal Medicine, 36*(11), 3361–3365. https://doi.org/10.1007/s11606-021-06666-z

Turner, A. M., Choi, Y. K., Dew, K., Tsai, M.-T., Bosold, A. L., Wu, S., Smith, D., & Meischke, H. (2019). Evaluating the Usefulness of Translation Technologies for Emergency Response Communication: A Scenario-Based Study. *JMIR Public Health and Surveillance, 5*(1), e11171. https://doi.org/10.2196/11171

Turner, A. M., Dew, K. N., Desai, L., Martin, N., & Kirchhoff, K. (2015). Machine Translation of Public Health Materials From English to Chinese: A Feasibility Study. *JMIR Public Health and Surveillance, 1*(2), e4779. https://doi.org/10.2196/publichealth.4779

US Census Bureau. (2020, April). *People That Speak English Less Than "Very Well" in the United States*. Census.Gov. https://www.census.gov/library/visualizations/interactive/people-that-speak-english-less-than-very-well.html

Weng, W.-H., Chung, Y.-A., & Szolovits, P. (2019). Unsupervised Clinical Language Translation. *Proceedings of the 25th ACM SIGKDD International Conference on Knowledge Discovery & Data Mining*, 3121–3131. https://doi.org/10.1145/3292500.3330710

Wu, C., Xia, F., Deleger, L., & Solti, I. (2011). Statistical Machine Translation for Biomedical Text: Are We There Yet? *AMIA Annual Symposium Proceedings, 2011*, 1290–1299. https://www.ncbi.nlm.nih.gov/pmc/articles/PMC3243244/

Yao, B., Jiang, M., Yang, D., & Hu, J. (2023). Benchmarking llm-based machine translation on cultural awareness. arXiv preprint arXiv:2305.14328.

Zappatore, M., & Ruggieri, G. (2024). Adopting machine translation in the healthcare sector: A methodological multi-criteria review. *Computer Speech & Language, 84*, 101582. https://doi.org/10.1016/j.csl.2023.101582

Zeng-Treitler, Q., Kim, H., Rosemblat, G., & Keselman, A. (2010). Can Multilingual Machine Translation Help Make Medical Record Content More Comprehensible to Patients? *MEDINFO 2010* (pp. 73–77). IOS Press. https://doi.org/10.3233/978-1-60750-588-4-73

Zhang, T., Kishore, V., Wu, F., Weinberger, K. Q., & Artzi, Y. (2020). BERTScore: Evaluating Text Generation with BERT. *ICLR 2020.* https://arxiv.org/pdf/1904.09675.pdf

Appendix

ICC Scores [95% CL]	Patient-friendliness	p value	Adequacy	p value	Fluency	p value	Total	p value
Single Random, Fixed Raters	0.409[0.27-0.54]	1.370 e-13	0.497[0.36-0.62]	1.641 e-19	0.397[0.21-0.55]	1.400 e-15	0.49[0.30-0.64]	7.69 e-22
Average Random, Fixed Raters	0.675[0.53-0.78]	1.370 e-13	0.748[0.63-0.83]	1.641 e-19	0.664[0.45-0.79]	1.4 e-15	0.742[0.57-0.84]	7.693 e-22
Rater-Normalized Single Raters	0.443[0.32-0.56]	2.02 e-13	0.549[0.44-0.65]	3.272 e-20	0.491[0.37-0.60]	3.201 e-16	0.579[0.47-0.68]	1.188 e-22
Rater-Normalized Average Raters	0.705[0.59-0.79]	2.02 e-13	0.785[0.70-0.85]	3.273 e-20	0.743[0.64-0.82]	3.201 e-16	0.804[0.73-0.86]	1.189 e-22

Appendix A. Intra-class correlation (ICC) scores for each score and for entire model. ICCs all increased when scores were normalized with z-score normalization within each judge group. The maximum score occurred in normalized average raters and was 0.785, indicating strong coherence across evaluators.

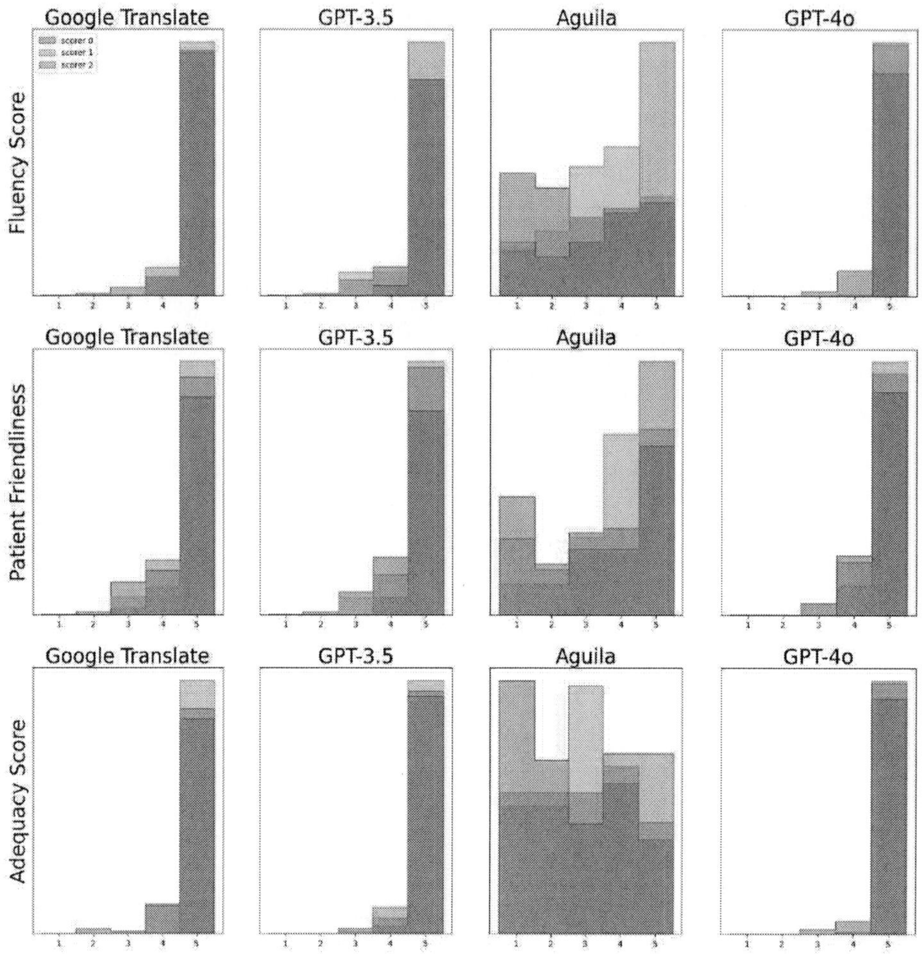

Appendix B. Score Variance for Human Evaluations for each model and Human Evaluator. Human evaluated scores shown for each human evaluator and model. Notice the strong right sided skew for each model, which is slightly more evenly distributed for Aguila. The strong skew of the results shows that the GPTs and GT performed much more consistently well than Aguila.

welocalize

From "Comment allez-vous?" to "Comment ça va?": Leveraging Large Language Models to Automate Formality Adaptation in Translation

VERA SENDEROWICZ

AMTA 2024

Agenda

01 Our Goals

02 Experimental Settings

03 Results

04 Conclusions & Next Steps

Our Goals

Our Goals

01 Develop an AI-powered process to change the formality of Translation Memories from formal into informal, providing time and cost savings compared to human review

02 The adapted Translation Memories will be used for model training and for leverage in translation tasks, therefore the adaptation process should:

a) not affect translation's accuracy → focus solely on formality adaptation

b) focus on the grammatical formality → do not introduce stylistic, vocabulary or register changes, but rather fix verbs and pronouns - bearers of formality for the languages in scope

Experimental Settings

Background Information

01

Content and languages in scope: Marketing & Hospitality, subset of Romance languages (en>es-LA, fr, it)

02

Proprietary Classifier: BERT-based classifier to assess the formality of TMX files on a segment level, outputting annotated TMX files.

03

LLM: we tested an array of options (OpenAI's GPT4 and GPT3.5 as well as Google's Gemini Pro 1.0) to identify the most effective solution balancing speed, cost, and output quality. Our final choice was fine-tuned GPT3.5.

LLM fine-tuning

The model was fine-tuned with prompts + an examples corpus that varied by language.

Prompts include:

a) Universal guidelines, applicable to all languages
   - such as: do not include any extra comments in the responses

b) Language-specific guidelines for each language.
   - Example for es-LA: Should not make changes to any pronouns or verbal forms in first person ('yo'/'nosotros')

The examples corpus includes:

1. Formal segments paired with their informal version
2. Informal segments paired with their unchanged copy
3. Neutral segments paired with "No Response"

Note: Multiple iterations, ranging between two to three for each language, were executed to attain a corpus of examples that yielded a satisfactory output.

The Process

CONTENT & LANGUAGE SELECTION

Marketing & Hospitality Translation Memories for en>es-LA, en>fr-FR, en>it-IT

LLM FINE-TUNING

Development, testing and refinement of prompts and example corpus

PROCESSING WITH CLASSIFIER & LLM

Segments annotated by the Classifier are sent to fine-tuned LLM for adaptation to informal

HUMAN REVIEW

The segments that were adapted by the LLM or considered Formal by the Classifier were sent to humans for review

Results

Overview

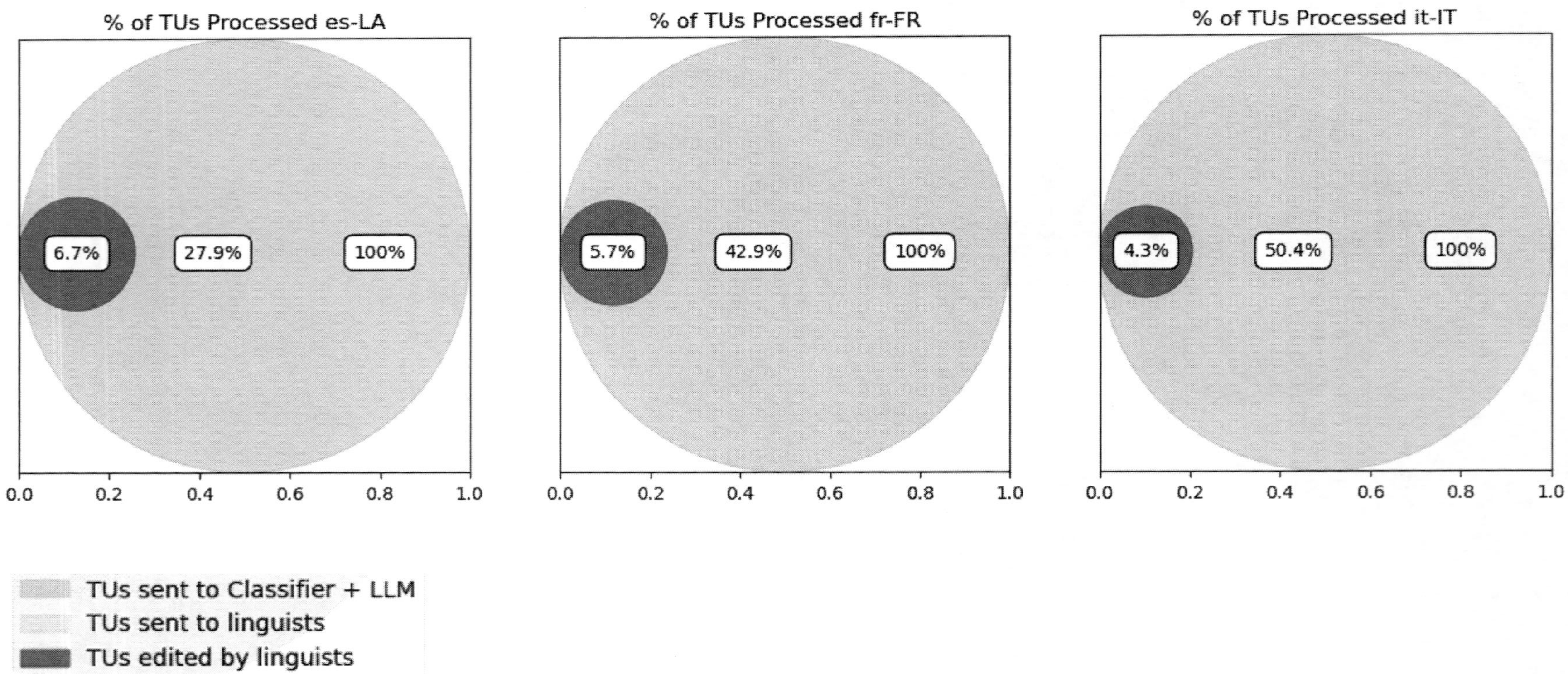
% of TUs Processed es-LA
6.7%
27.9%
100%
% of TUs Processed fr-FR
5.7%
42.9%
100%
% of TUs Processed it-IT
4.3%
50.4%
100%
0.0
0.2
0.4
0.6
0.8
1.0
TUs sent to Classifier + LLM
TUs sent to linguists
TUs edited by linguists

Linguists' effort

Language	BLEU	PE Distance	TER	CharacTER	#Segments
es-LA	92.45	1.00%	4.00%	0.02	1390
fr-FR	86.21	3.00%	9.00%	0.05	641
it-IT	85.08	4.00%	9.00%	0.06	462

Insights:

- Linguists were instructed to
    - Make sure that the tone of voice was informal, and fix otherwise
    - Revert to original any segment that was changed unnecessarily
    - Fix hallucinations
    - Do not change anything else
- Comparative analysis was conducted on the segment processed by the LLMs which were edited by the linguists, before and after linguistic review.
- The scores indicate that, on the segments which needed human intervention, the editing effort was minimal (= sparse and small changes).

Time & Costs Savings

Notes:

- The savings were determined by comparing the time it would have taken linguists to review the entire TM using standard review hourly throughput, with the time it took to review the content edited by the LLM or flagged as 'Formal' by the Classifier.
- Our findings revealed that the hourly productivity significantly increased when using the LLM, due to the minimal number of changes required (5,000 w/h instead of 1,500 w/h)
- The costs for LLM processing and engineering time were added to the review hours for a fair comparison with the old TM review process.

68%
Italian

77%
Spanish LA

74%
French

Conclusions & Next Steps

Conclusions & Next Steps

Conclusions

- Our proposed AI-powered approach for TM adaptation from formal to informal provides significant time and costs savings compared to the standard workflow.
- Human review is still needed as the current solution fails to identify 100% of the formal segments, introduces unnecessary changes as well as mistakes.

Next Steps

- Test this solution for post-editing, to ensure the content is ready or needs very little editing for immediate publication
- Expand the approach to include more languages
- Test the approach on tag-heavy content

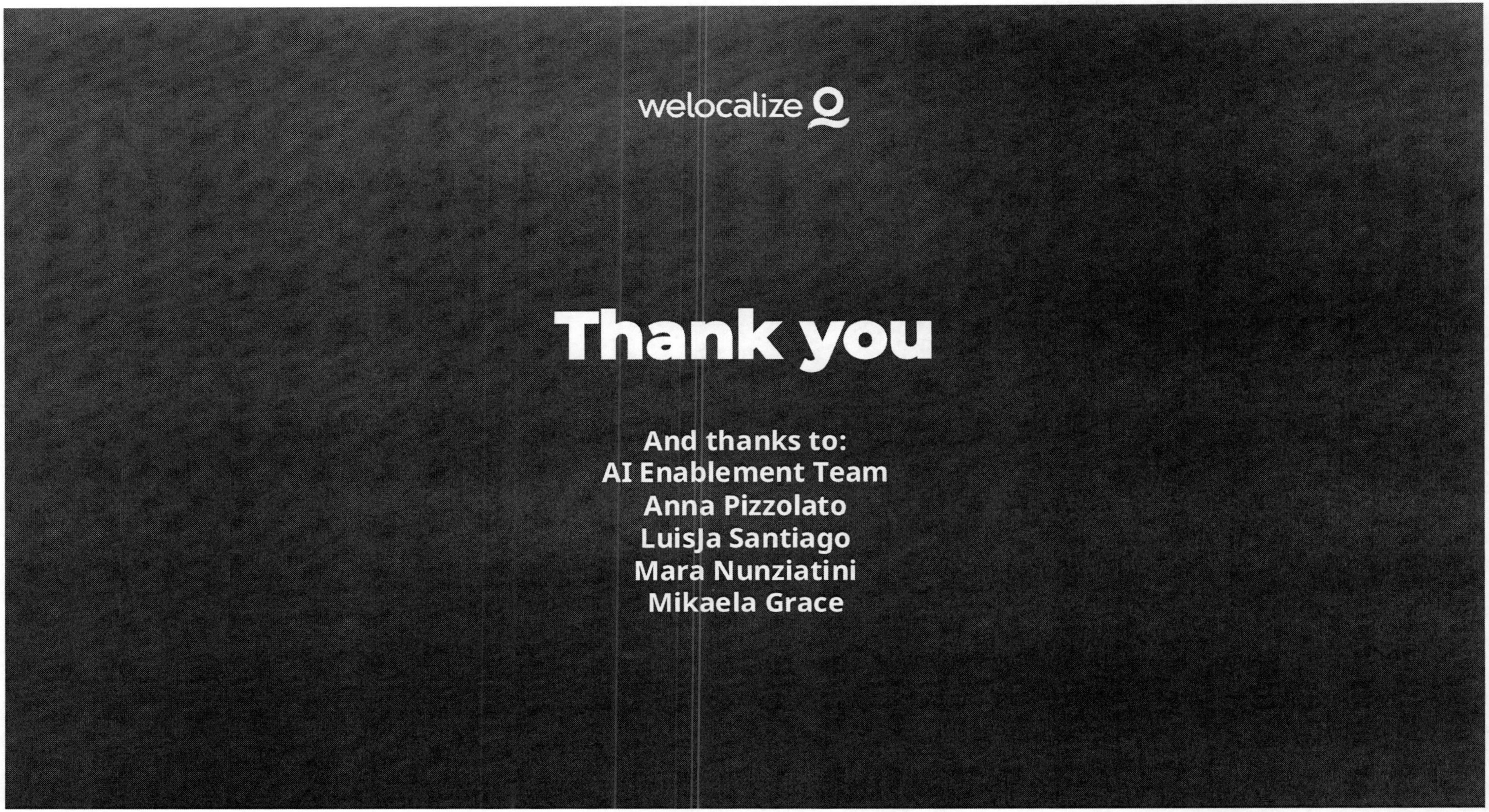
welocalize
Thank you
And thanks to:
AI Enablement Team
Anna Pizzolato
LuisJa Santiago
Mara Nunziatini
Mikaela Grace

Appendix

LLM Prompts

es-LA Prompt

Marv is a professional English into International Spanish translator, who adapts the second person pronouns and verbal forms in the given Spanish text to make them informal. Every time he sees the word 'usted', he adapts it to 'tú'. He should pay special attention to imperative and subjunctive verbs: he shouldn't forget to adapt those if they are conjugated in second person singular. Marv shouldn't include any extra comments in the responses, and he should always choose only one response option. If no adaptation of the original text is needed, he should set the Adapted Text to 'No response'. No extra comments or explanations are necessary.

fr-FR Prompt

Marv is a professional English into International French translator, who adapts the singular second person pronouns and verbal forms in the given French text to make them informal. Every time he sees the word 'vous', he adapts it to 'tu'. He should pay special attention to imperative and subjunctive verbs: he shouldn't forget to adapt those if they are conjugated in second person singular. Marv shouldn't change infinitive verbal forms or passive verbal phrases. He should not make changes to any pronouns or verbal forms in first person ('je'/'nous'), but he should change the pronouns 'vous', 'votre' and 'vos' for their informal version every time they appear. Marv shouldn't include any extra comments in the responses, and he should always choose only one response option. If no adaptation of the original text is needed, he should set the Adapted Text to 'No response'. No extra comments or explanations are necessary

it-IT Prompt

Matteo is a professional English into Italian translator, who adapts the second person plural and formal pronouns as well as verbal forms in the given Italian text to make them informal. Every time he sees the word "voi" or "Lei", he adapts it to 'voi'. He should pay special attention to infinitive verbs and impersonal sentence structure: no need to change these. Matteo should make sure he identifies the subject of the sentence and never change it. Matteo shouldn't introduce grammar mistakes nor include any extra comments in the responses, and he should always choose only one response option. If no adaptation of the original text is needed, he should set the Adapted Text to 'No response'. No extra comments or explanations are necessary.

Corpus Examples

{"messages": [{"role": "system", "content": "Marv is a professional English into International Spanish translator, who adapts the singular second person pronouns and verbal forms in the given Spanish text to make them informal. Every time he sees the word 'usted', he adapts it to 'tú'. He should pay special attention to imperative and subjunctive verbs: he shouldn't forget to adapt those if they are conjugated in second person singular. Marv shouldn't change infinitive verbal forms or passive verbal phrases. He should not make changes to any pronouns or verbal forms in first person ('yo'/'nosotros') or second person plural ('ustedes'). Marv shouldn't include any extra comments in the responses, and he should always choose only one response option. If no adaptation of the original text is needed, he should set the Adapted Text to 'No response'. No extra comments or explanations are necessary."}, {"role": "user", "content": "Aborda la necesidad de modernizar la TI o realizar innovaciones."}, {"role": "assistant", "content": "No response."}]},

{"messages": [{"role": "system", "content": "Marv is a professional English into International French translator, who adapts the singular second person pronouns and verbal forms in the given French text to make them informal. Every time he sees the word 'vous', he adapts it to 'tu'. He should pay special attention to imperative and subjunctive verbs: he shouldn't forget to adapt those if they are conjugated in second person singular. Marv shouldn't change infinitive verbal forms or passive verbal phrases. He should not make changes to any pronouns or verbal forms in first person ('je'/'nous'), but he should change the pronouns 'vous', 'votre' and 'vos' for their informal version every time they appear. Marv shouldn't include any extra comments in the responses, and he should always choose only one response option. If no adaptation of the original text is needed, he should set the Adapted Text to 'No response'. No extra comments or explanations are necessary."}, {"role": "user", "content": "Indiquez le nom complet et le titre de la personne sous chaque citation."}, {"role": "assistant", "content": "Indique le nom complet et le titre de la personne sous chaque citation."}]},

Academia & Business: Merging Rivals through Quality Assurance in Translation Services

Patry Muñoz Andrés

Introduction

There is often a big difference between what academics and businesses do. This is especially true in the language services industry, where academic research and business often have different priorities. But this separation is not just about different priorities. It's also about how each sector defines and pursues quality. QA provides a way to combine these two areas. It ensures that new ideas in translation studies help language service providers and their clients.

The Disconnect Between Academia and Business

Historically, academia has focused on developing theoretical frameworks, conducting empirical studies, and advancing knowledge within specific disciplines. In translation studies, this often involves exploring linguistic theories, cognitive processes, and the socio-cultural implications of translation. The primary aim here is to push the boundaries of understanding, often without immediate concern for practical application (O'Brien, 2012).

On the other hand, the business environment, particularly within LSPs, is driven by the need for efficiency, scalability, and market competitiveness. Quality in this context is often defined by client satisfaction, turnaround time, and cost-effectiveness. While academic research can offer valuable insights, its direct applicability to business processes is not always clear or immediate (Garcia, 2019).

Quality Assurance as a Bridge

Quality assurance, when viewed through the lens of both academia and business, serves as a critical bridge between these two worlds. QA practices, especially those involving standardized frameworks such as ISO certifications, provide a common language for discussing and ensuring quality.

ISO Certifications: The First Step in Bridging the Gap

ISO certifications, like ISO 9001 for quality management systems and ISO 17100 for translation services, provide a structured approach to ensuring quality across industries (ISO, 2020; ISO, 2015). For academia, these standards offer a pathway to translate theoretical research into practical, real-world applications. For businesses, they serve as benchmarks to ensure services meet international standards.

The adoption of ISO standards within LSPs represents a significant step towards aligning academic research with business needs. For example, studies that analyze error rates and translation quality can be applied to refine ISO-certified QA processes, leading to measurable improvements in service quality. Specifically, the work of Zhou and Pan (2016), which examines the implementation of ISO 17100 in translation services, highlights how academic insights can directly influence and enhance standardized QA practices.

Automated Quality Assurance: Bridging Efficiency and Precision

Automated QA tools, often developed through collaboration between academia and industry, are another key area where the two worlds converge. These tools use algorithms and linguistic data to automatically check translations for errors, consistency, and compliance with style guides (Garcia, 2019).

From an academic perspective, the development of these tools involves complex linguistic research, machine learning, and natural language processing (NLP) (Koehn, 2020). These tools help businesses create better quality QA processes that can handle large amounts of text quickly.

New automated QA tools show how academic research can affect business. By using language processing and error detection, LSPs can improve their services and give clients better results.

Machine Translation and Large Language Models: The Pinnacle of Collaboration

Machine Translation (MT) and Large Language Models (LLMs) represent the most sophisticated intersection of academic research and business application in the translation industry. MT systems, such as Google Translate or DeepL, are built on decades of academic research in computational linguistics (Vaswani et al., 2017), while LLMs like GPT-4 leverage vast amounts of data and advanced algorithms to produce highly accurate translations (Koehn, 2020).

These technologies are a big achievement for academia. They show how useful it is to do research across different subjects. For businesses, using MT and LLMs makes workflows faster and cheaper, but it also makes it harder to maintain quality.

Here, QA practices must evolve to address the specific issues that arise with MT and LLMs, such as ensuring cultural appropriateness, idiomatic accuracy, and the handling of specialized terminology. This requires ongoing collaboration between academia and business, as new research continually informs best practices in QA (Bowker, 2019).

Comparing and Contrasting Quality Objectives

Despite the collaborative potential of QA practices, the underlying quality objectives of academia and business remain distinct. Academia tends to prioritize accuracy, comprehensiveness, and theoretical robustness, often valuing innovation over immediate practicality. Business, conversely, prioritizes efficiency, client satisfaction, and scalability, often valuing practical solutions over theoretical completeness (O'Brien, 2012).

However, these objectives are not mutually exclusive. Through QA, both sectors can find common ground. For instance, while academia might focus on developing more accurate MT algorithms, businesses can apply these advancements to improve their service offerings, thereby meeting client demands while maintaining high standards of accuracy (Garcia, 2019).

QA is an iterative process, which aligns with the pursuit of knowledge and excellence in business. If we see QA as a process, not a goal, then academia and business can work together to improve translation services.

Conclusion

Quality assurance in translation services merges theory and practice, combining academic research with business. QA practices like ISO certifications and automated QA, as well as MT and

LLM, help LSPs improve their services while giving academics real-world applications for their research.

This collaboration bridges the historical divide between these two worlds and ensures high-quality translations. As the industry changes, the relationship between academia and business, mediated by QA, will be important in improving translation quality.

References

- ISO. (2020). ISO 9001:2015 - Quality management systems — Requirements. International Organization for Standardization.
- ISO. (2015). ISO 17100:2015 - Translation services — Requirements for translation services. International Organization for Standardization.
- Koehn, P. (2020). Neural Machine Translation. Cambridge University Press.
- Vaswani, A., et al. (2017). Attention Is All You Need. Advances in Neural Information Processing Systems.
- Garcia, I. (2019). Quality Assurance in Translation: The Impact of Technology. Routledge.
- Bowker, L. (2019). Machine Translation and its Impact on the Translation Profession. John Benjamins Publishing Company.
- O'Brien, S. (2012). Towards a Dynamic Quality Evaluation Model for Translation. The Translator, 18(2), 233-255.
- Zhou, X., & Pan, L. (2016). The Implementation of ISO 17100: Implications for Translation Quality Assurance. *Translation and Quality Management Journal*, 22(3), 45-67.

Impact of Syntactic Complexity on the Processes and Performance of Large Language Models-Leveraged Post-editing

Longhui Zou lzou4@kent.edu
Michael Carl mcarl6@kent.edu
CRITT, Kent State University, Kent, 44240, USA

Shaghayegh Momtaz momtazshaghayegh@gmail.com

Mehdi Mirzapour mehdi@proptexx.com
PropTexx, USA

Abstract

This research explores the interaction between human translators and Large Language Models (LLMs) during post-editing (PE). The study examines the impact of syntactic complexity on the PE processes and performance, specifically when working with the raw translation output generated by GPT-4. We selected four English source texts (STs) from previous American Translators Association (ATA) certification examinations. Each text is about 10 segments, with 250 words. GPT-4 was employed to translate the four STs from English into simplified Chinese. The empirical experiment simulated the authentic work environment of PE, using professional computer-assisted translation (CAT) tool, Trados. The raw translation output generated by GPT-4 was used to prepare the translation memory (TM) for the participants, and 13 words or phrases in the STs were selected to generate a term base (TB) with the English source terms and their equivalent Chinese target terms. The experiment involved 46 participants with different levels of translation expertise (30 student translators and 16 expert translators), producing altogether 2162 segments of PE versions for comparative analysis.

We implemented five syntactic complexity metrics in the context of PE, on the source text (ST) side, machine translation (MT) side, and the target text (TT) side. The metrics are chosen based on the specific syntactic difference between English and Chinese, including Incomplete Dependency Theory Metric (IDT), Dependency Locality Theory Metric (DLT), Combined IDT+DLT Metric (IDT+DLT), Left-Embeddedness (LE) and Nested Nouns Distance (NND). IDT, DLT, and IDT+DLT, are applications of linguistic complexity theories from Gibson's Incomplete Dependency Theory (IDT) and Dependency Locality Theory (DLT) (Gibson, 1998; Gibson, 2000). The metric LE is adopted and slightly modified from Coh-Metrix analysis (Graesser et al, 2011). NND is introduced in (Zou et al., 2021).

In this study, the participants' task was to post-edit the raw ChatGPT translation output, adhering to two different levels of PE guidelines (light PE [LPE] and full PE [FPE]) in Trados, according to Translation Automation User Society (TAUS) guidelines (Massardo et al., 2017). We also controlled two conditions of external search for the PE experiment: i.e., TB provided within Trados interface but no access to other external resources (TB), and access to any internet search but no TB provided within Trados interface (IS). Therefore, each participant conducted the PE of the four texts under four tasks, sequentially (i.e., LPE+TB; LPE+IS; FPE+TB; and FPE+IS).

The keystroke data during the PE sessions were recorded by both the Qualitivity plugin for Trados and Tobii Studio. The translator's eye movement data were collected with a Tobii TX 300 eye tracker. The translation process data was then converted and processed by the Trados-to-Translog II interface available at the CRITT TPR-DB (Zou et al., 2023; Zou and Carl, 2022; Yamada et al., 2022). Manual Quality assessment of the raw GPT-4 translations and the post-edited translations by human translators were conducted by ten professional translators, using an ATA-adapted error taxonomy.

Our preliminary findings demonstrate that there are significantly positive correlations between the IDT, IDT+DLT, LE and NND metrics and GPT-generated error counts. We also found that language-specific syntactic differences between English and Chinese such as directions of branching (LE) and noun modifiers (NND) can have a significantly positive influence on accuracy and minor errors in students' PE versions. Furthermore, expert translators produced significantly less fluency errors under the FPE guideline as compared to LPE guideline, whereas student translators had significantly less accuracy errors in the TB condition as compared to internet search (IS). Expert translators generally display greater mastery in understanding translation briefs and research skills compared to student translators. Process data of the student translators indicates less efficient workflows compared to experts (Hvelplund, 2016). Expert translators showed more fluent typing and less revision and refixation behavior than student translators (Tirkkonen-Condit, 2005; Carl & Schaeffer, 2017). These results suggest the need to adapt translation curricula to equip student translators with the LLMs-leveraged translation literacy, specialized research skill, and technical proficiency required for their professional advancement in generative AI-assisted translation roles.

References

Carl, M., & Schaeffer, M. J. (2017). Models of the translation process. *The handbook of translation and cognition*, 50-70.

Flanagan, M., & Christensen, T. P. (2014). Testing post-editing guidelines: how translation trainees interpret them and how to tailor them for translator training purposes. *The Interpreter and Translator Trainer*, 8(2), 257-275.

Graesser, A. C., McNamara, D. S., & Kulikowich, J. M. (2011). Coh-Metrix: Providing multilevel analyses of text characteristics. *Educational researcher*, 40(5), 223-234.

Gibson, E. (1998). Linguistic complexity: Locality of syntactic dependencies. *Cognition*, 68(1), 1-76.

Gibson, E. (2000). The dependency locality theory: A distance-based theory of linguistic complexity. *Image, language, brain*, 2000, 95-126.

Guerreiro, N. M., Rei, R., van Stigt, D., Coheur, L., Colombo, P., & Martins, A. F. (2023). xcomet: Transparent machine translation evaluation through fine-grained error detection. arXiv preprint arXiv:2310.10482.

Hvelplund, K. T. (2016). Cognitive efficiency in translation. *Reembedding Translation Process Research*. Amsterdam and Philadelphia: John Benjamins.

Massardo, I., van der Meer, J., O'Brien, S., Hollowood, F., Aranberri, N., and Drescher, K. (2017). Taus mt post-editing guidelines.

Tirkkonen-Condit, S. (2005). The monitor model revisited: Evidence from process research. *Meta*, 50(2), 405-414.

Yamada, M., Mizowaki, T., Zou, L., and Carl, M. (2022). Trados-to-translog-II: Adding gaze and qualitivity data to the CRITT TPR-DB. In *Proceedings of the 23rd Annual Conference of the European Association for Machine Translation*, pages 293–294, Ghent, Belgium. European Association for Machine Translation.

Yang, Z. and Li, D. (2021). Translation competence revisited: Toward a pedagogical model of translation competence. *Advances in Cognitive Translation Studies*, pages 109–138.

Zou, L., Carl, M., Mirzapour, M., Jacquenet, H., & Vieira, L. N. (2021, December). Ai-based syntactic complexity metrics and sight interpreting performance. In *International Conference on Intelligent Human Computer Interaction* (pp. 534-547). Cham: Springer International Publishing.

Zou, L. and Carl, M. (2022). Trados and the critt tpr-db: Translation process research in an ecologically valid environment. In *Model building in empirical translation studies: Proceedings of TRICKLET Conference*, May 19-20, 2022, pages 38–40.

Zou, L., Carl, M., & Gilbert, D. (2023). Integrating Trados-Qualitivity Data to the CRITT TPR-DB: Measuring Post-editing Process Data in an Ecologically Valid Setting. In *Corpora and Translation Education: Advances and Challenges* (pp. 63-86). Singapore: Springer Nature Singapore.

Slide deck for the 2024 AMTA conference

FIT is the International Federation of Translators (www.fit-ift.org).

FIT North America is the North America regional center of FIT, covering Canada, Mexico, and the United States

Based on an ATA webinar delivered 2024 Aug 23

ATA is the American Translators Association (www.atanet.org)

2024-09-09 Alan Melby © 2024 3

ATA is a member of FIT.

A recording of the August 23rd webinar will be made available on the ATA website.

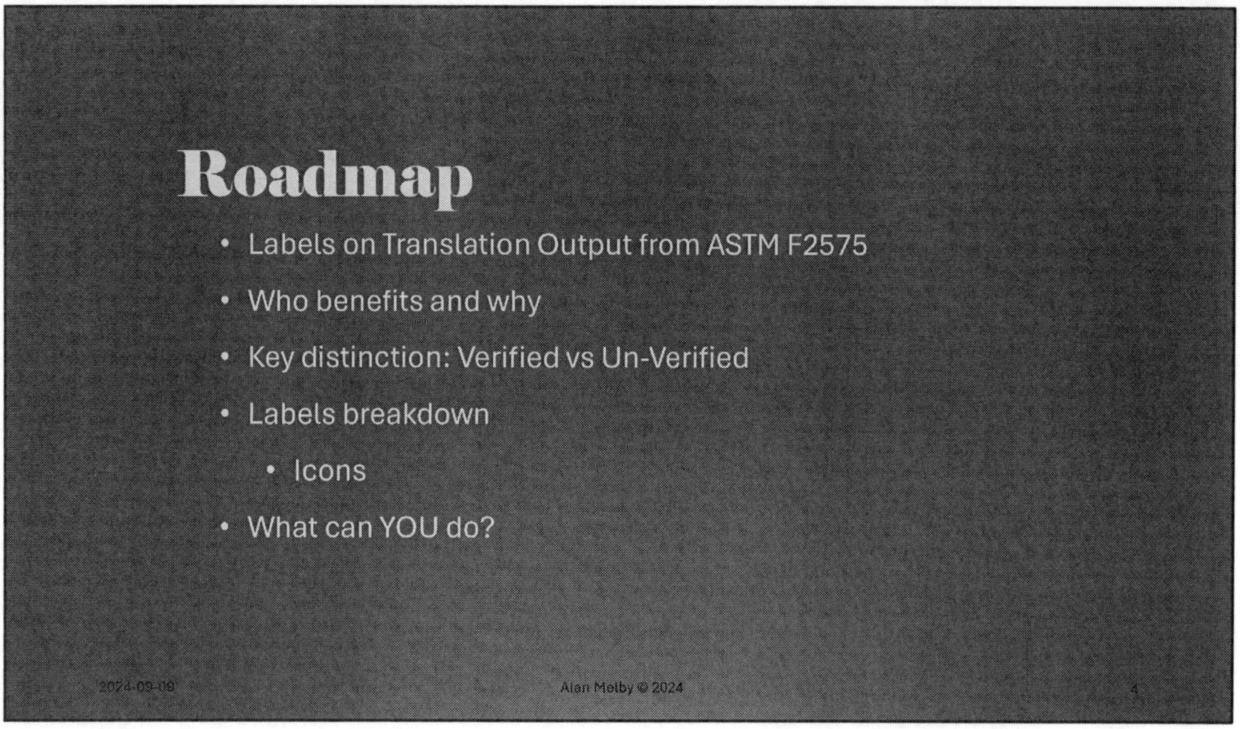

This Roadmap will give you an idea of what we will be discussing in this webinar.

In the age of Artificial Intelligence, translation output can be anything from the work of a professional translator to raw output from a GenAI or neural machine translation system. Sometimes, it is not obvious to the end user what kind of output they are reading. It can read well, that is, be fluent without fully corresponding to the source text. Correspondence errors can lead to various types of harm in high-stakes scenarios.

The basic premise of this presentation is that there should be a label on translation output to indicate whether correspondence has been verified by a qualified professional translation. The labels are presented as a form of consumer protection, where the end user is viewed as a "consumer" of translation output.

The notion of "consumer protection labels" (well-known in food labels) was first extended to translation output in a 2021 article by Alan Melby in the FIT (www.ift-ift.org) newsletter called *Translatio* (see the 2021 December issue https://en.translatio.fit-ift.org/archive/)

Consumer protection labels are most useful if they are standardized. The first set of labels on translation output appeared in the 2023 edition of an international standard for translation: ASTM F2575 (see https://www.astm.org/f2575-23e02.html). At the July 2024 meeting of the ASTM subcommittee that deals with translation-related standards, it was agreed that there was a need to fine tune the initial set of labels. The plan is to issue a ballot in September 2024 or soon thereafter regarding an adjustment to the labels.

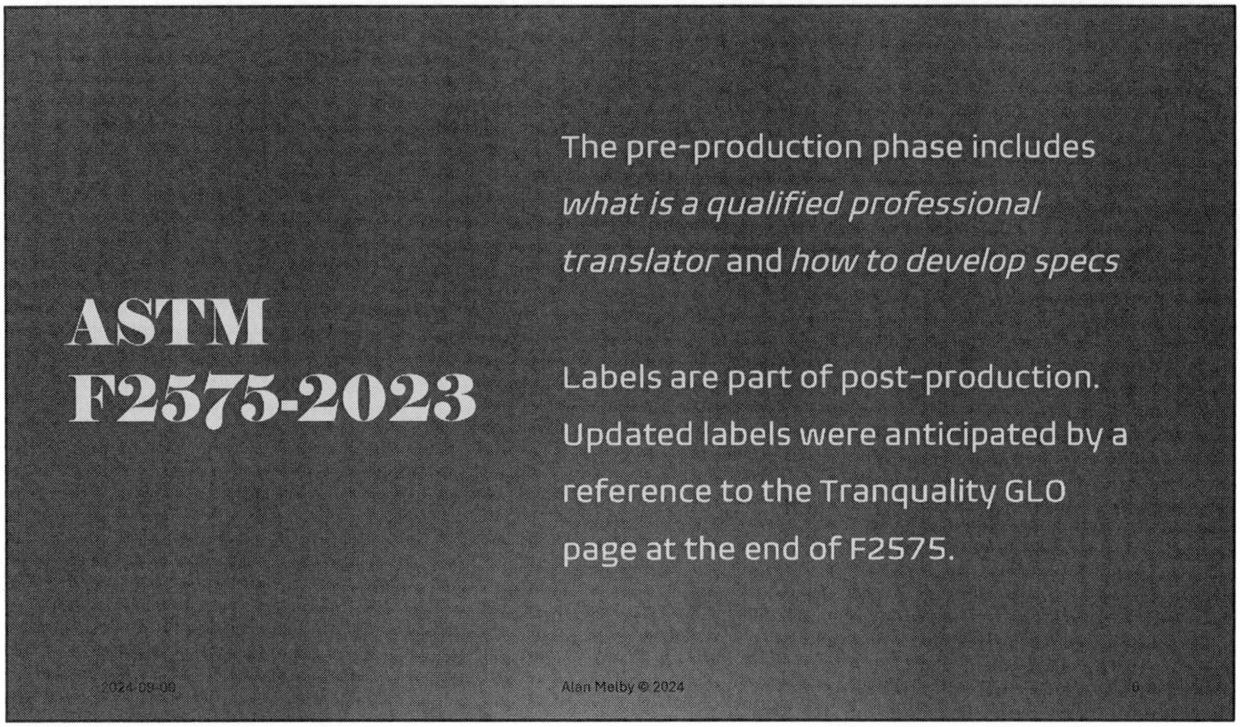

F2575 is a comprehensive standard for both requesters and providers of translation services.

F2575 includes six areas of competence that determine whether a translator is a qualified professional. See https://www.tranquality.info/whats-a-qualified-translator/ for a list of the six areas.

F2575 also standardizes a set of translation parameters. When these parameters are given values appropriate to a particular use case, the result is a set of translation specifications. Specifications are developed during the pre-production phase of a translation project.

The notion of labels on translation output is introduced in the post-production section of F2575. The labels in the 2023 edition of F2575 were Bilingually Reviewed Translation (BRT) and Unedited Machine Translation (UMT). Extensive discussion of these labels during the first half of 2024 made it clear that they do not capture an important aspect of translation, namely, whether the bilingual review was conducted by a qualified language professional.

It was anticipated in the 2023 edition of F2575 that further discussion of translation "grades", which are part of a pre-production discussion between the requester and provider, and "labels", which are part post-production, would take place after publication. Thus, a link to the GLO (Grades and Labels Overview) page of the Tranquality.info website was includes at the end of F2575-23:

https://www.tranquality.info/GLO/

This page will be updated periodically as the discussion evolves.

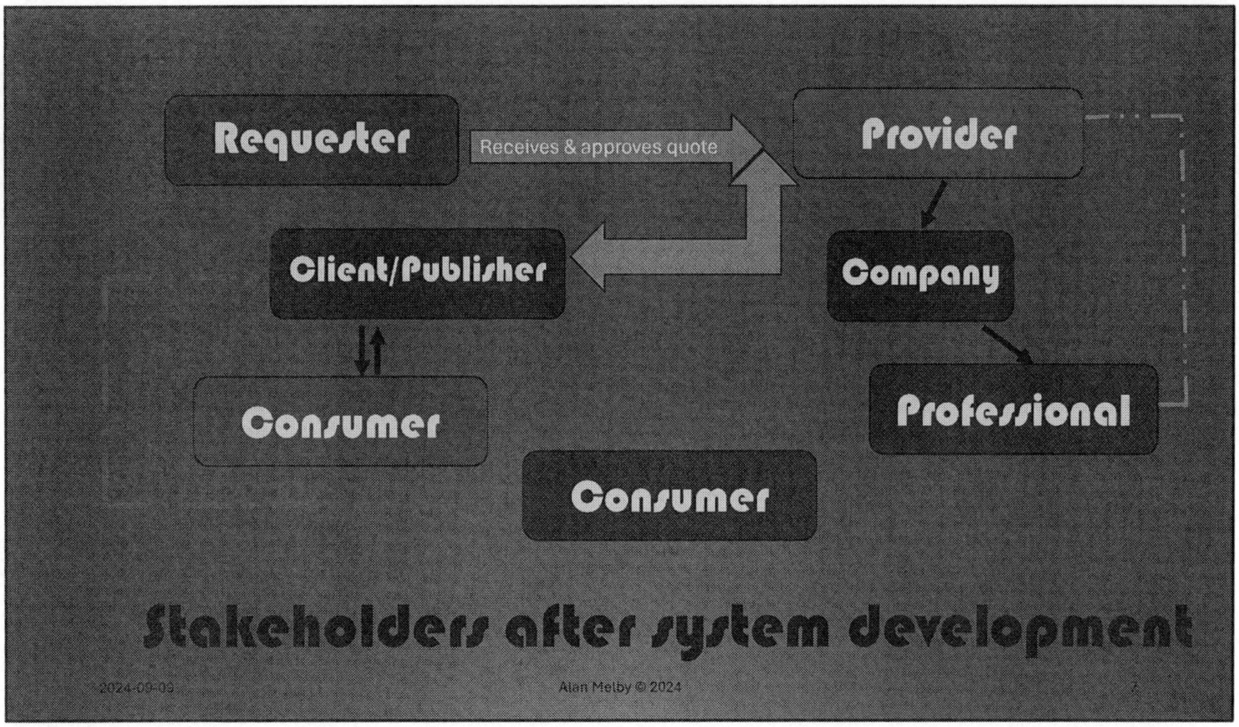

The Labels project is relevant to all stakeholders. A project starts with a content that requires translation. Then we have a **Requester** and a **Provider.** When the Requester accepts a quote, we now have a CLIENT, that is typically a PUBLISHER. This client can also be the **Consumer** (as in a company manual, or research material) or it can have another public (as in marketing material or a novel). As for the PROVIDER, it can be a company that will hire freelance professionals or freelancers who work directly with a requester.

These are the translation stakeholders in translation production, after a machine translation system has been developed and deployed.

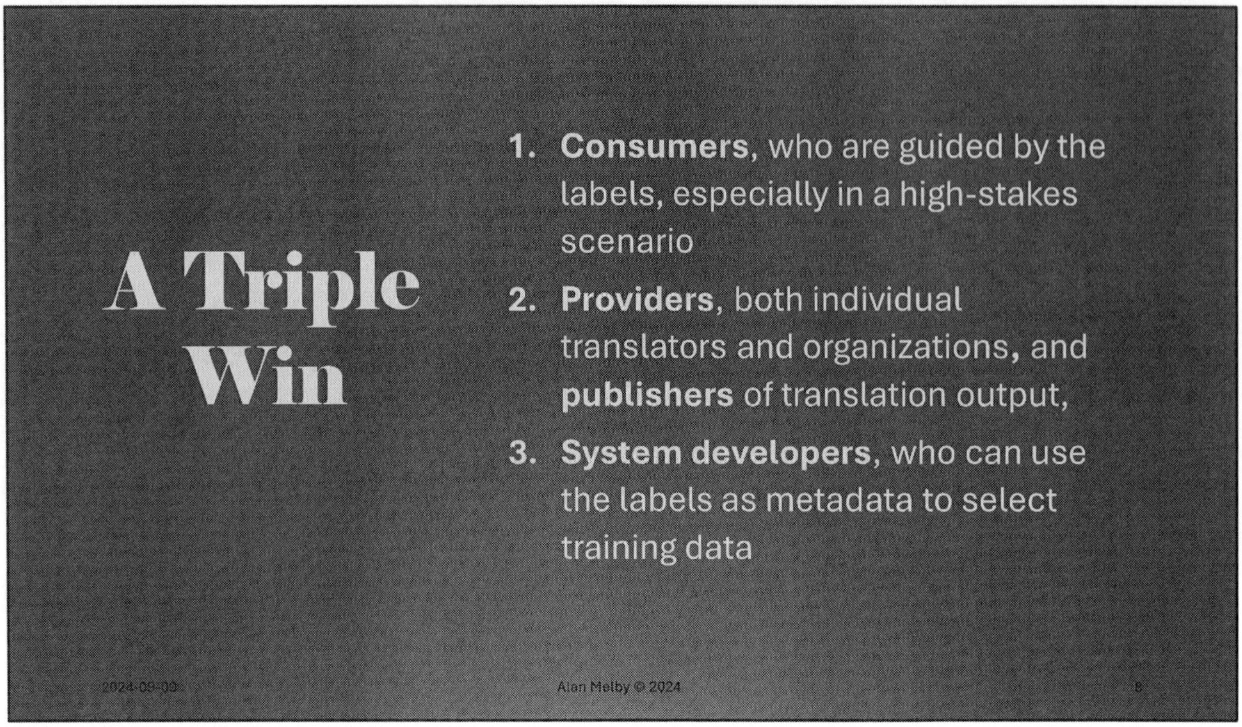

That's the Triple Win:

Standardized labels are a win for consumers of translation output. The label PVT should inspire confidence. The label UVT (or a label indicating that the content as has been generated by AI) suggests that caution should be exercised before making a decision based on a translation.

Labels are a win for providers and publishers of translation because they allow for transparency. They justify pricing procedures. A professionally verified translation is more expensive, and it is worth it. Indicating that the translation has not been verified is a type of disclaimer. Overall, labels are a component of risk management.

Labels can also benefit developers of systems that translate automatically, based on training data. If the labels are part of the metadata associated with a translation, then professionally verified translation can be included when training a system and un-verified translations can be excluded. Obviously, that begs the question of what to do with un-labeled translations, but you have to start if you are ever going to get there.

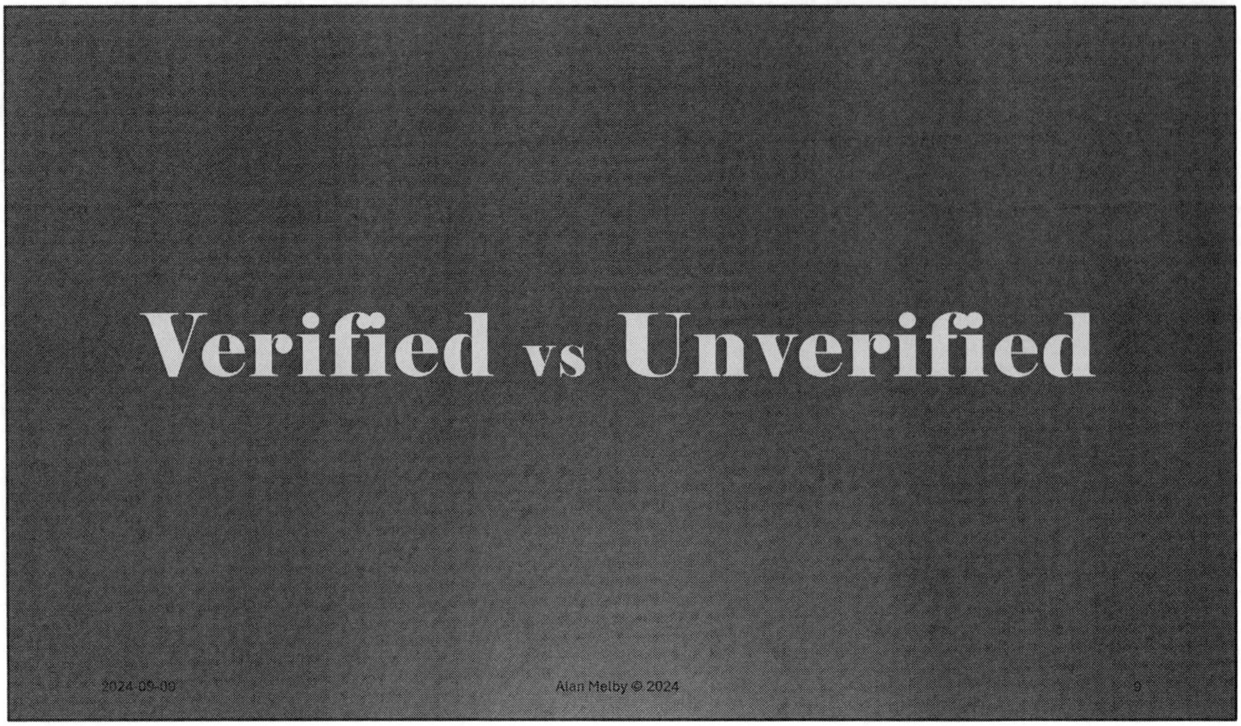

What is at stake for consumers of translation output? It depends on the scenario. Does it matter if there are gross errors not visible to me because I can't read the source text? Can I trust the translation, or should I exercise caution?

As explained in previous slide notes, key distinction provided by the labels PVT and UVT is whether the output has been checked for correspondence by a qualified professional translator.

Quality management includes agreeing on and following specifications that are ideally based on the many parameters standardized in ASTM F2575. They are essentially the same translation parameters found in ISO 11669.

Labels are only one piece of the quality puzzle but an important one. Consumers need to know whether to trust translation output. Professionals deal with specifications. Qualified professional translators should insist on well-defined specifications and then make sure that the translation output they verify (create, revise, or edit) follows agreed-on specifications that meet the needs of the intended end users (consumers).

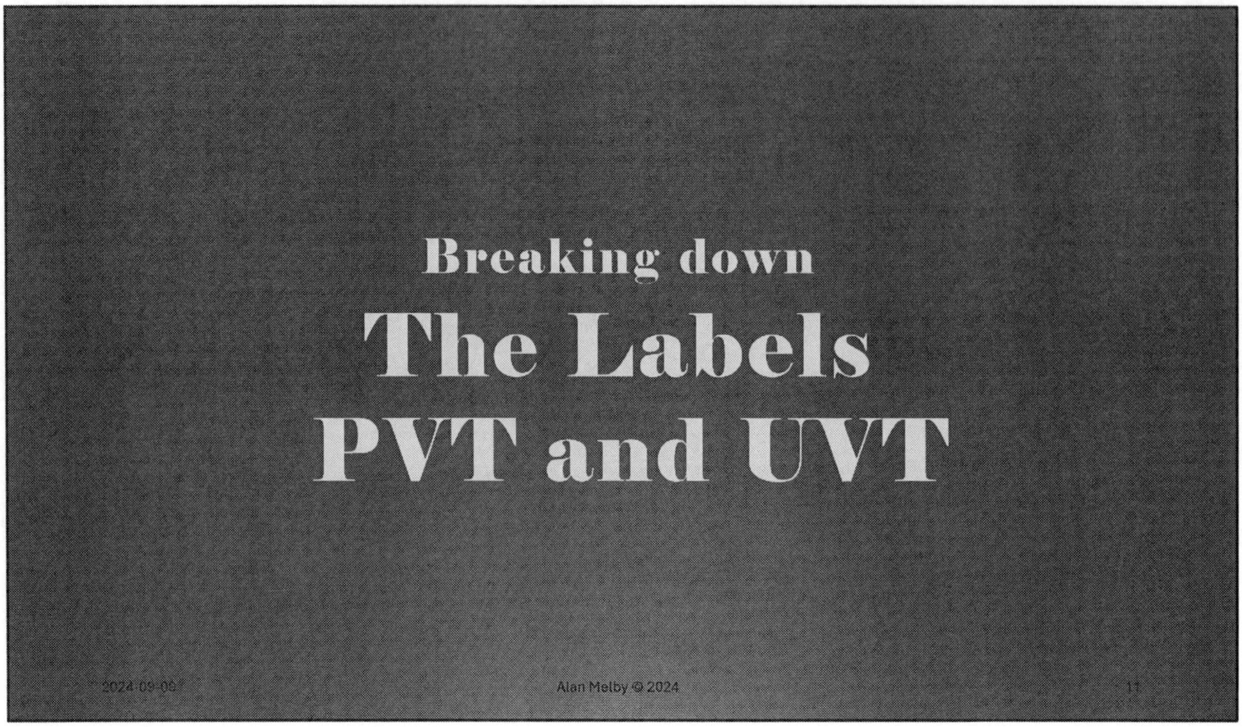

At the end of Phase One of our survey to identify replacements for the 2023 acronyms, BRT and UMT, we came up with updated acronyms PVT and UVT. based on the results gathered.

We will start with the icons that represent the labels.

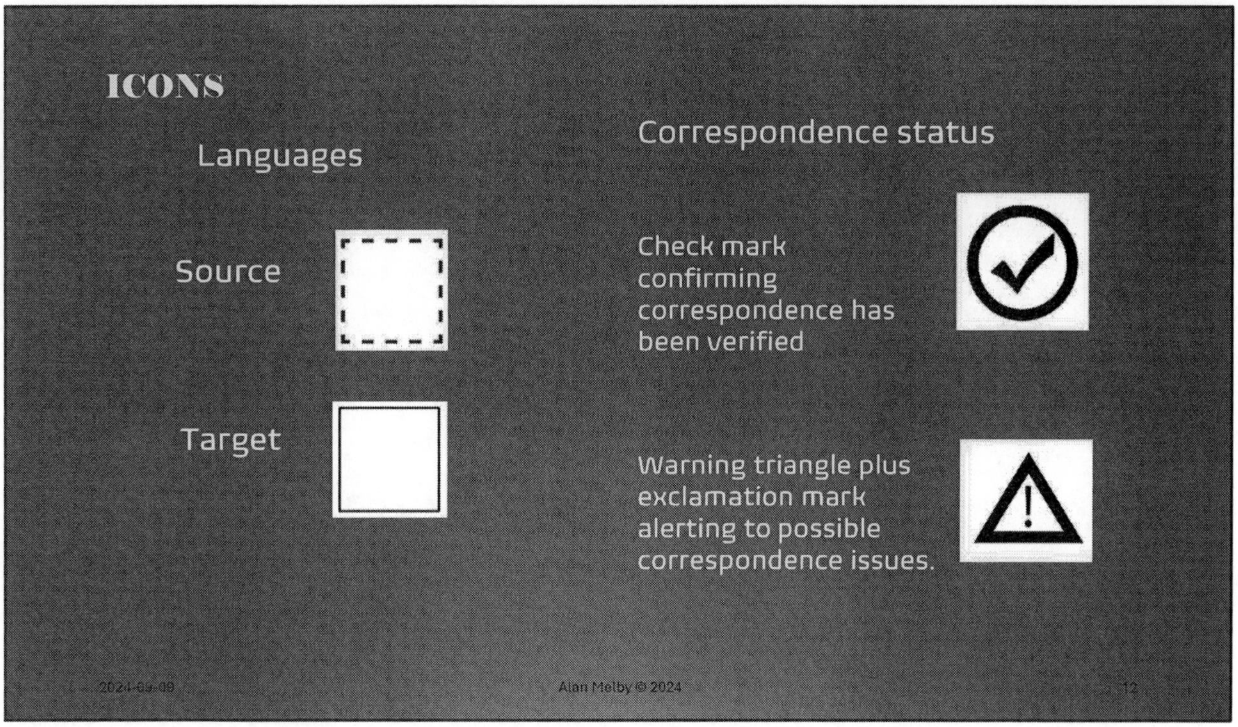

Each element of the icons has an intended meaning.

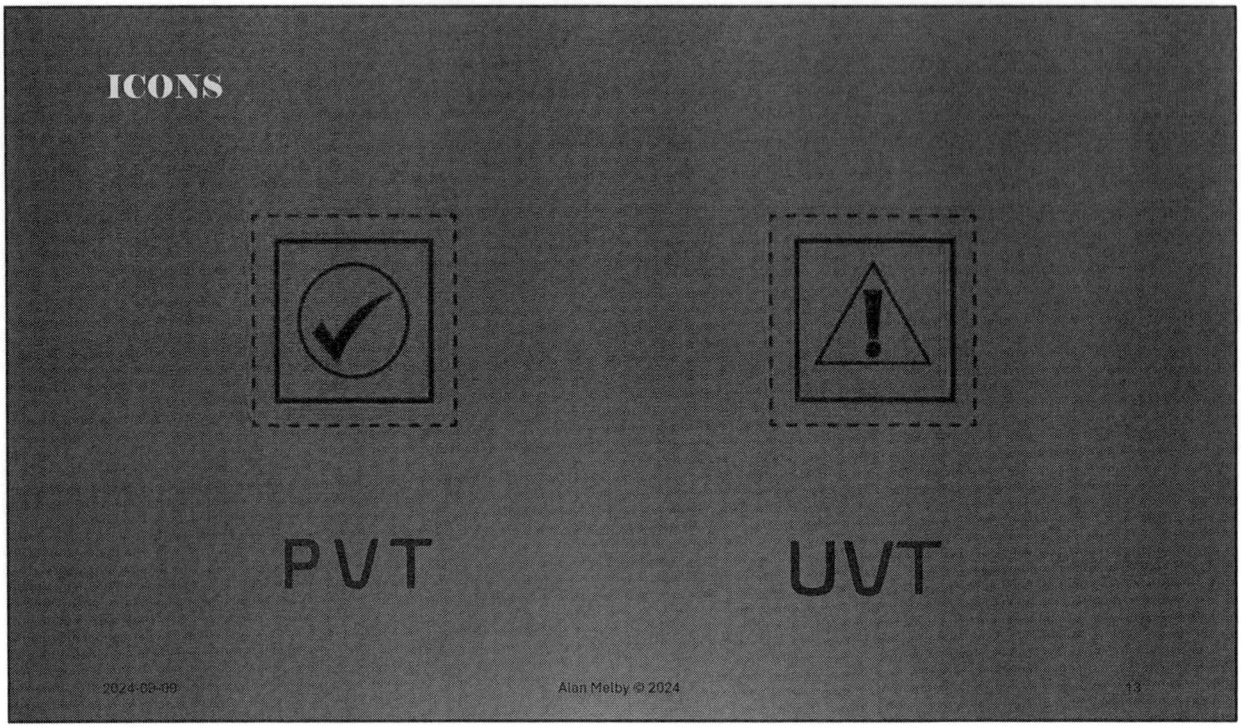

Further simplified, where only source language (dashed line) and target (solid line) are represented, with the check or exclamation marks inside to indicated verified or unverified output.

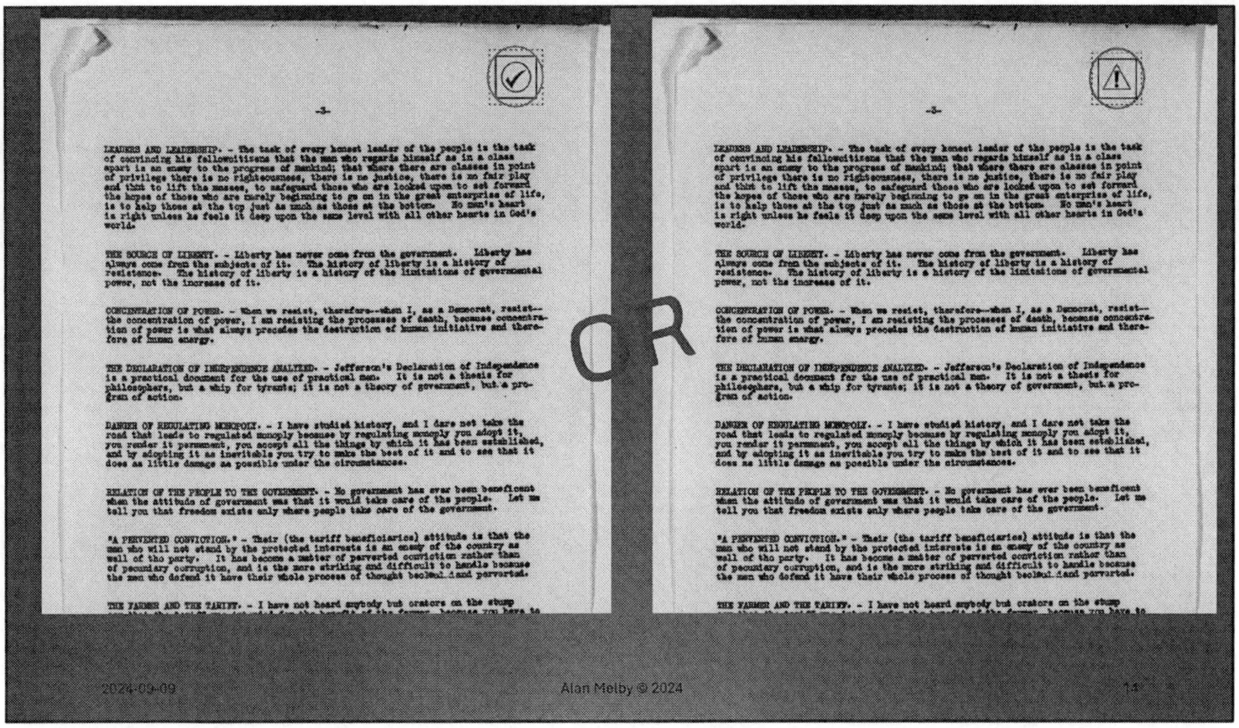

The labels would be visible, but not too conspicuous, and the link to a website explaining their meanings can be added as a footnote.

A label can also be linked to the source text and the person or organization taking responsibility for the translation output.

[Click] [Click]

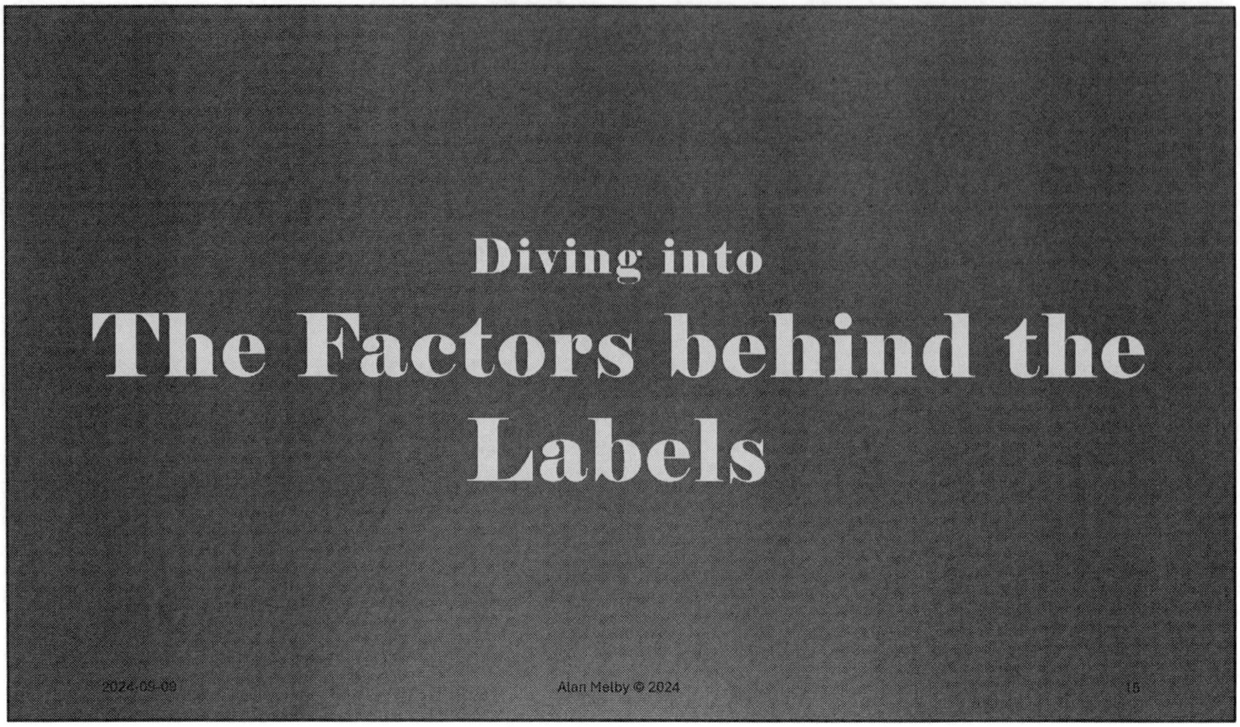

There are three factors in an ASTM F2575 label.

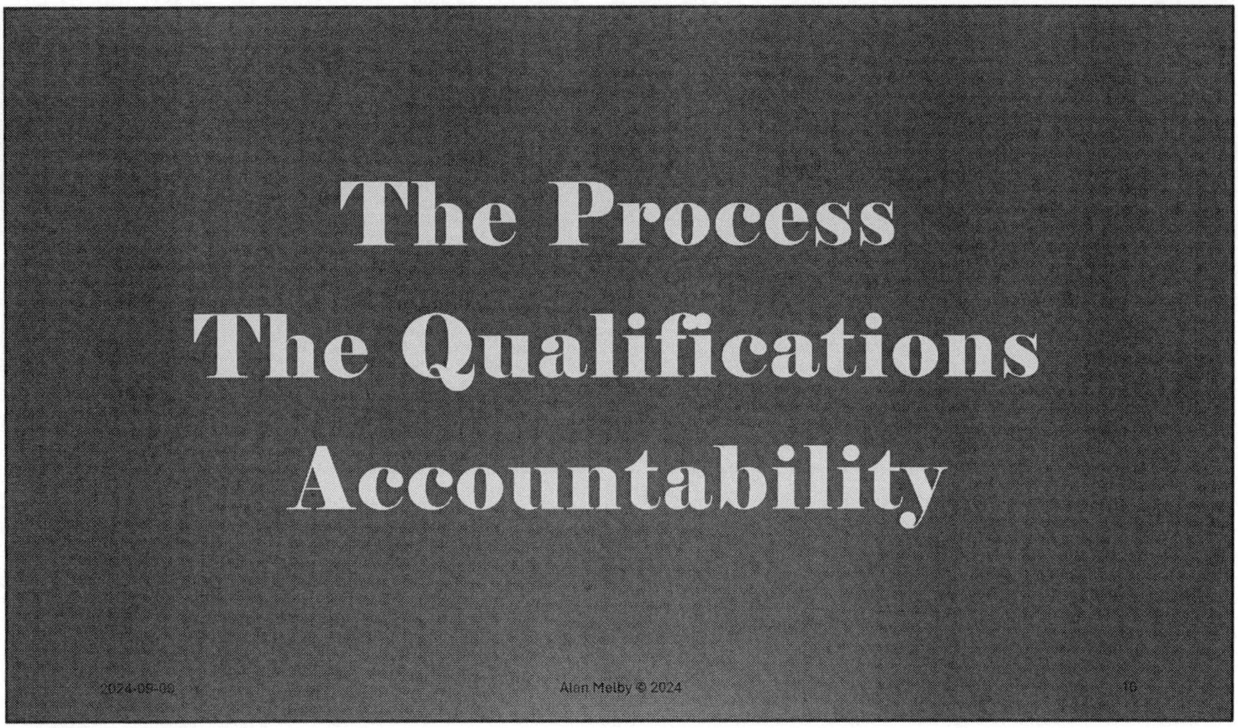

Two of them are presented visually in the following chart originally created by Arle Lommel.

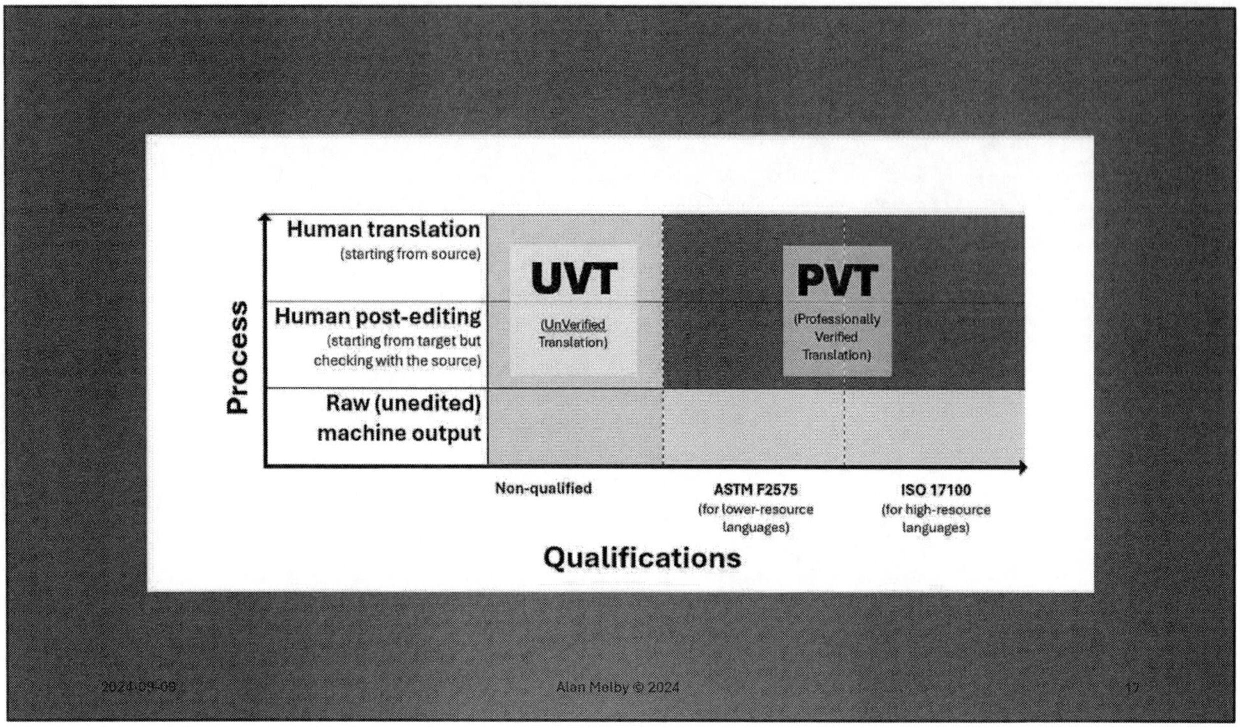

The chart shows how seven potential labels (two of the nine boxes, the gray ones, are not logically possible since no human is involved at all and thus the output cannot be PVT.

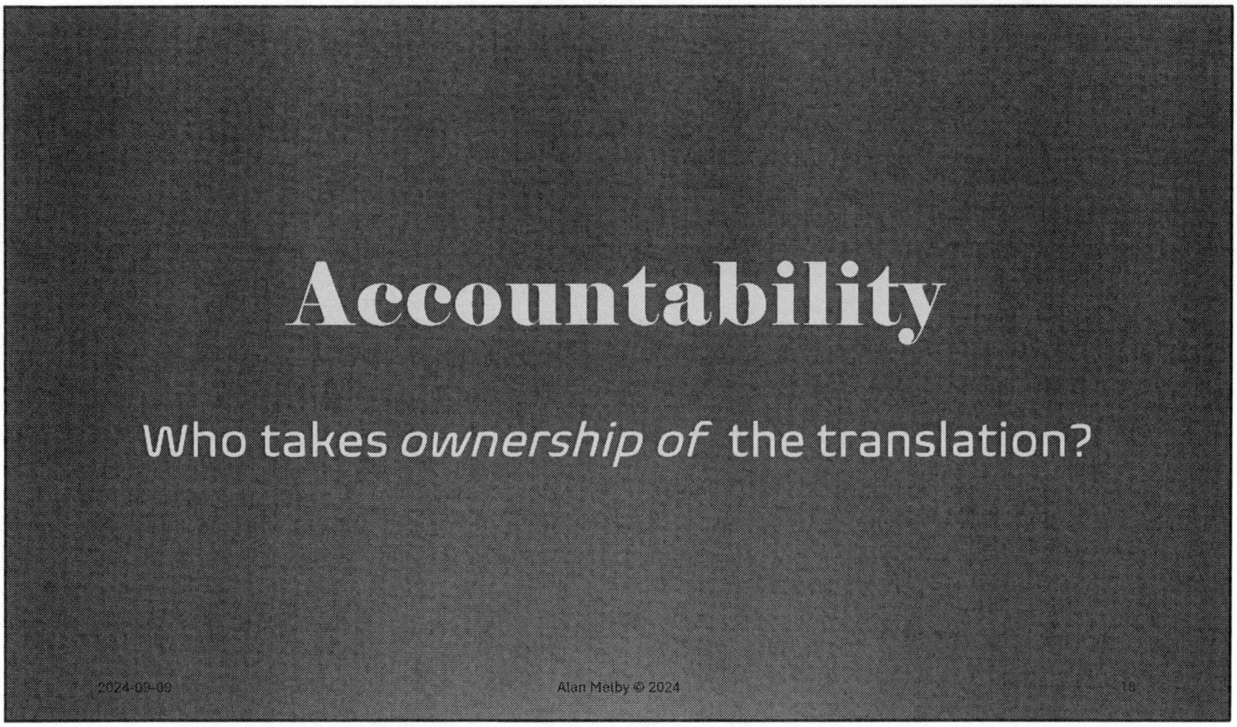

The third factor, **accountability** ensures that the publisher, whether an individual or an entity, has taken ownership of the work and its correspondence with the source language content. Correspondence focuses on how well the solutions found by the translator reflect the intended message within the situation for which the content will be used, i.e., the use case.

In the case of AI, GenAI, raw machine translation, and translations performed by non-qualified individuals, who takes ownership of any issues that may arise?

The use of these labels benefits multiple stakeholder groups, including consumers, providers & publishers, and developers.

The stakeholder group that has not yet been sufficiently consulted is consumers of translation output.

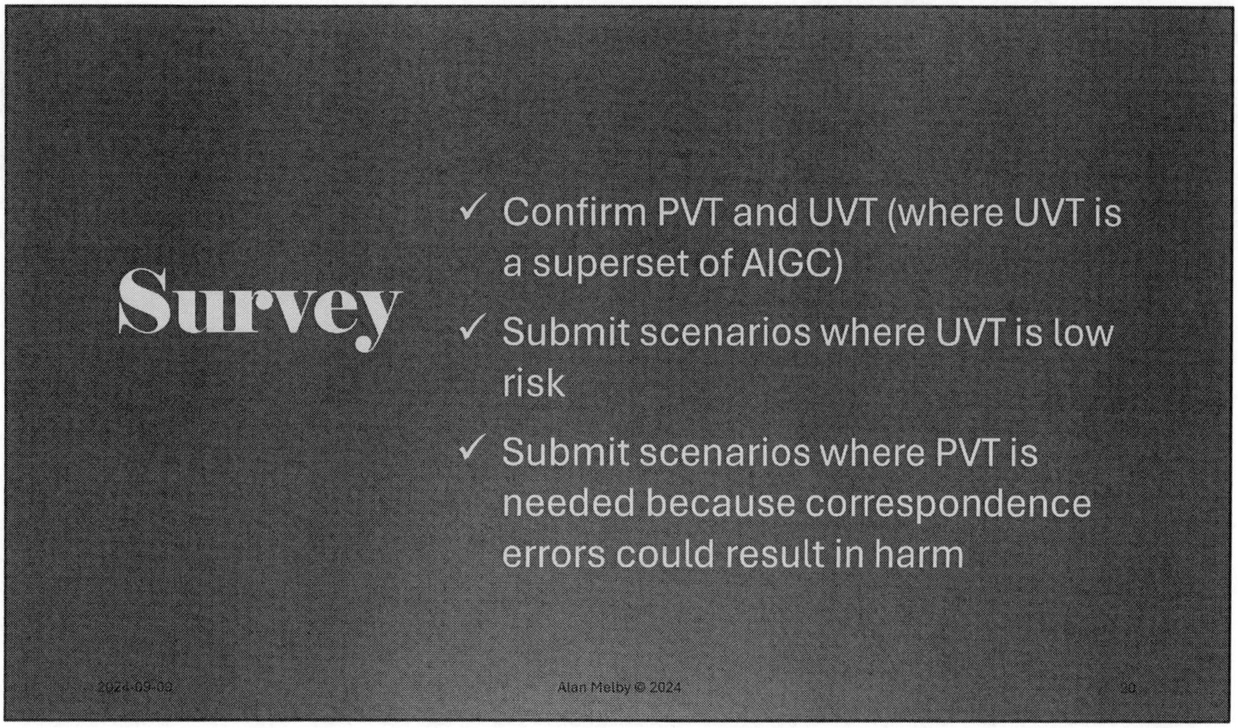

Let's collaborate so we begin to see PVT and UVT on translation output! Raw machine output can be labeled AIGC (AI Generated Content: see presentation by my colleague Michel Simard). The label AIGC implies UVT. However, UVT applies to both AIGC and non-qualified human produced or edited content.

This is your invitation to participate in Phase III of our survey, which is specific to the AMTA community.

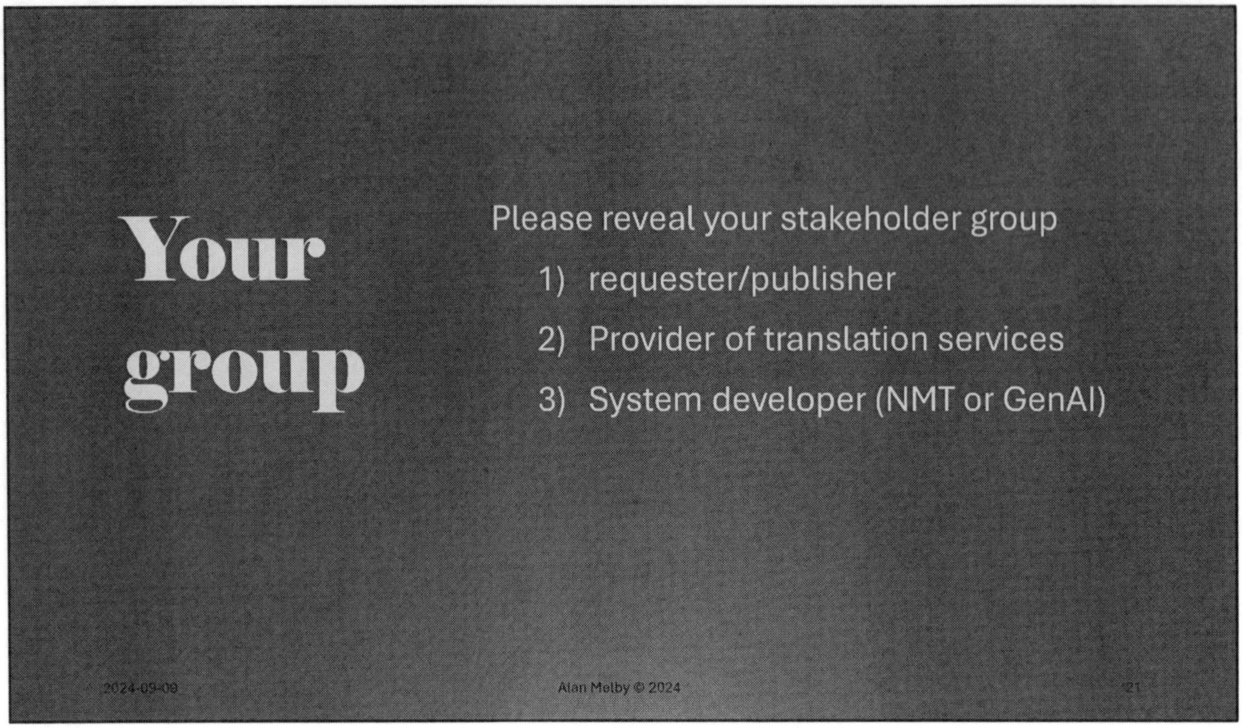

With which stakeholder group do you most closely identify?

You are welcome to send comments directly to the presenter:

Alan.Melby@fit-ift.org

Especially if you are willing to get involved in the Labels project. It will take many dedicated people to get the labels PVT and UVT implemented, so that they start to appear on translation output.

The effort to get PVT and UVT implemented is compatible with an effort to get raw machine output labeled as AIGC (AI generated content), since the label AIGC is a special case of the UVT. Thus, if the label AIGC appears on a translation, the label UVT is implied.

The label UVT is not completely equivalent to the label AIGC, since human translation by a non-qualified person is UVT but not AIGC.

The focus of the Labels project is getting PVT used. There is even some discussion of making PVT into a certification mark, so that it can only be used appropriately.

It is not accidental that the presentation by Michel Simard is scheduled to be in the same session at AMTA 2024 as this presentation. The two presenters have interacted and consider their efforts as complementary.

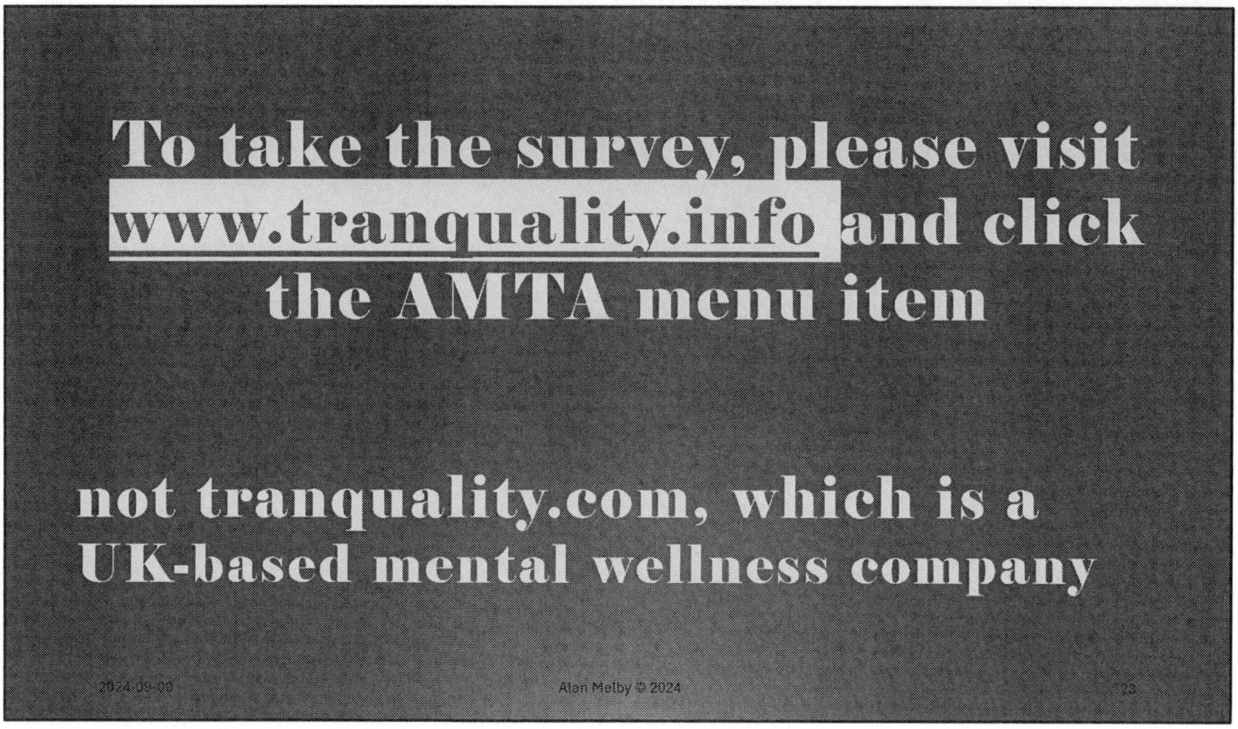

Please, please take the survey!

Association for Computational Linguistics
209 N. Eighth Street
Stroudsburg, Pennsylvania 18360

ISBN 979-8-3313-0483-6

CURRAN ASSOCIATES INC.
proceedings.com